Praise for
THE CONNECTED PARENT

"Palfrey and Gasser offer a thoughtful and necessary consideration of the difficulties of parenting digital natives, and how to contend with them. They show us how to remain connected to our kids, and to our humanity, in an age in which our kids live, learn, and struggle as much online as they do in the physical world."

—Jonathan Zittrain, Harvard University

"*The Connected Parent* comes at a time when the practice of parenting has been made much more challenging as children spend increasing amounts of time with screens, technology, and the world around them. Parents have been overwhelmed by fearmongering, misinformation, and confusion when it comes to their children's engagement with the digital world. *The Connected Parent* is a book that many parents will find refreshing, informative, and grounded in the familiar realities of daily life. Drawing from some of the best research in the world and their deep subject matter expertise, John Palfrey and Urs Gasser make a significant contribution to the ongoing conversation about how to help our children use technology more effectively while also supporting their health, happiness, and readiness for the future."

—S. Craig Watkins, author of *The Digital Edge:
How Black and Latino Youth Navigate Digital Inequality*

"I can't imagine a more important book for a caretaker or parent of a child or young adult. Many parents think they understand the online world their children navigate for hours every day, but this moment is more complex than any other in the digital age. Children and young adults experience ideas, emotions, and feelings of belonging based on how they experience their online world. Palfrey and

Gasser offer clear direction and vital insight on understanding their digital space and making it safe, fun, and productive. *The Connected Parent* is a must read for anyone with a child (and those preparing to have one)."

—Farah Pandith, author and former US diplomat

"This book is the must-read guide for parents as they navigate their children's journey in all things digital. No duo is more suited for the task—as esteemed educators, prominent researchers, and as parents of teens themselves, Palfrey and Gasser help guide parents on their shepherding of their kids through responsible, thoughtful, and rewarding uses of digital tools. The book is filled with tips on how to be effective partners and interlocutors in the process of working with teenagers as they game, learn, befriend, and experiment online. The book illuminates on questions about privacy, safety, and overuse of digital tools. This is the guide that I wish I had when I was parenting teens."

—Danielle Keats Citron, author of *Hate Crimes in Cyberspace*

THE
CONNECTED
PARENT

THE CONNECTED PARENT

An Expert Guide to Parenting in a Digital World

JOHN PALFREY AND URS GASSER

BASIC BOOKS
NEW YORK

Basic Books
Hachette Book Group
1290 Avenue of the Americas, New York, NY 10104
www.basicbooks.com
Printed in the United States of America

First Edition: December 2020

Published by Basic Books, an imprint of Perseus Books, LLC, a subsidiary of Hachette Book Group, Inc. The Basic Books name and logo is a trademark of the Hachette Book Group.

The Hachette Speakers Bureau provides a wide range of authors for speaking events. To find out more, go to www.hachettespeakersbureau.com or call (866) 376-6591.

The publisher is not responsible for websites (or their content) that are not owned by the publisher.

Print book interior design by Linda Mark.

Library of Congress Cataloging-in-Publication Data
Names: Palfrey, John G. (John Gorham), 1972– author. | Gasser, Urs, author.
Title: The connected parent : an expert guide to parenting in a digital world / John Palfrey and Urs Gasser.
Description: First edition. | New York : Basic Books, [2020] | Includes bibliographical references and index.
Identifiers: LCCN 2020014346 | ISBN 9781541618022 (hardcover) | ISBN 9781541618008 (ebook)
Subjects: LCSH: Internet and children. | Internet and teenagers. | Parenting. | Parent and child. | Internet—Social aspects.
Classification: LCC HQ784.I58 P33 2020 | DDC 004.67/8083—dc23
LC record available at https://lccn.loc.gov/2020014346

ISBNs: 978-1-5416-1802-2 (hardcover), 978-1-5416-1800-8 (ebook)

LSC-C

10 9 8 7 6 5 4 3 2 1

For the quite wonderful parents and grandparents
in our lives and the lives of our children

Contents

Introduction   1

Part I: Growing Up in a Hyperconnected World
One   Screen Time   15
Two   Social Life   41
Three Privacy   69

Part II: Some Topics Parents Worry About Most
Four   Safety   91
Five   Anxiety   109
Six   Addiction   129
Seven Gaming   141

Part III: Engaging the World Beyond the Home
Eight Diversity   159
Nine   Learning   187
Ten   Civic Life   215
       Conclusion   231

       Acknowledgments   243
       Further Reading   245
       Notes   265
       Index   279

Introduction

ONE SATURDAY MORNING, Matthew comes home after a sleepover party celebrating his friend Alex's twelfth birthday. Once Matthew has thrown down his coat and sleeping bag in the kitchen, his mom greets him and asks, "What'd you guys do at the party?"

"Oh, you know, we stayed up late playing video games," Matthew says.

His mom doesn't let that go. "How late were you up?"

"I don't know . . . late."

She follows up. "What games?"

"You know . . . the usual. Mostly *Call of Duty*."

"You do anything else?" his mom asks.

Matthew replies, "Yeah, well, we watched a movie."

"Did you guys talk to one another?" she asks. She knows she is starting to push her luck asking so many questions of her twelve-year-old son, but she is anxious to know the answers.

"Well, we texted a bunch, in-game," Matthew says, impatience creeping into his voice.

"While the movie was going on?"

Matthew looks at her funny. "Yeah, kind of, always."

"Didn't you do anything else?"

"Not really," he says. "We ate. They ordered pizza. Before you ask: it was pepperoni. Okay?"

His mom laughs. "You're right. I *was* going to ask what kind of toppings. Okay, well, be sure to get some sleep tonight."

Later, Matthew's mom is on the phone with Alex's mom. As they discuss the prior evening, they figure out that the entire party, from the 5:00 p.m. arrival time through the eleven o'clock departure the next morning—minus a few hours of sleep in the wee hours—was spent on the boys' devices. The kids at the party are all well behaved, do well in school, and have strong friendships. But as their parents can't help but see, their kids' experience of childhood is highly mediated by digital devices.

Nothing seems to be going wrong for Matthew or Alex—and the boys certainly aren't bothered. Should their parents be worried?

YOUNG PEOPLE ARE growing up in a world that is significantly different from the one that most of their parents experienced during childhood. Even compared with the time when millennial parents were growing up, the world is more complex, more interconnected, and faster-paced.

Technology is a key driver of these changes. Today, virtually all children in well-off societies are growing up with a phone in their hand, access to much of recorded knowledge at their fingertips, and a whole lot of questions in front of them about what life will be like. While there are exceptions—the children from low-income families or from remote areas may lead a more analog-oriented, less digital life—the lives of children are increasingly mediated by digital devices around the world.

We have written this book for parents who wonder what they should do about the role of technology in the lives of their children. Parents today are facing urgent new questions: How much time should kids be allowed to spend staring into screens? At what age should we let them have their own social media accounts? What about playing video games—how much is too much? How can we keep them safe from harm online? Are our children going to grow up less socially able if they've had their nose in a screen for too much of their childhood?

We address these common fears in this book, but we also want to illuminate the possible benefits young people can gain from their use of new media and technologies. We take up these topics and offer advice in a simple, straightforward way that is nevertheless grounded in the most reliable research.

WHY SHOULD YOU READ THIS BOOK?

You might wonder why you shouldn't just google an answer for each of these questions as they arise instead of reading an entire book. After all, you can find plenty of advice online about how to handle every parenting question, especially when it comes to technology and kids. Some of that advice is very good. There are some terrific blogs and websites out there. We read Sonia Livingstone's *Parenting for a Digital Future* blog regularly, for instance. We are devotees of the Family Online Safety Institute's guidance as well as much of what Common Sense Media and the American Academy of Pediatrics offers parents. We will point you to many of these excellent resources and others that we have found to be reliable over time. They are all easy to find online.

Through this book, we offer two main benefits that you just can't get from googling. First, we share parenting suggestions that are grounded in the best research about kids and technology—the best research we've been able to find, be it our own research or that of others. We have been studying this topic for years, since long before social media became a thing. And second, we offer these suggestions in the context of a consistent philosophy about raising children in this digital age. We call this philosophy *connected parenting*. While you might not always agree with us on each topic, you will always know where we are coming from and why.

We approach this topic as researchers, educators, and parents. For more than a decade and a half, we have been researching kids and technology. Together, we have co-led a series of research projects through the Youth and Media Lab at the Berkman Klein Center for Internet & Society at Harvard University. We have overseen research centers on technology in the United States and in Switzerland. We have taught high school, college, and graduate students. John has been the principal of a residential high school (Phillips Academy in Andover, Massachusetts) with more than a thousand students from every state and from dozens of countries around the world. And in what we consider our most important role, each of us is the parent of two kids, all of whom are now in their teenage years.

This book builds on our previously published work. In 2008, we wrote *Born Digital*, a book that has been published in ten languages and updated in multiple editions over the years.[1] The idea for this new book comes out of the many presentations and school visits we have made since *Born Digital* came out over a decade ago. At every one of those events, parents would ask for our advice. Parental advice wasn't the main purpose of the original book, which had more of an academic focus and explained our and others' research on youth and media. We hadn't intended to advise parents.

This new book presents an answer to the question we heard again and again: In light of all this research, what advice can we offer to parents? Put another way, in the midst of all this change and complexity, what's a parent actually supposed to do? How can the research help people do their incredibly important jobs as parents? How can a parent support a child in enjoying the benefits of the digital age while managing the risks?

For *The Connected Parent*, we base our observations on the research that supported *Born Digital* and the reams of sound research published since then. Our research has primarily taken the form of surveys, focus groups, and structured interviews conducted between 2005 and 2020. In addition to our own research, we draw extensively on the work of other researchers from around the world. We recommend that anyone who wants a deeper dive into the research consult the many books and research reports we cite in this book.

OUR PHILOSOPHY: CONNECTED PARENTING

As mentioned earlier, we call our overall philosophy in this book *connected parenting*. The idea is for you, as a parent, to engage positively with the young people in your life when it comes to digital issues.

The connected parent understands the basics of how the digital world works; you don't have to be an expert, but you do have to roll up your sleeves and stay abreast of the technology. As a matter of fact, it's fine to recognize that your child will know more about the technology while you will know more about life. What we share about technology in this book, plus what you would learn from occasional use of the internet, including email and social media, is plenty. We think that the right idea is to be engaged in social media enough so that you can remain credible in these conversations.

Connected parents seek to establish—and then keep open—a positive line of conversation about technology with their children. A parent can help kids make sound choices about their use of technology as they grow and as circumstances shift. Instead of always looking for the exact answer, the connected parent looks for a good conversation starter and a way to engage with a child in helpful ways. We do know how tough this effort can be, especially in families where everyone is working hard and where time (and patience, for that matter) is short. We hope this book can help prompt conversations in any family, even as circumstances dictate that parents will sometimes need to make their own unique decisions.

The connected parent keeps the line of communication open especially when things get difficult. That's when your input is most crucial. Whether or not they ask for it, your children need your good common sense and your love, even tough love—particularly when they are struggling. They will have an easier time hearing it when the advice is part of this long-running conversation, rather than a one-off. By keeping the lines of communication open, you will have established a track record of listening to your child and giving sound advice on good days as well as bad.

Connected parents understand the ways that digital media now touches every aspect of a young person's life. Especially since computing went mobile, children have technology connected to their bodies most of the time. All too often, they sleep next to it and turn right to it the moment the alarm on the phone wakes them up. Their social lives course through it. Their schoolwork is often accessed from their phones—as are their grades and feedback from their teachers, if they are lucky enough to get feedback. They learn about health, sex, politics, and fashion online. They do much of their shopping through a mobile phone or laptop. For some, the most fun games are experienced through a screen. We have to come to grips with the ubiquity and the power of digital media.

The best news about connected parenting is that most of the sound parenting practices from the past still work in the digital age. That's not to say nothing has changed. In fact, a lot has changed. But not so much that the job of the tech-savvy parent should be overwhelming.

Connected parents don't let fear guide their approach. They need to establish a sense of balance for the complex issues in a child's life today. The research clearly shows the many benefits of technology use for young people as they are growing up. These benefits include the potential for social and emotional growth, increased creativity and productivity, new avenues for learning and for engaging with the world, and opportunities to connect with a more diverse group of friends. As a connected parent, you are open to these ideas and possibilities—especially the possibility that your child will grow and benefit from experiences with digital media and new technologies.

The connected parent understands, too, that some youth behaviors are risky and others are decidedly mixed. Some young people can share too much information about themselves through digital devices. Many of the most popular services, using advanced psychological research, are literally designed to encourage them to do so. Some young people also put themselves in harm's way through apps and websites. And some young people struggle with the seemingly inexorable pull of games and social media online—especially when they are supposed to be doing their homework.

To boil this philosophy down, you'll want to keep these five key elements in mind as a connected parent:

- Keep a constructive conversation open with the young people in your care about digital issues and all the important topics in their lives.
- Engage with the technology yourself so you can remain credible and model good behavior.
- Seek a sensible balance between providing support and offering independence, shifting this balance over time as appropriate.
- Embrace the positive aspects of digital culture while helping young people develop the skills they need to mitigate the risks.
- Keep an open mind about what sound data can teach us rather than succumbing to fears about new technologies.

Most of the questions and concerns facing parents today are not completely new. Many of today's parents—especially millennial parents—have grown up with these same technologies themselves. That's a big change from ten or fifteen years ago. Connected parents continue to stay abreast of the different ways in which their children are growing up.

More recently, however, there have been profound changes in how children relate to one another, how they read and learn, and how they engage in civic life. We have an awesome responsibility to help them take advantage of what is great and good about the digital world and to navigate the parts that are confusing and, occasionally, downright scary. The positive news is that many researchers, educators, and parents are putting their heads together to come up with strategies to help guide the way.

Our guiding philosophy of connected parenting grows out of the idea of connected learning.[2] A network of researchers formed the Connected Learning Alliance and developed the connected-learning paradigm as a guide for educators, parents, and policy makers so that they can find better ways to use technology to enhance children's education. We were among those who have developed and championed these ideas of connected learning. This field of research was funded by the MacArthur Foundation, where John now serves as president. In this book, we extend the idea of connected learning directly into recommendations for how all of us parents and others caring for children can take advantage of the things the digital world has to offer our young people, while we also address the risks they face as they grow up.

A GUIDE TO THE BOOK

The Connected Parent is organized around the questions we most frequently received from parents over the years while we were on the road discussing our research. We have also heard versions of these questions from tweens and teens themselves—especially the many incredible research assistants who have been working in the Youth and Media Lab.

Our advice, like our work, has primarily focused on children aged thirteen through to their adolescence, which, as research shows, now extends into a young person's twenties. We comment where appropriate on issues related to younger children as well, to the extent that there is sound research to provide guidance. But the focus of this book falls on youth during their tween and teen years.

The ten topics often find their way into conversations in the form of a parent's worries:

Screen time: How much time online is too much?

Social life: Are kids less social these days because of technology?

Privacy: Is it true that kids no longer care about privacy?

Safety: How do we keep our kids safe from harm in a digital age?

Anxiety: Why do our kids seem more anxious than ever?

Addiction: Is it possible that my child is addicted to technology?

Gaming: Should I be worried about all the violence in popular video games?

Diversity: Is technology affecting our kids' abilities to engage with others across differences?

Learning: Are our kids learning less than we did? Do they read less and cheat more?

Civic life: Are young people more apathetic than we were?

We don't have all the answers to these questions. Sorry to disappoint right at the start, but it's true. Some of these questions lack an easy answer. In each case, we offer you our point of view in light of what we consider the strongest available evidence. Sometimes, the research isn't yet all that clear. In other cases, the question leads to a judgment call. And as any parent knows, the hardest issues facing kids as they grow up can feel intractable. We will honestly admit when we believe that the research is still ambiguous as well as when we think the findings are incontrovertible—and which advice lines up best with what the research shows.

The effects of digital media on young people are still unclear. Parents we have talked with over the years have had wildly divergent views about whether media and technology use is fundamentally positive or negative. Parents vary enormously in how concerned they are about digital media use and how they wish to address it. On the flip side, many parents are excited about the possibilities for learning, socializing, and civic engagement online. Researchers, too, can disagree as to whether and to what degree we should be worrying about certain issues, especially relating to screen time.[3]

As a result, each chapter includes a mixture of fact and opinion. We have drawn facts from the most reliable research we can find on each given topic. Sometimes, we have conducted that research ourselves; most of the time, we draw on the research that others have done. Then we offer our opinions in the form of advice. We approach each topic in the knowledge that every family is different. The answers to the hard questions of parenting in a digital age are going to depend on many factors. Each young person is unique. Kids need different things at different ages. Every family's available time and financial resources are also unique. What's going to work in a household with two parents, one of whom is home full time, will not work in a household with a single parent who is barely staying afloat while holding two jobs.

Given this diversity of experience and needs, we aspire to offer general principles that can work in a range of situations, but we also know that sometimes, you will have to deviate from the script. Sometimes, a family will need support that goes far beyond the advice this book can offer. While the book's recommendations about intergenerational learning and joint family activities might apply to all families, we're of course acutely aware that parents and children from less resourced communities might have very different experiences and struggles in both their offline and their online environments. Schools, libraries, after-school programs, and other institutions often play a special role in supporting families from less privileged backgrounds. And we can all find ways to help raise awareness in our larger communities about issues of our children's technology use.

The book's chapters follow a simple format. First, we define the chapter's central topic and the related issues that worry parents the most. Then, we set forth the most salient data on that issue, making clear the degree of certainty that we have in the facts available to us today. Third, we present a philosophy that guides our approach to each topic. The core of the chapter takes the form of practical advice based on these data and our experience as educators, parents, and researchers. We organize ideas around parents' frequently asked questions in the "Common Questions" section near the end of many chapters. And we conclude with a short recap section with the most important takeaways from each topic for easy reference. As your children grow up, you might not want to reread the whole book or even an entire chapter, so these recap sections might serve as a quick resource to which you could return as time goes on.

Along the way, endnotes point you toward some of the most important research on each respective topic. We encourage you to read the original studies for topics of particular interest and to draw your own conclusions about the right choice for you and your family as your child grows. We do not pretend to have the only—or even the best—advice for every child and every family situation. At the end of the book, a "Further Reading" section suggests books and other resources that we have found especially helpful in our own research and parenting.

In this book, we intend to provoke your thinking and prompt good conversations with your kids. So, let's jump in—and connect with the ways young people are growing up in this increasingly digital age.

PART I

GROWING UP IN A HYPERCONNECTED WORLD

CHAPTER ONE

Screen Time

JAMIE, AGE FOURTEEN, wakes up around 6:30 a.m. on school days. The first thing she does is reach for her phone, the one that's buzzing to wake her up. It's on the floor right beside her bed.

Her eyes only half-open, Jamie flips through a series of applications that indicate she's got messages. Snapchat, Instagram, Facebook, Twitter. School email can wait till later. (As she often explains to her mom, email is what *adults* use—it's not for kids.) One Snap story catches her attention. She gets pulled into the narrative and from there into other stories. She loses track of time as she scrolls. It's thirty minutes later before she makes her way to the shower.

Smartphone back in hand, Jamie spends breakfast flipping through her Insta feed. On the bus to school, earbuds in, listening to music, she plays games until she arrives. The school day doesn't involve too much screen time in the classroom, but every break spent walking through the hallways allows for a check of her phone and her various feeds.

After school, she's at the library for an hour or so, online for a research project. By late afternoon, she's on a friend's couch, each of them on their phones, chatting with friends elsewhere, listening to music together. She comes home, and her phone is still out during a quick dinner. Jamie turns to Netflix in the evening, bingeing on her favorite show of the moment (reruns of *The Office*). Her mom comes into her room at 11:00 p.m. to tell her to shut down her computer and go to bed. Jamie objects but eventually gives in, and she's asleep by midnight.

Does Jamie's routine sound excessive? Actually, her daily screen exposure is probably below average for a teenager in the United States. If her total media usage is under nine hours a day, she's below the norm in this country today. Yet her relationships with other young people and the outside world, every day, seven days a week, 365 days a year, are mediated by technology.

THE IMAGE OF a young person staring into a smartphone is a sign of the times. Adults are no different. This image will be one of the most enduring aspects of this era. Given how quickly technology and behaviors are changing, it is likely that this image will look hilariously dated not too long from now. The interface and our kids' practices are bound to change. Someday a person staring down into a phone will look the way a 1980s hairstyle does to a teenager in 2020. But for now, the face-in-phone image is ubiquitous.

Many parents have concerns about their kids and their screen time. How much time should a child spend looking at a screen? Starting when? How much is too much? At what point should I insist that they put away their phones? Should I be monitoring what they're doing on their phones? They seem so infatuated with their device—is that healthy?

A screen is often a highly reliable babysitter, as every harried parent of young children knows. You have a long car ride? Plane ride? A long wait at the grocery store? Dinner with friends? The best way to get some peace is to put some kind of a device with a game, movie, or Netflix subscription in front of your child. We get it. We have been those harried parents.

It's not easy to know how hard you should work to resist what seems like the inexorable pull of these technologies. You might wonder, as we do, whether there is a way to flip the script and make some of that screen time turn from a concern into a benefit for your kids. Though this topic is never an easy one, you do have options and there are ways to support your children as they grow.

WHAT THE RESEARCH SHOWS

The data confirm your impression that Jamie and her friends are experiencing much of their childhoods through their digital devices. These screens connect them with each other and the rest of the world. Living a digitally connected life, as virtually all our children do in the United States and other wealthy countries, means that a screen is turned on somewhere near them for hours every day. It is completely reasonable to wonder if your child is spending too much time staring into screens.

The research on screen time may surprise you, though. A moderate amount of time engaged in digital activities is not inherently harmful. In fact, moderate use of devices can bring many opportunities for socializing, self-expression, exploration, and creativity. Large-scale studies, such as a study of thirty-five thousand young Americans and their caregivers, have shown that one to two hours of screen time a day can lead to higher levels of social and emotional well-being for young people than levels found in their peers without this screen time.[1] Concerns about social and emotional behavior only arise in the cases of the relatively few young people whose use of digital devices fall outside the typical range of reported screen time.

Put another way, the relationship between screen time and well-being in childhood is not linear. More screen time does not simply mean more harm to kids. The harmful effects of screen time come only from *excessive* engagement in digital activities. What constitutes excessive can be tricky to define and can differ by person, type of activity, and other circumstances. The research suggests that the Goldilocks principle should guide the connected parent: Not too little, not too much, but some kind of a balance is right for most young people in most situations.

Let's start by digging into the data about how much time most young people are spending on screens. The most important piece of technology in a young person's life is typically the mobile phone. Through this mobile device, a young person accesses the latest social media feeds, interacts with friends, watches movies, and plays games. More often than ever before, children either own or have access to smartphones that they use to go online, watch Netflix or YouTube, do their homework, post on social media, and chat with their friends. They also use their mobile phones to ask for help when they need it, as the extraordinary results of Crisis Text Line—a mobile service that connects those in need with help—have demonstrated.

Getting a grip on the precise numbers for how many young people have devices and how much time they spend on which activities can be tricky. The numbers vary according to which study you read, but overall they show a clear upward trend in recent years. According to a 2018 report by Common Sense Media, 89 percent of teens owned their own smartphone, compared with 41 percent in 2012.[2] A 2018 study conducted by the Pew Research Center found that 95 percent of young people aged thirteen to seventeen in the United States have or have access to a smartphone.[3] Data from other parts of the world also reflect high rates of access to devices. For example, 56 percent of children in the United Kingdom use smartphones to go online daily, and 82 percent of children in Brazil use phones to access the internet.[4] In Canada, nearly 60 percent of young people own a mobile phone.[5] In Switzerland, it's 98 percent.[6] The exact rates reported in these studies will vary a bit, depending on the exact question the researchers asked. But the message is the same across cultures: most kids in wealthy countries have regular access to digital devices and use them a lot—more and more over time.

There is reason to worry about inequities in the digital world, but access to phones is fairly widespread in wealthy countries. According to the 2018 Pew report, "smartphone ownership is nearly universal among teens of different genders, races, ethnicities, and socioeconomic backgrounds" in the United States.[7] The same is true in many other countries, such as those in Western Europe and East Asia. But smartphones are not the only screens young people use. The Pew study also found that 84 percent of all teens say they have or have access to a game console at home, with higher shares (92 percent) among boys than among girls (75 percent).[8] While wealthier families are more likely to own game consoles, ownership among lower-income families is catching up in recent years. Another screen that facilitates the digital lives of young people is a desktop or laptop computer, with 88 percent of teens reporting access to such devices at home; the percentage is higher for wealthier families with advanced educational degrees.[9]

Taken together, the data suggest that young people are spending a lot of time each day on digital devices. Over the past few decades, the amount of time spent online has been steadily increasing. Nearly half (45 percent, to be exact) of teens say they use the internet "almost constantly," according to the 2018 Pew Research study.[10] That number has nearly doubled from a survey a few years before, when

24 percent said they were using the internet "almost constantly."[11] Another 44 percent said they go online several times a day.[12] These responses are consistent with the findings of other large surveys and qualitative research: nine out of ten teens go online at least several times a day. Several researchers have been studying this phenomenon for decades and writing reports about it every few years. Their findings have been borne out time and again: as the years pass, tweens and teens spend more time, on more devices, doing more things. The same is true for adults. Nevertheless, these basic numbers are only part of the story about the question of screen time and parenting.

If you remember just one thing from this chapter on screen time, it would be this: the *way* young people use their screens is more important than simply *how much time* they spend on those devices. Young people are using digital devices in various ways that are often surprising to adults. Digital activities and usage patterns differ widely and can include watching shows, gaming, messaging, learning, and activism.

To get started, we offer a few data points on two activities that parents often seem particularly curious about when it comes to screen time: entertainment and social media usage. Teens spend about nine hours a day using entertainment and social media, according to the most recent large-scale study in the United States.[13] Tweens are not far behind, at about six hours a day.[14] These figures do not include any time at school or doing homework. The kids' digital time could be spent watching TV or movies (whether on a traditional TV screen or streamed on a laptop over Amazon or Netflix), playing video games (on a separate console, a smartphone, or a PC), hanging out on social media, or listening to music.

This study, conducted by researchers at Common Sense Media in 2015, shows that many types of behavior and usage patterns are masked by these overall numbers. Among both teens and tweens, about 6 percent report no time spent using entertainment and social media. On the other end of the spectrum, 11 percent of tweens and 26 percent of teens spent more than eight hours a day with this kind of digital media. That's more than a full-time job for these kids—and seven days a week rather than the typical five-day workweek.[15]

Social media drives some of the concerns parents have about screen time. Adoption of social media platforms has grown steadily over the years but is now slowing down in the United States, according to the latest statistics. Young people have been a key driver of social media and platform diversification, with Instagram and Snapchat gaining popularity recently since around 2017. Teens and tweens express a range of views about their experiences using social media. On the positive side, 81 percent of teens aged thirteen to seventeen say social media makes them feel more connected to friends, and 68 percent report that these platforms make them feel as if they have people who will provide emotional support in difficult times. On the negative side, 45 percent of teens state they feel overwhelmed by all the drama on social media, and a slightly lower percentage say they feel pressured to post certain types of content to make them look good to others. Not all young people can step back and think critically about their use of media, but some do—and most young people surveyed recognize that the effects of social media are neither uniformly good or bad. Their recognition of the dual nature of social media is an opening for discussion.[16]

One clear finding to emerge from these data is the ubiquity, the scale, and the increase in screen time for tweens and teens over the past few decades. The *way* that young people spend this large amount of time, outside school and on top of homework, has obvious consequences. The messages that they are receiving, how they interact with one another, the data they are creating about themselves, the risks they are running—all of these things matter a great deal to their development. At a minimum, it is incumbent on us as parents, along with the children's teachers and other mentors, to help them contextualize what they are doing and learning. And it makes sense that we would help them use this time productively where possible.

Younger children tend to have much less screen time per day. The data relating to this measure have been relatively stable since around 2010. A similar study by Common Sense Media, tracking the use of media by children from infancy to eight years of age, found that it averaged a bit over two hours per day.[17] While TV was still the most common screen type in this 2017 survey, mobile devices have been gaining ground fast. Two 2019 studies showing that very young children tended to spend more time online than was recommended laid the cause for this tendency at the feet of their parents.[18]

Although the gap is narrowing with time, wealthier parents are still more likely than poorer families to have access at home to high-speed internet. Other divides, including racial divisions, also persist for broadband service at home. As Pew reports, "Racial minorities, older adults, rural residents, and those with lower levels of education and income are less likely to have broadband service at home."[19]

A small majority of parents in the United States (55 percent) say that they set some limits on the amount of time that their children spend online during a given period. Some parents report that they set time restrictions as a consequence for bad behavior, but many others simply apply across-the-board limits on time online. Parents of younger children, including younger teens, are more likely to set time-based limits than are the parents of older teenagers.[20]

You might reasonably wonder how certain we are about the research on any given topic. For screen time, the amount of time our kids are spending online is very clear. In this respect, we are extremely confident. A few great researchers have spent more than a decade studying this issue and updating their research over time. The methodologies they use are sound, and the studies tend to find nearly the same results for similar populations. And the exact numbers don't really matter; what matters is the order of magnitude of screen time. In other words, we know that more and more of most kids' lives are mediated by devices.

So what's a parent to do about all this screen time? And to what degree is it a problem? These are thornier questions. The data are not as helpful in this respect. The short version is that moderate use of screens can be a benefit for most young people. On the other hand, there can also be a connection between high levels of screen time and anxiety, addiction, and aggression among young people. Higher levels of screen time can also be associated with obesity, unhealthy diet, depressive symptoms, and lower quality of life.

We understand that families are very different, from one to the next, in terms of their circumstances. Families with a great deal of privilege and means—and that includes our own households—have greater ability to manage the time spent online in their household. Families with two parents and fewer children have logistical advantages in this respect, too. For a single-parent household with multiple children with a wide range of ages, the advice in this chapter on limiting screen time may be much harder to follow. We get that. And there aren't easy answers in those cases, as the parents involved know, even with the best of intentions.

THE CONNECTED PARENTS' APPROACH

It may help you to know our basic philosophy of parenting with respect to kids and technology before we dispense any advice. We both have teenage children. We've sought to align our own parenting at home with what we've been learning from our work with the Youth and Media team at the Berkman Klein Center for Internet & Society.

For both of us, our work in this field has stemmed in part from trying to figure out the best way to parent our own children as they were growing up. John's spouse was in graduate school studying early childhood development when their first child was born. As researchers of the internet and digital media, both of us see the benefits of using technology in learning, connecting, and growing up. But those who study early childhood development, in particular, have some real concerns about screen time, especially for the youngest of children. So who's right?

Our philosophy has been to seek to gain the greatest benefits from digital media while mitigating its downsides. We have seen and experienced how technology can be a tool of empowerment that has sometimes allowed children to participate in civic life and engage with ideas and other people in ways otherwise not possible. And young people can use the technology as a lifeline to get the help they need in key moments. We seek a balance in terms of the approach we take with our children and our students.

We have found that most one-size-fits-all rules for screen time don't work well. We want young people to embrace the creativity and innovative spirit of the internet, the fun and vibrancy of (some) social media, and the excitement of the digital era. Young people can use new technologies to create new forms of art, develop skills that may earn them jobs in the future, and start new political and social movements that change the world. At the same time, many young people get pulled into counterproductive activities online. They don't always spend their screen time well or act using their best judgment. They can put themselves at risk in a variety of ways.

Connected parents work from the premise that children do need limits, both for technology usage and for other activities. Young people benefit when we define and enforce those limits, even as they press (and sometimes rage) against them. Rules and guidance need to change with the child's age and circumstances. While they can take different forms, rules always need to be clear and fairly enforced. Kids see through our ambivalence and lack of integrity faster than we realize. They have an amazing meter for recognizing insincerity and hypocrisy. We need to think through our approach in advance, communicate it as clearly as we can, stick to our beliefs as long as it's appropriate to do so, and adjust along the way.

Rules are much more easily set than enforced. Both of us are parents of young people with busy and complicated lives. Even as the data suggest that we should set some limits, especially for young children, we know that the complexities of life often get in the way. And if we can't always live up to the ideal and need to accept limitations on enforcement, some research suggests that the key is not only to set standards but also to have ongoing discussions about the reasoning and concerns behind them. At least then, young people are better informed about the risks they are taking if they decide to take advantage of the weak spots in their parents' monitoring abilities.

Connected parents listen to their children and discuss issues such as screen time and appropriate limits with them. When we pose questions to young people in national surveys and in focus groups, we include space for teens and tweens to share their own concerns about technology use. Young people themselves can and should have a voice in helping us understand their practices in an ongoing way that provides texture and context for the data that we collect more formally. For this reason, we urge connected parents to listen carefully to the lived experiences of the young people in their care.

We need to be the adults who set and enforce the rules. But our kids can help guide us along the way. They don't always get the decision-making authority, but we can learn a lot from them. They also appreciate being heard and understood, even when we end up disagreeing with them. Technological change has broken down certain boundaries and hierarchies. When managed with care, this change can form stronger connections between us and the young people in our lives. We should embrace these connections, which can help us improve how we ourselves teach and learn.

Technology isn't a separate category of parenting. The way our children interact with media is part and parcel of their complex lives. It is connected to nearly everything else: formal and informal learning, friendship, the development of civic life, the preparation for the workforce, and the way kids relate to institutions and one another. Your rules about technology will make sense to your children when the details are part of a coherent philosophy. The philosophy should be grounded in a real-world understanding of how much your kids value their digital devices and the connections they enable—especially whenever our adult perspectives differ from our children's.

Finally, our philosophy on how much time young people should spend using digital technologies turns in part on what they are doing when they are online. The studies of screen time help give us a sense of overall scale of kids' day-to-day exposure. But there's a difference between a ten-year-old spending several hours playing *Minecraft* and the same kid spending those same hours watching reruns of a sitcom on Netflix. The time spent on Netflix isn't necessarily harmful to our kids, but other activities just might be more creative and challenging and might lead to a happier, healthier childhood. This philosophy, grounded in sound research and years of practice, sets the frame for our specific advice.

OUR RECOMMENDATIONS

When you think about whether to set rules for your children in terms of time spent on digital devices, we urge you to consider this question more broadly: do you generally set any rules for your children? Unless you follow an extreme parenting philosophy, your answer is almost certainly yes. You don't let very young children use the hot stove. Young children can't cross the street on their own or walk to day care without you. You require them to get a certain amount of sleep (or at least you try really hard to get them to sleep). You ensure that they periodically eat something.

The connected parents' answer to whether young people need rules about their engagement with technology is yes. The real answer is a bit more complicated than that, but we start with the premise that too much of anything can lead to problems down the line and that you want to maximize the good things while minimizing those that cause harm. If your child spends half the night on the phone texting with friends and scrolling on social media, he won't be rested enough for school the next day. Or if your child spends the whole afternoon playing *Fortnite* rather than doing homework, her grades may suffer.

We have found that students actually want you to set some boundaries on screen time and the types of things they can do online. Even if (or more likely, when) they push back in the moment, they are well served by carefully set, consistently upheld limits. You have no doubt seen this phenomenon over and over again in parenting. Most young people need adults to limit their excesses and to show them a good pathway forward in life.

Let's start with the most basic of questions: How much time should they spend online? The answer depends a lot on the age of your child. Most experts suggest that virtually any kind of screen time for the very youngest children is not a good thing. Over time, it makes sense to give young people more freedom as they demonstrate that they can handle it. The American Academy of Pediatrics published an important revision of its screen time guidelines in 2016, and we agree with their latest recommendations for the youngest children:[21]

Birth to eighteen months: Avoid all screen media—phones, tablets, TVs, and computers—where possible. The academy and other researchers have found that lasting negative effects on children's development of language, reading ability, and short-term memory are possible at this age. Studies have also shown problems associated with sleep and attention. One caveat to this basic rule: video chatting or phone chatting with grandparents or far-away family or friends is fine. In fact, it is to be encouraged, for all sorts of good reasons unrelated to technology.

Eighteen months to two years: If you like, introduce some short clips, fifteen minutes a day at most, of some high-quality children's media. Watch them with your children. Whenever possible, don't use these devices as an electronic babysitter. We know that this advice is easier said than followed, especially for folks who have little backup parenting support and few childcare options. Children will recognize what you are doing with your devices, and they will want to participate, too. Your modeling from the start makes a huge difference.

Two to five years: The academy recommends that parents set a limit of no more than one hour a day of high-quality programming for children, though we would advise focusing more on the quality of the programming and your interactions with your children than on the precise amount of time involved. When they are watching, be sure to watch shows with them. Talk to them about what they're seeing. Give them context for what they are watching and how it connects to the world around them. Try to break up the exposure into discrete doses, rather than a solid block of time, and be sure to intersperse discussion, reading time, and other forms of direct human engagement with the screen time.

Our advice is to prioritize creative, unplugged playtime for your very young children, at least up through the toddler age. No evidence convinces us that extensive screen time at a very early age affords any advantage. And there are definitely reasons to think that sharp limits for babies and toddlers are likely to serve them well over time.

Some parents marvel at their toddler's seemingly innate ability to interact with technological devices. It's true. A very young child can zip through the interface of an iPad in a way that seems much more natural than a grandparent's first attempts. The child's facility has to do with many factors, one of which is the way that Apple and other big technology companies approach design. They design pathways that feel intuitive for younger minds.

As amazing as a toddler's ease with an iPad can seem, that's not a reason to believe that kids need to learn to use an iPad at age one, for fear that they will never get a job in Silicon Valley or will never compete in an increasingly digitized workplace. We've in fact been struck by how many of our colleagues who work in Silicon Valley and other tech hubs keep their kids far away from technology for as long as they can.[22] Some parents go as far as to enroll their children in Waldorf or Montessori schools, where tech is kept from kids for the entire school day. These parents know something about what it takes to succeed in the technology field, and early exposure to the latest apps doesn't make the list. Though not a scientific study, these decisions by Silicon Valley parents should at least make others reconsider their children's tech exposure.

Even from the very beginning of your child's life, you'll want to imagine how your child's technology use will progress throughout childhood. The connected parent doesn't necessarily have it all plotted out exactly, but having a general game plan makes sense. This exercise is particularly important for a reason that all experienced parents and teachers know well: it is much easier to set tighter limits early on and then relax them over time, as kids' behavior warrants, than it is to impose harsher limits after allowing certain freedoms.

The connected parent's strategy teaches and guides a young person along the trajectory of childhood. For virtually everyone born today, there will be a time in their infancy when they are not yet using screens themselves. And then one day, probably nearer the end of adolescence, they will have unfettered access to screens and all manner of digital technologies. Our job as the adults in their lives is to teach them good habits along the way so that they will be ready for the freedom they will enjoy as adults.

The parents' job is to adjust those boundaries over time. If the period from age zero to six is really about tight limits, you could consider the age range from about six through a child's tween years as a time to introduce some decision making. This idea may not seem totally feasible to you, but we started in our own households with the idea of half an hour a day of any type of screen time for our young kids and then scaled up from there over time. By the time they are in high school, it's almost impossible to restrict their activity. They will just route around your controls, and you will undermine their trust. Spend the time up till then helping them develop the skills they need to make good decisions in their digital life. Here are our suggested approaches to the next age ranges.

Six to Twelve

Start small and work your way up. Thirty minutes a day for a six-year-old may be reasonable, heading up toward two hours a day (especially on a weekend day) for a twelve-year-old. Keep in mind that this is the age range when many schools will start to require your child to do things online, including doing homework and submitting it online. Many students will obtain their first mobile device during this time—or will see their friends get one and wish for one of their own. As the limits change, consider the various ways in which the limits might work. For example, you may be more permissive with time on screens over the weekend or on long bus trips. Rules that are clear and flexible in the right ways can help you build and maintain a trusting relationship with your child. Again, the quality of their time online is just as important as, if not more important than, the sheer time. For a ten-year-old, two hours spent on learning-related game apps may be more productive than two hours spent watching reruns of *iCarly* or, in the case of Jamie in the vignette at the start of this chapter, *The Office*.

Thirteen to Fifteen

Parents can scale up from two hours per day to no more than four hours per day. Research shows that one to two hours of screen time per day is often associated with positive social-emotional behavior, with problems reported in some instances when the amount goes above four hours a day.[23] You still need some rules during this period, but they are much harder to enforce. This age range is probably the last one for which you can actually manage any type of real limits on young people's activities (and many kids by this point feel that their period of freedom is long overdue, but every child is different).

Many kids have mobile devices at this stage. Kids in their early teens often begin using a wider range of applications, games, and social media. Many students first join social media sites in this age range, in part because most major social media companies often require users to state that they are at least thirteen years old before they can create their accounts—though, obviously, companies have limited ability to enforce these age restrictions. This age range is often the time when online trouble first occurs for young people. For example, they might experience their first bullying (either as the one who bullies or the one who is bullied).

Nevertheless, adults find it much harder to monitor mobile devices today than did parents of an earlier era, when the family might have kept a shared desktop computer in a common area of a house. Even as it becomes harder to enforce limits, you still need some rules if you can enforce them well. Many parents will retain the right to log in to their children's accounts and check their text messages. Such a practice is likely to be unpopular with your children and conflicts with their need for more privacy as they grow older. But you may have some opportunities to engage in productive conversations about online behavior as a result of having these sometimes-fraught interactions with your children over your ability to log in to their accounts. Gradually, these conversations about screen time and device usage will become more important and effective than strict rules and enforcement schemes.

Sixteen and Onward

In a child's life, there's a point at which most parents won't be able to enforce many, if any, controls. For many parents, that point is somewhere around age fifteen or sixteen. At this stage, the connected parent focuses on providing advice and context for what their teens are experiencing. You might also want to share your own struggles with limiting your digital device usage—a great conversation starter in our own parenting experience! By seeing what your child's friends and their parents are posting, you may also learn about important things happening in your child's life. This knowledge may help you have good conversations with your child. You are still a crucial person for your children, even if they seem to want you to act more like a potted plant in the corner of a room than as an active and visible participant in their lives. Whatever your situation, don't abdicate too soon.

WE HAVE TWO final pieces of advice. First, we have emphasized rules and enforcement quite a bit throughout the chapter. But the connected-parenting approach means you need first and foremost to keep communication channels open. In our experience, it is as important to have conversations about the rules and the rationale behind them as it is to set them. More often than not, listening carefully, empathetically, and with an open mind to our children can help parents gain surprising insights.

An anecdote from Urs's family might illustrate the point. One of the norms in Urs's home is that he and the rest of his family put down their phones during family dinners. They never stipulated it as an explicit rule, but it became the default over time. One evening, however, Ananda (a teenager at the time) asked for an exemption to this unwritten rule, with the explanation that she wanted to be there for her friend, who was not doing well. As this story shows, the best uses of digital technology sometimes require parents to see things from their children's perspective and occasionally to make exceptions to the rules.

Second, for children of all ages, we urge you to emphasize one rule about time and screens: kids need to get off devices an hour before they intend to fall asleep. The absolute minimum is that they shut off their screens at least a half hour before bedtime. One of the clearest findings from the research is that excessive media use can lead to too little sleep for kids. This issue is most acute among teenagers, who tend to get far less than the steady nine hours and fifteen minutes of sleep that they need each night. Screen usage is a major culprit. You have to set a firm rule that favors sleep over late-night binge-watching and video game playing. And then you have to follow the rule yourself, or it will backfire on you.

Now that we've set out some rules of thumb, let us acknowledge the many reasons you might choose to deviate from this overall plan. For example, you may need to adjust your screen-time limits for your child's overall development picture. Some young people are thriving everywhere—they have plenty of good friends, enjoy a positive and appropriate sense of self, are doing well in school and activities, and are connected to family and teachers. For these kids, more permissive limits may be appropriate. But for other young people, who are struggling in one area or another, some firm redirection of their time may be in order.

What if your ten-year-old child attends a school with a 1:1 iPad program (a school program in which each child has an iPad), where all the schoolwork is done on tablets? Or what if your school has gone all virtual, as many schools around the world had to do during the COVID-19 pandemic that began in early 2020? Plainly, an hour or even two hours a day may not be sufficient for your child to do all the homework. Kids need time to get their homework done. Likewise, a young person who has a challenge seeing or hearing may need a digital device for much of the day for assistance.

The connected-parenting approach doesn't call for absolutes with exceptional circumstances such as these. Parenting arrangements may be part of the equation, too: with a single parent working two jobs, the enforcement of any kinds of limits may be more challenging than in households with multiple caregivers and more flexible work schedules. Homeschooled students and those who are autodidacts (kids who teach themselves really well) may be learning a ton on YouTube—and that may be just exactly how they should be spending much of their time.

As with most things in life and parenting, it's about finding a healthy balance and then staying true to your word. Think through a series of questions as you review your plan for online time. Are your children doing well in school? Do they seem to have a healthy and positive social life? Are they getting the recommended amount of sleep, exercising regularly, and eating healthily? When they are interacting with media, is it generally a positive experience? If things are generally going well, you probably don't have to worry too much about how much time they are spending online. If any answers to the preceding questions seem off to you or to other adults in your child's life, then you should go back and review their screen habits. And when you set a plan in place, stick to it—consistency is essential—and avoid hypocrisy at all costs. We are big believers in the importance of consistency in rule-setting and explaining any appropriate variances from the norm. You need to live by the rules you set for your kids, or they will see right through you.

COMMON QUESTIONS

You might still have some related questions on your mind, so we offer some answers to these common questions on hot-button topics.

At what age should a young person get a smartphone? How about a computer?

In John's house a few years ago, when his children were still young, he and his wife made a family decision that twelve was the right age to get a mobile device and that the start of high school (roughly age fourteen in the United States) was the right age for the kids to get their own laptop. John and his wife based their decision about these ages on the Goldilocks principle that this book advocates for connected parents. They wanted their children to be reachable when the kids were traveling between home and school and other activities and to be able to connect with friends and mentors online. But they didn't think the children needed to be glued to their phones earlier than that. There was no magic to the age John and his wife selected; they just applied their best judgment based on the data available to them and the circumstances of their family.

In light of some of the most recent data on mobile phone access, your children may start asking about a phone at around age nine. The right age for access will, of course, be up to you and your situation. This issue is as much about a family's finances as it is about anything else. For many families, another mobile phone on the plan is going to be prohibitively expensive. A good plan that many families use is for a student to get a mobile phone at the age that he or she can do a bit of work outside the home to contribute to the cost of the service plan.

What kinds of screen time are more beneficial for young people?

We take a broad view of the benefits that young people can derive from their time using screens. For young children, TV programs such as *Sesame Street* have been designed to teach them empathy and the skills needed to thrive in a complex, diverse world. We consider this time well spent, especially when children and caregivers watch together and talk about each lesson during and after the show. We are also fans of *Dora the Explorer*, whose adventures teach kids about problem-solving, sensible risk-taking, and human kindness. The *Curious George* TV series and movies are classics that promote children's curiosity and exploration and a greater understanding of right and wrong. *Minecraft* is a building game, a bit like Lego blocks, that can entertain kids for hours while engaging their creativity. Scratch, a visual programming language designed for kids, has taught many millions of young people to code. Moreover, time spent independently exploring topics of interest online, texting friends, and engaging in identity play can all be hugely valuable to young people as they grow older. For teens, their exploration of the world of online activism and their abilities to seek out information, including how-to videos, can lead to lifelong value. For many more ideas, consult Common Sense Media, which reviews screen time options by age and type.

What are the best practices when it comes to using devices at night?

This one is really simple: using a digital device close to bedtime can undeniably delay anyone's ability to sleep soundly. What's also abundantly clear, most kids, and nearly all teens, get less sleep than they need to thrive. Their brains need the special kind of downtime that sleep affords. The rule in our families is that there are no screens allowed for a half hour before one's set bedtime. (Some researchers argue that an hour, or even longer, before sleep is better.) We also urge charging your devices in a place other than right beside the bed, to avoid temptation!

What about family contracts and community contracts related to screen time?

Family contracts are a common idea: all the family members enter into a contract, agreeing to each person's screen time limits, before access is granted to the network or a new device makes its way into a child's hands. These contracts can work, but we've observed that parents seldom limit themselves enough, so the contracts seem one-sided to kids. Lopsided agreements rarely work. In fact, they usually backfire. So if you do try a family contract, then be sure to give your-self equal treatment!

Another idea is the community contract: a group of families or an entire grade at school enters into an agreement. For example, everyone agrees that no child gets a mobile phone until, say, age twelve or the seventh grade, whichever comes later. You can imagine many variations on this theme. If you think such a contract might work with your friend group or extended family, go for it. Remember how important the peer group is for young people, especially in the tween and teen years. By helping your child build a positive peer group, you will help ensure that every day, your messages about screen time and online activities will be reinforced by positive peer role models rather than undercut at every turn.

It's tricky to judge the best quantity of time spent online, since the quality of the digital material varies so widely. For sure, some amount is too much at every age. You probably agree, or you wouldn't have picked up this book. Our central message is that it helps to make a plan early, make sure that it's clear to your children, carefully explain any deviations from the rules, and stick to your plan.

One final note before we move on: remember that our kids are watching us. All the time. For many young people, the most powerful role models through childhood are their parents. We hope so, anyway. That means that your own digital practices matter a great deal. So put down the phone, grab your child by the hand, and head outside for a walk or a game in the park. It'll be good for everyone.

KEY TAKEAWAYS

The Goldilocks principle should guide the connected parent's approach to screen time.

Large-scale studies show that few young people regularly use digital devices so much that their usage has harmful effects. Precise guides are hard to come by and vary according to the age and experience of the young person.

Common sense is a wonderful guide when it comes to screen time. If your children are thriving in other areas of their lives, and their screen time strikes you as moderate, then all is probably well. If your children are having other kinds of problems in their lives and spend a very large amount of time online, then a conversation is in order about cutting back or setting limits.

Limits on screen time should be based on age and other contextual factors. We agree with the American Academy of Pediatrics that the youngest babies should not be exposed to screens for extended periods, other than for the purposes of connecting with distant friends and relatives or the like. As they grow, screen time can increase. Set limits early, and relax them over time.

Except for the smallest babies, quality of screen time matters much more than the sheer quantity. We are much less focused on precise amounts of screen time than with the context surrounding the use of screens. With younger children, the connected parent will watch TV or use screens with the child, engaging together with programming that is age-appropriate. For older children, keep an eye on the types of activities as well as the quantity, and remain in conversation about screen time and usage.

Technological limitations on screen time can work at younger ages, but these controls are much less effective with tweens and especially with teens. Most internet service providers offer technical ways to limit the use of the internet, for instance. These parental controls allow you, mostly for free, to limit the amount of time someone spends online and the user's type of use in your home. In the teen years, technological limits are virtually useless and, worse, tend to undercut the relationship between caregiver and child. Avoid technological controls that undermine trust; instead, work to develop positive habits that will persist after the child has left your home.

Screen time is not necessarily all bad! A moderate amount—say, an hour or two a day—has been shown in large-scale studies to be associated with positive social and emotional behavior.[24]

CHAPTER TWO

Social Life

"WHAT'S UP WITH all the typing?"

"I'm just texting with a friend, Dad."

Rachel is on the couch, staring into her phone, smiling occasionally. Every few moments, she taps a message into the phone. Her headphones are in, so her dad has to ask her again, louder this time, to get an answer.

"Who are you texting with?"

"I'm texting with Deanna, Dad."

"Who's Deanna?"

"Oh, just a girl I'm talking to in a game I'm playing."

"What do you mean? You met her during a game?"

"Well, she was in a group chat I'm in with a bunch of other kids. We were messaging each other within a game. She's super nice."

Ding. Ding. Ding. Rachel's iPhone keeps pinging away.

"You mean to tell me you've never met her?"

"Dad. I've met her. Just online."

"You've never seen her face-to-face?"

"Well, no. But I know a lot about her."

"You'd better watch yourself. You don't know if she's really a girl your age. You don't know what she really wants from you."

"*Dad . . .*"

OUR CHILDREN FIND it unremarkable to meet others and maintain relationships solely online. The group chat in which Rachel met Deanna happened to be a messaging function within a game. Sometimes, kids will first make friends online and chat on screens long before they ever see one another face-to-face. Sometimes, kids will conduct the relationship entirely online, without ever meeting in person. Much of the time, relationships have both an online and an offline component to them, but not always. These modes of interaction strike most parents as foreign at a minimum, if not downright risky.

When you see a group of teenagers gathered on a street corner, it is often a curious sight. All five of them might be staring into their phones, never exchanging an audible word with each other, even though they stand next to one another. Same thing if they are clustered together in a restaurant or in someone's living room. How could this be? Wouldn't it make more sense to put down their phones and talk to one another? What's their rationale for not doing so?

The amount of time kids spend online with their friends can baffle us as adults. They even stay glued to their screens when they are *with* their friends, sharing the same physical space. WhatsApp group chats, Snaps (the messages created and sent on Snapchat), Insta messages (the messages created and sent on Instagram), instant messaging within a game . . . the number of ways that young people connect online these days can seem hard to keep up with.

Many parents worry that all this time online makes their children less social and less able to interact with one another offline. Some adults worry that kids will lose the ability to connect face-to-face. That's a difficult concern to study—social ability is difficult to measure—but it's on many people's minds. We are more optimistic about the situation than many parents we hear from, but we understand where these concerns come from.

One insight can help parents see things a bit more the way our children do: we as adults often break things down into screen time and face-to-face time. That breakdown doesn't make as much sense to young people. For kids, it is not online life and offline life. It's just life. It's one overall experience. For many young people (particularly those in well-off countries), online and offline are more or less seamlessly connected. Remember, many children have never known anything different from life with smartphones that instantly connect them to billions of other humans and platforms, whereas we as their parents grew up fearing the costs of long-distance phone calls and remember the funny noises made by modems and the dial-up internet. Kids are used to connecting with people online. Much of the time, they are used to engaging with their friends through social media *more often* than they do face-to-face. That's the backbone of many friendships these days.

There is some good news to alleviate at least some of this worrying. The time spent engaging with screens may often seem excessive, but it isn't necessarily undermining kids' social skills. Our children are learning, connecting with one another, and creating important friendships through those screens. Of course, most parents will find it helpful to set some age-appropriate guidelines on screen time, as we argue throughout this book. What's more, young people must learn to avoid risky online habits in the social context—things that would put their safety or their privacy at risk. And no doubt, you should be a part of their social life online (especially if your kids are younger) to help them navigate this tricky period in their lives—which can be more complicated in the digital era than in the past. But we can't declare that this generation of kids will lack social skills because they grew up with social media.

WHAT THE RESEARCH SHOWS

Before we dig into some of the data that inform our thinking about young people's lives in the age of social media, let's take two steps back to examine what we mean by *social life*. We use the term as a shortcut to describe young people's interpersonal relationships with people in their immediate surroundings or the public. This broad definition includes relationships between a child and family members, teachers, and peers, to name just a few. As in the case of relationships with parents, teachers, school friends, or sports teammates, these social connections are often initiated offline, but are increasingly mediated—and even formed, as Rachel's story illustrates—through digital technology and online interactions.

A wealth of research from different disciplines provides deep insight into the social life of young people today. It describes the various types of interpersonal relationships that young people form; how such relationships play out across gender, age, and socioeconomic backgrounds; how interpersonal factors define friendships; and how interpersonal relationships influence a young person's mental and physical health. For the purpose of this chapter, we narrow things down by focusing on peer relationships (specifically friendships), how social media shapes our children's social lives, and how young people feel about their tech-mediated relationships. This frame of reference yields some of the data points underlying the advice offered in the next section.

Big Picture: Technology, Social Life, and Digital Friendships

Common Sense Media offers a starting point for learning how social media is shaping young people's lives. Here are two highlights from its "Social Media, Social Life 2018" study (which focuses on thirteen- to seventeen-year-olds):

- Digital devices and social media play a key role in teens' social lives today, with usage growing dramatically over the years. In 2012, when a previous survey was conducted, 34 percent of teens used social media more than once a day; in 2018, that number rose to 70 percent, with 16 percent reporting that they use it "almost constantly."[1] The increase in smartphone ownership and access has propelled this growth.
- When asked about their preferred way to communicate with friends, teens put texting (35 percent) over face-to-face communication (32 percent), followed by social media (16 percent) and video chatting (10 percent). The trend is clear: the proportion of teens who say their favorite method of communication is "in person" dropped from 49 percent in 2012 to less than a third in 2018.

Some additional interesting clues come from a 2018 UK Safer Internet Centre report titled "Digital Friendships." The report confirms the importance of online activity for young people:

- The most popular platforms eight- to seventeen-year-olds used to communicate with their friends on a daily basis are YouTube (41 percent), WhatsApp (32 percent), Snapchat (29 percent),

Instagram (27 percent), and Facebook or Messenger (26 percent). Teens are more likely to communicate with friends online than are younger children.

- Some 67 percent of thirteen- to seventeen-year olds say they would feel isolated without having access to digital technology that allows them to connect with their friends, and 49 percent state that they have made friends online that they wouldn't have met otherwise.[2]

The report also makes a few interesting points about how young people express themselves online. Perhaps unsurprising to parents, emoji are the most popular expressions, followed by slang terms and facial expressions in selfies. Furthermore, the report highlights how social media shapes the expectations of young people's offline relationships. In particular, the survey responses highlight how important it is for young people to be included in group chats by their friends and to receive a friend's response once the friend has seen a message they sent.

Given the increasing significance of social media usage by young people and the possible effects on their social life, let's take a closer look at some of the dynamics at play.

Zoom In: Social Media Platforms, Usage, and Diversification

The social media services and apps that young people prefer change every few years, with some platforms persisting longer than others. For example, Facebook, founded in 2004, has experienced some recent declines in relative popularity among young people, particularly in the United States, yet it still has a huge presence and today boasts more than a billion users worldwide. In contrast, some parents may remember MySpace. Consider the difference between MySpace's trajectory and Facebook's. MySpace was founded only a few months before Facebook (in the fall of 2003) and was more popular for a while, yet it has since completely fallen off the map.

Facebook is a particularly important example because of its reach, persistence, and power in the online marketplace. The platform has been a staple of social life for the past decade and a half. In 2018, however, it fell in the United States from first place in terms of services used down to fourth place, according to Pew Research Center. Facebook ranked behind YouTube (number one), Instagram (number two—a service that Facebook owns), and Snapchat (number three). Twitter, Tumblr, and Reddit round out the list of the top seven social media services used by teens in the United States in 2018. Internationally, platforms such as WhatsApp and WeChat play a large role as well. The point is obvious: the nature and use of platforms by young people changes over time. Researchers at the Pew Research Center have been conducting excellent long-range studies that show this change very clearly.[3]

When it comes to young people's social lives, the trend that researchers call *platform diversification* is one of the most interesting developments in the social media space. As Sandra Cortesi at the Berkman Klein Center explains, young people are now using different social media platforms for different reasons. For example, young users consider the audiences they want to reach, the experiences they want to have, their own and others' preferences across social contexts, and the features of the platforms—including the perceived intimacy and privacy associated with them. As parents, we should pay attention to the diversity of platforms our kids use, too. Research shows that young people engage in a wide range of activity online. Sometimes, they are expressing the same identity that they present when they are face-to-face with someone. At other times, they present a different facet of their identity online. They may also curate different features of their personalities and lives on separate platforms.[4]

Young people may even curate multiple identities within the same platform, as the Youth and Media team at Berkman Klein Center has shown. For instance, it is common for a young person to have multiple accounts on Instagram. One account may use the person's real name, or a close approximation, and map more or less to the kid's customary public identity in day-to-day life. Another account might be a *finsta*, or fake insta, and feature, say, a meaner or tougher or more sarcastic personality. This finsta is typically shared with only a small, private audience of that young person's closest and most trusted friends.

For some students, this multiplicity of platforms and accounts allows them to try out expressions of different forms of sexuality or gender. Nonbinary young people (those who do not identify with a gender binary of masculine or feminine) can find support and room for crucial self-expression as they explore their gender and sexuality in ways they feel they cannot at home or in school. Especially for young people who perceive their parents, teachers, faith community, or peers as intolerant, these online communities can be affirming— even lifesaving.

Social Life Online and Experiences

What experiences—both positive and negative—are young people having with social media? Over the past few years, researchers from many disciplines have started to look into this question, approaching it from different vantage points. Several studies have examined the role of social media on youth's well-being, for instance, by investigating the relationship between social media usage and depressive symptoms, or understanding how social media usage is linked to cyberbullying and the very serious consequences it might have. This section will focus on what young people themselves say about their experiences with social media, social life, and digital friendships in particular.

Some of the key insights come from the Pew Center study we described in Chapter 1. The study reports that teens generally say that social media helps strengthen friendships and can offer a resource for emotional support, but it can also lead to drama and the pressure to post certain types of content. Overall, teens associate their social media usage with more positive than negative emotions, more feelings of inclusion than exclusion, and more feelings of confidence than insecurity, according to the survey.[5]

Data from the 2018 UK Digital Friendship report also show that the majority of young people have positive experiences and interactions online. For instance, 68 percent of young people said that chatting with their friends can cheer them up, and most teens reported that something online made them feel happy (89 percent), excited (82 percent), or inspired (74 percent) in the last week.[6] However, like the data from Pew, the UK report also confirms that many young people have negative online experiences, including bullying or feeling excluded by others.

To round out our survey, let's take a look at a study published in 2019. It examines whether the increasing amount of time young people spend on social media affects their well-being.[7] Using a large-scale representative data panel, the researchers conclude that social media use *is not* a strong predictor of life satisfaction among adolescent users.

Taken together, these studies should give some relief to all of us who worry about the negative long-term effects of social media on the well-being of the next generation. That said, we need to keep in mind that social media can hurt the mental or physical health of a child. As with all statistics, even if the numbers might look encouraging at the aggregate level, they are of limited help in predictions about the experiences of a single individual.

Social Life and Skills

Watching their kids spending so much time on digital devices and online, many parents are worried that young people are largely driven by instant gratification (for instance, the number of likes generated by a certain image-and-caption combo on Instagram). Parents fear that their children might not acquire the social skills necessary to successfully deal face-to-face with adults like teachers and employers later in life. Catherine Steiner-Adair, a clinical psychologist and author, is among the cohort of experts who contend that kids who spend so much time with texting and online communication are missing out on acquiring critical social skills. Most of these communications take place in what Steiner-Adair calls a "nonverbal disabled context," where body language, facial expression, and small vocal reactions are largely muted.[8]

Other researchers approach the topic from a different angle by taking a broader look at social and emotional skills. Experts in social-emotional learning often refer to the *big five* model of skills that students need to learn: conscientiousness, agreeableness, emotional stability, openness, and extraversion. These skills are more often learned by young people through a range of interactions rather than merely taught in a top-down way in school. Arguably, social media can help with the development of each of these categories of social-emotional skills. Social media and other online interactions, including gaming, can contribute to a young person's development of these big five skills by helping them with open-mindedness, task performance, and engagement with others.[9]

Beyond the question of social skills, navigating one's social life extensively through digital technologies might help with a different set of skills: those that might be relevant for young people as they become participants in the digital economy down the road. To be sure, young people differ in their online abilities and activities, and, for instance, those from more privileged backgrounds incorporate digital technology often in a more informed way. Our focus group interviews also reveal that young people from a variety of backgrounds have developed sophisticated social media strategies.

For example, they curate content for different audiences, select their social media platforms according to context and purpose, and experiment with various forms of creative expression to build their own audiences.

The Disinhibition Effect

Let's return briefly to the topic of social skills. One of our behavioral blinds spots in social media is due to a phenomenon called the *disinhibition effect*.[10] One of the simplest rules of online life is the hardest for people of all ages to learn: that they may do things on a screen or another device that they would not do when another person is right in front of them. We all are capable of being less inhibited if we are typing something into a device rather than facing someone. We are capable of typing or posting something that we will later regret, that is meaner or harsher than we would be comfortable saying directly to someone else.

For teenagers, this disinhibition effect is exacerbated by the fact that their brains are not yet fully formed. They can be inclined to take more risk than they should, especially in the heat of the moment. Combine this risk-taking, a youthful inability to think through long-term consequences, and the general disinhibition effect, and you may have an occasionally unhealthy dynamic. In their social lives, young people today can run risks, to others and to their own privacy, in ways that previous generations could not.

Social media and messaging apps are always at hand for our young people today. School-age children used to have to sleep on an interaction before they saw the person the next day. That's no longer the case. If there's an altercation during school, then the response might come during the afternoon and a counter-response that evening—all in an online, semipublic space for an entire social group to observe (but potentially not for any *adults* to observe). Young people have difficulty understanding that their public interactions have greater consequences than their private exchanges do. What they say to another person in one moment can easily be shared with others and spiral into a much larger issue than was initially intended.

That said, the young people we have spoken to in focus groups and interviews are often somewhat aware of the issue. Some of them have developed interesting strategies to deal with challenges in the heat of the moment. These strategies include turning off their phones, logging out of an app, calling a friend, and taking a screenshot and showing it to a person they feel close to. The most sophisticated young people are aware of how long-lasting and shareable things online can be. Still, when the moment is right, a conversation with your kids about the potentially long-term public dissemination of their interactions might provide an opportunity for some helpful guidance.

"Smartphones Are Destroying a Generation"

A few years ago, much of the advice about kids revolved around the idea that they were somehow not as smart as the previous generations. We did not find this theory compelling then, and we do not find it compelling today. A prominent line of thinking today takes a similar tack: smartphones are destroying a generation. This theory considers the rising popularity of the iPhone and connects that rise to various other trends: kids dating less often, having less sex, feeling more lonely, and getting less sleep. Other observers link the use of the smartphone to the rise in anxiety among young people and the increase in rates of suicide. Some of these dynamics do show up in the data. There is little doubt that kids in the United States are more anxious today than in the past, more prone to depression, and more likely to take their own lives. These are terrifying facts. We should— and do—worry about them.

The weakness in the theory that pins all these social ills on the smartphone lies in the lack of evidence of causation. No doubt some of these correlations look very strong. Some of the theory is compelling. And some of it may prove to be true over time. But there is much more work to be done before we pin, say, the changes in teenage sexuality on kids' use of the smartphone.

Social media can certainly contribute to anxiety and depression for young people. The feeling that everyone else's life is much better than yours—as seen on Instagram or Facebook—can be challenging for a young person. But other factors are at play here too: the stress of college admissions and the challenges of a changing job market, for instance, no doubt play a role as well. As researchers, we study this topic because we care about kids and their development. We seek to understand these dynamics and to track them as they change. Along the way, we resist hyperbole (such as "dumbest generation" and "destroying a generation"—even as we know this language does sell books and attract clicks!). We know that older generations have fairly consistently feared and derided the practices of younger generations, especially in terms of their social lives. Rather than succumb to fears, we prefer to draw with care from the soundest data we can find to guide parents and teachers. We defer to you, as parents, in terms of what you decide to do with the data and advice we offer.

The Bottom Line

Research shows that parents use a wide range of approaches with their children when it comes to social media use. They try methods like sharp limits on time, technical controls, shared use of the technologies, and lots of talking about what works best. Research also shows that the young people best able to cope with the challenges and opportunities of digital life are most likely to have parents who have used a balanced approach featuring a combination of strategies. It is this combined approach that lies at the heart of the connected-parenting theory we advance throughout this book.

THE CONNECTED PARENTS' APPROACH

Our philosophy on the social lives of young people online today is the same as what we'd say to an adult: a balance makes sense. In a fulfilling friendship, you might imagine a mix of ways to interact with someone you care about. Depending on life circumstances, you might meet a friend for a walk, a coffee, or dinner in real life. You follow what's going on with your friend's family on Facebook and smile at the photos posted on Instagram. Texting or calling occasionally might help you to reconnect or plan for the next time you'll see that person in real life. Our children should pursue something similar in their social lives—most likely, they already do. Of course, this type of approach is much easier for young people of privilege to pursue than it is for those whose circumstances are much more challenging from day to day.

The ability to socialize (online and face-to-face) is itself a skill that our children will need to master. Like it or not, their lives are being led in part online. Their peers (and their bosses and those who report to them later in life) will expect them to interact via a digital device. The exact format and application may change, but the basic mode will probably be the same. They need to gain positive skills as they are growing up, as they do in any other arena. The modes of engagement are getting more sophisticated over time as platforms multiply. Youth have begun to learn how to manage audiences and reputations across different platforms, just as we as adults must if we are engaged in professional life today.

We want our children to have healthy, good, strong, lasting social relationships. It is essential that we give them the time and space to develop their identities in a healthy way as they grow up. If a healthy social life is our overarching goal in this regard, we must also note that the space where these relations are formed, lived, and reconfigured has shifted—in part—for our children's generation. The space in which they do this dynamic and important work of growing up has moved from the exclusively physical realm to an interconnected series of spaces.

This logical progression leads to the conclusion that we must also adjust our own expectations of what *balance* means. We may start out thinking that the balance should be very heavily skewed toward the face-to-face. For some of our children, this may not be the right balance. Each generation must face up to these changing realities for their children. The parents of kids growing up in the 1980s in the United States had to cope with how much time kids spent at the mall; perhaps for a previous generation or in other cultures such as Europe, it was the cinema or the dance hall. These realities must shape our philosophy too, even if our preference from our initial instinct or experience might be slightly different. Put another way, our view of the right thing needs to be carefully examined in light of the lived experiences of our kids—just as our parents had to do when it came to our own generation.

OUR RECOMMENDATIONS

A key to connected parenting is to keep an open line of communication with our children to the greatest degree possible. This advice is easier for some parents to follow than for others. It is easier with some children than with others, even in the same household. Before you roll your eyes, please recall that even the most recalcitrant kids do want their parents' help and approval on a deep level. You have more to say about their social life and social media usage than you may think. And you may have more to learn from them than you think, too.

Find ways to talk to them about their social life online, just as you do with other important topics of growing up. Your children might not want to talk to you about it, but you have to keep the line of communication open. Even if you can't get a conversation going about specific friends, talk in generalities and help them to think through the role that social media plays in their social life. Help them think through the first impression they will make when they meet someone online before they meet them in person. That will happen over and over in their lives if they go to a new school, a camp, even a new job later on in life.

You don't need to be an expert about each new app to give good advice about their online social life. Engage your children by using your common sense. Help them see how, socially, online life is a mixed bag. For some children, online experiences help a great deal with developing relationships; for others, the experiences can lead to misunderstandings and hurt. You do need to be credible in the conversation and to know at least the core facts that we present here about what is going on for kids online. We hope that this book, and the website and Facebook groups associated with our work on the Youth and Media team, will provide some data and talking points that you might use to seed conversations with your children and keep you credible.

By knowing the basics we have shared in this chapter, you at least have some openings for discussion. You might ask about how their friends might be curating messages for different audiences on these social media platforms. You might talk about how you notice that your own friends on Facebook only present the beautiful pictures from their life and not the challenging moments.

Just as important, be sure to listen as well as talk. Your children undoubtedly know more about the latest applications and how they and their peers are using them than you do. No matter how much you read about the research, you are probably not spending as much time on screens and trying out new apps as they are. When you ask questions and listen, your children might be inclined to reveal insights about their experiences growing up partly online, partly offline.

All of us, as adults, can learn a lot from young people about social media—about their lives, how the technologies work, and how to parent effectively. You also have much to contribute to their learning. You could perhaps tell your children about interesting people you've been following or reading about online. And we urge you to report back to your fellow parents on the Youth and Media Facebook group to share what you are learning!

The Monitoring Debate

Parents have long argued about whether to monitor their child's social media use. That argument has raged not only among parents, but also between parents and their children. Of course, most young people want the independence that comes with an unmonitored social media experience. Parents want to be able to check in on what their kids are doing, mostly for the right reasons of keeping them safe and to offer good guidance when things get sticky. (And let's face it: you may just be curious to know if they are dating someone new or if their friends are getting into trouble.) We've had the same debates in our own households.

The data show that many parents do find one way or another to monitor their children's use of social media—some methods more technical than others. Some parents (a small majority, in a recent Pew Research Center study) will occasionally scroll through the messages on a child's phone or check the web history of their visits to sites on the internet. Others—particularly those who may be on social media as well—may befriend their children online and through it may get a better sense of what's going on. A minority of parents may use online monitoring services or location-tracking tools to determine precisely where their children are at all times.[11]

Our advice is to trust your instincts in this area, up to a point. With younger children, say, up to age twelve, the use of technical tools to monitor usage and track activity and whereabouts can make sense if the right safeguards are in place. Once children enter their teens, however, these tracking activities tend to lose their effectiveness and create privacy issues—and, ultimately, are likely to backfire on you. Teens can often find one work-around or another. They go to a friend's house, a library, a school computer; they manage to get a second phone; they create multiple accounts and share one with you but not the others—in the end, their evasive techniques can get quite sophisticated.

This type of technical monitoring also tends to undercut the trust that is so crucial for you to maintain with your teenage child. If the child either doesn't know about the monitoring and figures it out, or if your child knows you are doing it and finds ways around it, then the trust that you've worked so long and hard to establish with your child erodes. Particularly during the teen years, this insight about maintaining trust rather than seeking to exercise a level of control that will prove illusive is important.

Now, when your kids first open their own social media accounts, it makes good sense to establish the premise that you can access their accounts anytime. Federal law protects children's privacy by making it illegal for social media companies to collect certain data from people under the age of thirteen—so usage agreements on major sites require that users state that they are above the minimum age before they can open accounts. Especially given our legal backgrounds, we recommend that you and your children stick to the rules. At the same time, we understand that it can be difficult in reality as your child may start asking about having a social media account many years before that age requirement. You can make a deal with them: they need to allow you to have access to their account as long as, say, they live under your roof and you pay the bill for their phone and data usage. Your child can agree to leave their username and password somewhere secure and offline in the home. But just as you would give your children some privacy in offline spaces, you also need to consider and respect children's online privacy needs and expectations as they grow older.

Even if you don't ever actually intend to check their accounts, a shared understanding that it's okay for you to do so at any time might be a useful tool in a rare moment of crisis. Knowing their username and password to key accounts, even if you never use them, can be smart. If you establish that deal right up front, when they most want the access to the social media accounts, the conversation will be much easier than if you try to establish this monitoring arrangement later on.

Support a Healthy Social Life

Parents can support their children in many ways and help them build a healthy social life, including meaningful relationships with family members, teachers, and friends—both offline and online. At a basic level, you can help your children develop a moral compass as they learn how to navigate and shape their digitally connected social lives. You can model appropriate moral behavior and share your own struggles. You can help your children register acts of kindness and set them apart from unkindness. You can be active listeners when your children share their experiences and questions and help them think through moral dilemmas. You can demonstrate how you care about others; children will witness their parents' interactions and treatment of the people around them. You can set expectations for your children's responsibilities toward others. You can teach your children kindness and empathy from an early age and reward such behavior as they get older. These parenting techniques have been around for a long time. We now encourage you to use these insights and apply them to the digital realm in which your children are growing up. What happens daily on the internet and over social media should provide ample opportunity for you and your children to engage in the kinds of conversations we propose here.

Skills such as empathy and kindness are also important tools for building resilience in the face of the challenges of a digitally mediated social life. Again, the things parents can do to support the building of resilience in children are not new: Teach your children how to make friends; encourage them to help others. Maintain a daily routine, including unstructured time to be creative. Teach the importance of self-care, and nurture a positive self-view. Show how to set reasonable goals and move toward them, and help your child keep things in perspective.

Resilience can be learned over time. We recommend that you create a plan for how you can use face-to-face time and digital tools to empower and support your child in building resilience. Teachers often think about teaching resilience in a series of four simple steps: First, young people need to identify what makes them stressed. Next, they figure out what they typically do to react to these stresses. Third, they should brainstorm with you the range of possible ways to react to these stresses. And finally, you can ideally help them practice, in real time, with a range of reactions to the things that cause stress in their life. This simple four-step approach can help them build resilience—and a growth mindset—that will serve them well throughout life.[12]

How to Handle the Disinhibition Effect

Here's one useful piece of advice regarding your child's social and emotional skills: Talk with your children explicitly about the research on the disinhibition effect. Help them see that they need to take a breath before they write something in anger. Rash acts can get them in trouble; many of us have experienced messing up in this way offline. Mistakes that we ourselves have made, or make, represent an opportunity to share and to demonstrate a growth mindset that our children can emulate. By exposing your own shortcomings, up to a point, you can help your children learn—at least to make their own mistakes.

One approach we have used works like this: Ask your child about a time when they were upset by some unfair comment that someone had posted about a friend online. Your child will almost certainly have observed something that struck them as unjust on social media. After pointing out to them how it can help not to respond right away, you could talk them through how they might draft something and then sleep on their response before posting it online. Often, just the passage of time can help young people avoid the biggest problems that they can create for themselves. By getting them to think through the long-term consequences of a post, a text, or an image that they've shared in the heat of the moment, via a screen, you may save them much pain and trouble in that instance and in many more down the road.

Taking a Break from Social Media

As enthusiastic as people can be about the potential of new technologies, young people also need time away from their devices and social media. In this spirit, we offer two pieces of advice. First, focus on ensuring that the children in your life make time for face-to-face encounters and activities that are distinct from social media. Second, we recommend specific rules related to homework and social media.

We are fans of the concept of device-free time for young people. Such time means that they affirmatively decide to set aside their devices and do something else for a while. Of course, life circumstances differ greatly from family to family and even from child to child, so no single prescription will work for everyone. Consider setting times of day, such as the breakfast or dinner table, when devices are in a cabinet or set aside. For others, taking a walk without a phone or making a trip to the public library or local park might be a way to spend time with others but without devices mediating the relationship. Many summer camps require campers to leave their phones at home; if such a camp is a possibility for your family, it can be a boon for the social development of young people. We have also made little deals with our children about screen time: spend thirty minutes gaming, then spend thirty minutes reading an actual book or doing math exercises with a pencil and paper. This matching approach can work surprisingly well.

We also encourage you to set clear rules about social media use during the time that students are doing homework. A very high percentage of students engage in social media when they are doing their homework. The main problem with this practice is distraction. They are not going to do their homework as well as they would if they were just paying strict, focused attention to the task at hand.

We suggest having your children refrain from using social media during the time that they are doing homework. If their school requires the homework to be done on a device, use an application that blocks social media during that period, or at least create an agreement that they won't engage in any social media while doing homework. If your child has a smartphone, it should be out of sight and with the sound turned off.

The rule shouldn't ban the use of all technological devices during homework but rather should focus on social media usage. For many students, the use of online services such as Khan Academy can be a lifeline. At Phillips Academy in Andover, Massachusetts (the school that John led), the faculty and staff have partnered with Khan Academy to develop excellent supplemental teaching materials in mathematics, for instance. If a student is struggling with a concept in math, the individual can go online to Khan Academy and get access to a clear explanation of the idea and then a series of exercises to test understanding. If the student gets several problems right in a row, it means the student has mastered the idea and can move on.

Many other websites offer credible, useful supplements to classroom and textbook learning for kids. PBS Kids games, the National Geographic educational materials in science, and the BBC Schools games sites are all excellent resources—none of which should be banned during homework time just because they are online. Wikipedia can be a terrific source for what we call *presearch*. The online encyclopedia is not a formal source itself, but it is a place to get an overview of an idea and to direct students to primary sources. The Digital Public Library of America offers free primary source sets that are popular with high school students of history and their teachers. Local libraries, such as the Carnegie Library of Pittsburgh, also offer exceptional online resources such as language learning tools and online research aids.

Your children are likely to explain to you that they can multitask. "It's no big deal, Mom," is a common refrain, and perhaps, "You don't know what you are talking about." We assure you: you *do know* what you are talking about. Students cannot multitask. (And neither can anyone else, for that matter.) What they are really doing is switch-tasking. That means switching between tasks rather than completing two tasks at once. And the switching back and forth is not instantaneous. There are costs to switching like this—costs in terms of the adjustment time and the refocusing it takes to move from task to task.

We suggest that you require your child to undertake the following experiment. Imagine that your child is reading a book for English class. The assignment is to read fifteen pages per night. Set a timer, and have your child read the fifteen pages in the ordinary way—with the browser on the computer open to Facebook and your child's smartphone at hand. Time how long the assignment takes. Then, the next night, take away the computer and the smartphone or whatever device is often at hand, and have your child read the fifteen pages with no plausible technological distractions close by. The devices should not be in your child's line of sight; we recommend placing them in a drawer or in another room altogether. If this experiment goes the way it customarily does, the time will be one-third to one-half as long to read the fifteen pages. If you really want the experiment to work, give a reading quiz after each assignment. We'll bet that the child's retention is *much* higher without the distractions, too. For motivated students, or at least kids who value their free time, this type of experiment can be life-changing.

The Constant: Modeling

As in all other cases, parents need to model the behavior they want to encourage in their children. We adults frequently underestimate how much our children (and our students, if we are teachers) are watching us and emulating our approach. If we spend the entire time we are at the dinner table staring into our phones, our children will do the same. If we use texting to interact with people in the same house or building, our children will do the same instead of getting up to go talk to that person. It's incumbent on us to check our own behavior—and to modify it as needed—before we turn to dispensing advice to our kids. Modeling the right behavior is crucial in part because kids are so fantastic at sniffing out hypocrisy; that's a key teenage specialty.

COMMON QUESTIONS

But surely our kids must be less able to have good social relationships these days because of all the time they spend online. What can we do?

There's really no sound evidence to back up this claim. Of course, it's fair enough to worry about it and you can find plenty of articles claiming that kids' social decline *must* be true. But for a moment, let's assume that you're right and that kids are less socially able these days because of social media. Perhaps a brilliant study in ten years will prove it to be so. What then? Is your approach going to be to ban your children from ever going online? Isn't it better to help them develop positive relationships that have both an online and an offline component, since that is what they are likely to experience for the rest of their lives?

What are schools doing to help parents educate kids on these topics?

In most places, not enough. Some kids will roll their eyes at you when you raise these concerns about social media, because they will have already had an annual session or some other lesson about safety and citizenship online. If so, that's a great sign. But for most schools, there's just not enough time in the day to cover all the material mandated by the state or school district. That some states and districts do mandate this sort of material is good, but many do not. Nor are there sufficient educators who know enough to teach digital literacy well.

The short answer is this: Don't assume anything about what your kids are getting in school. Talk to your children about it. Ask them what they are learning at school and from whom. Fill the gaps that you have to fill—no one else will do it if you don't—and urge your schools to do more if you find they are not doing enough.

Most of the time, the parenting advice I see focuses only on the risks that kids run when they use social media. Do the possible negative consequences outweigh any social benefits?

Children run very real risks these days. And for many reasons, some kids are more anxious, more prone to suicide, and better able to cause long-term harm to themselves and others online. We can and must educate our kids about these concerns and give them the skills to navigate the complex world they inhabit.

It's natural for parents to worry—that's a big part of what you do! Worrying is a core aspect of your job description as a parent.

But as researchers, we also see the substantial good that can come from kids' relationships and the things they learn and do online. That's why we do not advocate a total ban of the technologies in a child's life but rather promote the idea of connected parenting. The connected parent places an emphasis on conveying the skills young people need today, both on and offline. We seek to support parents in guiding children away from the very real risks out there and toward the opportunities afforded by this new, emerging world in which they are growing up.

KEY TAKEAWAYS

The use of screens is an integral element of the social life of most young people today. While you may be tempted to think of it as all or mostly bad, the data simply don't lead to that conclusion. Bear in mind that many older generations have feared the strange ways of the younger generations, whether the strangeness had to do with changes in religious practice or the advent of rock and roll. Sometimes, the older generations might be right, but much of the time, the change is not as bad as they fear. The connected parent believes that young people will need to conduct some of their social lives through screens.

The connected parent also keeps a line of communication open. The healthiest relationships that young people have with adults are those built on trust and the sharing of good news as well as concerns. When it comes to social life online, you can be a huge help to the children in your life if they know that you are available to them, that you will listen, and that you will give good advice and encouragement.

You can only give good advice about social life online if you are informed and credible. The connected parent doesn't need to be online 24-7 to be credible—and in fact should not be. But it is smart to use the same services that your child spends a lot of time on, just so you know how they work. If something comes up, you'll understand some of the structural dynamics at play and be able to advise using your hard-won common sense.

Ensure that your child puts a lid on social media during home-work time. Of course, children might need to use the internet to consult a source or touch base with a friend—about the work. But if they think they can Snapchat on random matters and learn math effectively at the same time, they can't. Time spent on screens for social purposes can be a good thing in moderation, but it should not be done at the same time as homework.

Modeling, modeling, modeling. Recall that your child is watching you all the time, including how you treat other people in real life as well as online. Your Facebook account is almost certainly fair game for your child to see how you are interacting with others, just as your mode of interacting with bus drivers and teachers in front of your child is fair game. Remember, the kids are watching us! Being a positive role model can powerfully influence our children in this area of social life online.

CHAPTER THREE

Privacy

"I'M SO PSYCHED!"

Two high school students, both in their late teens, sit across from one another on a couch. They're talking to each other while scrolling and posting on Snapchat on their phones.

Sam leans over to her backpack, pulls out an opened envelope, and explains her excitement: "I finally got my first debit card!"

Sam's friend Brennan replies, "Wow—that's great. Congrats."

Sam pulls the card from the paper it's stuck to, holds the card next to her face, and takes a selfie with it.

"Dude, what are you doing?" Brennan gasps.

"I'm posting a picture of my new debit card to Snapchat," says Sam. "I told you, I'm psyched!"

"Sam, wait . . ."

"Wait what, Bren?"

"I'm not so sure that's a great idea . . ."

THE CONNECTED PARENT

THERE'S A COMMON saying among observers of Silicon Valley: "Either you pay for the product, or you are the product." People who lead technology companies tend not to like the saying, but there's much truth in it. As parents, we need to consider what this observation means for the privacy of our children—and ourselves, for that matter.

As kids lead their lives partly online, spending hours and hours a day tapping information into their phones, they are using a variety of services that are "free." Have you ever gotten a bill for your child's extensive use of Instagram or Facebook? (It's the same company, in case you didn't know.) How about Google or YouTube? (Again, they're owned by the same company.) How about from Snapchat? Or Twitter? We'd be shocked if you ever did receive such a thing— and it might be a fraudulent bill if you had. Instagram, Google, and so forth, are all "free" services that allow us to use them without any kind of up-front payment.

Have you ever thought about how they actually make money?

And make money they do. In the third quarter of 2019, Google had more than $40 billion in revenue.[1] Let us repeat this statistic: it earned this much in a quarter—one-fourth of one year. In the same quarter, Facebook's revenue topped $17 billion. Facebook's success came despite a year that was marred by a crisis related to its handling of private data and growing concerns about its role in the manipulation of elections. We're guessing that you didn't pay any of that money to Google or Facebook—directly, anyway—and yet you probably used both services or something else the companies owned.

The primary way that these gigantic companies, and many smaller ones too, make money is by collecting lots of information about lots of people and then selling targeted advertisements. If we all stopped giving our comments, conversations, photos, preferences, locations, search information, and other data to Google, Facebook, and other companies, they would have absolutely nothing to sell.

The simple truth is that much of the highly profitable internet economy depends on the sharing of lots and lots of personal data. The next wave of technology development—which has been called by various names, such as artificial intelligence, machine learning, and deep learning—likewise relies on massive sets of data about people, things, and places to make decisions and predictions, which in turn can be sold in many ways.

What does this have to do with your child, you may ask? *Everything*. Your child, and each of us, *is* the product in the internet economy. We are simultaneously the producers, the consumers, and the products (the consumed!) of the internet economy.

At a minimum, our job is to make our children aware of the possible consequences of their decisions. These choices to give up personal information are sometimes obvious. Other times, our kids are completely unwitting. It's unlikely (probably impossible, actually) that anyone engaged in the modern economy will be able to completely avoid sharing information about themselves in digital formats. So developing the awareness and skills that come with experience will be essential for all our children growing up in this digital era.

Perhaps the greatest challenge for parents when it comes to information privacy is modeling good practices ourselves. We tend to share far more information with our peers and the world at large than we ought to when we use social media services, in particular on dating applications and platforms such as Facebook. Our children watch everything we do. If we record what we are doing and share it for all the world to see, our children will see it, too. And we in turn need to remain credible so that we can give good advice to our kids when they have questions of their own about information privacy. We often give up that credibility too easily.

Back to the debit card example with Sam and Brennan. If you don't believe us that people actually post pictures of their brand-new debit cards—without blotting out the numbers—just go online. We don't want to shame anyone in particular, but let's just say that even with minimal effort or expertise, you'll have little trouble finding such photos.

WHAT THE RESEARCH SHOWS

Parents worry that kids leave too many digital traces of themselves online which, in turn, might have negative consequences for the kids down the road. Against the backdrop of how the internet economy works, that's a reasonable fear. Considering the sheer amount of time that kids are on their devices and sharing information with one another, there are abundant opportunities for mistakes to lead to problems later on.

The potential for problems starts early. At the ripe old age of two years, the vast majority of children in wealthy countries have an online presence. In the United States, that number means 92 percent of kids.[2] Of course, it's very unlikely that the children themselves have set up their own online presence.

It turns out that most of the time, *we the parents* are the start of the problem. The data are clear: we are the ones who are getting our children started in sharing too much about their lives in digital form. We are the ones who share the pictures and other information about them, even before they have the chance to make up their mind about how much to share. What's even worse, we tend to be terrible role models when it comes to sharing information about ourselves. The track record of many adults on the privacy front can be *worse* than the behavior of young people. That's one of the key data points to consider: our own role in the process that leads to kids' lack of data privacy.

Once they are old enough to make up their minds about sharing information online, young people do often continue to share a good deal of information about themselves. They exhibit a wide range of behavior, from the painfully naive to the impressively sophisticated. This range often cuts along socioeconomic lines. Young people with higher socioeconomic status tend to be more sophisticated about sharing information than are kids with lower socioeconomic status, who tend to be less knowledgeable about sharing information. Tweens and teenagers with engaged parents and schools that teach digital literacy and digital citizenship year after year are similarly more cautious about sharing personally sensitive information online. And young people from higher socioeconomic backgrounds are more likely to ask their parents for advice about privacy settings and technological controls than are young people from lower socioeconomic backgrounds.[3]

It's not that kids don't care about privacy. That generalization is a myth, and not a terribly helpful one at that. They just have a different understanding of privacy than adults do—and they don't want to share things with you. Young people do tend to share information with their friends, often information that you wish they would not. Especially as they get older, they tend to find platforms and mechanisms to share information with friends beyond the reach of their parents' gaze. If parents regularly check the text messages of their teenagers, the young people are highly likely to switch over to another platform to message their friends. Snapchat is a popular alternative, since the messages are auto-deleted over time—so even if parents cotton on to a teen's strategy, the history will not be evident unless the child's messages to friends were very recent. Facebook's Messenger product (pulled out from the Facebook service into its own related product) is another mechanism that young people use to avoid the parents-looking-over-their-digital-shoulder routine.

What young people tell us as researchers in focus groups and interviews can be a leading indicator of their future behavior. For instance, in a 2013 report that our Youth and Media Lab produced along with Pew Research, we found the following: "Focus group discussions with teens show that they have waning enthusiasm for Facebook, disliking the increasing adult presence, people sharing excessively, and stressful 'drama,' but they keep using it because participation is an important part of overall teenage socializing."[4] A few years later, we saw a falloff in usage of Facebook; as of May 2018, overall teen usage on Facebook had fallen to just over 50 percent, behind usage of YouTube, Instagram (a part of Facebook in corporate terms), and Snapchat.[5]

In the same 2018 Pew study, teens reported that Snapchat was the service they were most likely to use most often.[6] One of the features of Snapchat is that the material posted is, in theory, ephemeral. In other words, what you post on Snapchat—unless someone has purposely recorded your posting in some way—goes away after a short period. Teens report that this feature of Snapchat is appealing and one of the reasons for its rise in popularity. Snapchat does not rely on the idea of a public profile, as Facebook and Instagram do, for instance. Snapchat functions as a messaging service—one that is not likely to keep the conversations around. Most content is sent privately from the sender to one or more receivers. Editing is strictly limited. And the feel of Snapchat content is often much more spontaneous and authentic than the curated feel of Facebook and Instagram posts, which are expected to persist.

Young people are most likely to ask their peers for advice on privacy; a close second group they ask is their parents. In focus groups and interviews, students have been very clear with us that they are less likely to ask their parents or teachers if the kids believe that the adults are not up to speed on computers and the internet.

Although we have no definitive across-the-board proof, our read of the data about information privacy is that young people are sharing more and more about themselves over time. This increase corresponds to the rise of the mobile internet, social media, and the overall increase in time spent online. At the same time, relatively

sophisticated young people are coming up with interesting strategies to control and manage information about themselves—often in
cleverer ways than how their own parents manage privacy. Rather
than worrying that kids don't care about their privacy, we need to
be worried all of us—at all ages—care too little about our privacy.

The data about young people and privacy are fairly well established at this point. For more than a decade, we have been asking
detailed questions of hundreds of teens about their thoughts and
approaches to information privacy in the digital realm.[7] Clearly,
many young people make terrible choices, while others are quite sophisticated about how they navigate digital privacy. The research is
inconclusive about how to help young people make better choices in
their online behavior. Part of the answer is, of course, education, but
who should provide the education? For young people with a strong
family unit and friends who are thoughtful and kind in their online
behavior, the privacy concerns are comparatively low; for kids who
have to figure everything out on their own, the privacy concerns of
the digital realm are quite high.

THE CONNECTED PARENTS' APPROACH

Connected parents handle data privacy as we suggest they do for
the other issues in this book: with a commitment to balance, conversation, and paying attention to the data. We take a skeptical view
of our knee-jerk fears. Despite the privacy risks of extensive media
usage, we do not advocate that you keep your children away from
all digital devices and services while they are under your roof. Such
a strategy is impractical and unhelpful for their social and emotional
development.

Parents should, however, teach their children from an early age
to make sound choices about the personal information they share.
Young people are capable of thinking, learning, and choosing things

that will be in their best interests—even if they don't always listen, learn, or make good decisions.

Connected parents know that the most powerful force for tweens and teens is the culture of their peers. Adult modeling and advice come in a close second. Courses in school on digital citizenship and other skills can be helpful to a degree, but the most important and effective way for young people to learn is by example, through experiences, and listening to peers and adults they trust. While you might wish that you could "outsource" this type of teaching to the schools your children attend, the job of teaching about privacy is primarily going to fall to you as parents, to families, and to friend groups.

OUR RECOMMENDATIONS

In our research, kids tell us that the best way to get them to pay attention to concerns such as data privacy is by sharing real-world examples with them, ideally about people they know or people they can relate to. Often, if you know of people in your community who have already run into problems with oversharing online, you may already have all the examples you need. On Google, you can find lots of other examples.

We'll give you a few examples you might use. These are true stories but composite versions with the names removed, so we're not compounding the problem for the young people involved by outing them in this book. Young people's oversharing of information about themselves can lead to problems that fall into many categories. We will offer examples in two buckets: (1) sexting and (2) college or job-related.

Sexting

More young people than you think share sexually explicit images of themselves during their adolescence. Studies show that the number of US youth who engage in some form of sexting during their teenage years probably falls at least between 15 and 33 percent.[8] Because of low self-reporting of all sexually related behaviors, those numbers might even be on the low end. That means there is a good chance that one of your children has engaged in, or will engage in, sexting during adolescence or knows someone who has.

Here's how it tends to go. Kids report to us that one person, more often than not a boy, will ask a girl to send sexually explicit photos of herself to him. It's often during a flirting phase of a relationship. The girl will (though not always, of course) send one or two pictures—or sometimes many dozens of photos—over a text-messaging app or Snapchat. She may think that these pictures will be kept safely between her and the boy to whom she has sent them. Very often, the boy will then show them to others—perhaps just by flashing the phone, or by forwarding the image, or by letting someone else take a photo of the image on the original boy's phone. Either way, the images often make their way to others, unbeknownst to the girl. This sharing can take place right away or, sometimes, after a long relationship ends.

This scenario presents many problems. It is cruel to the girl and can be deeply embarrassing. Further, many of those activities are illegal in most parts of the United States, depending on the ages of the people involved. It's often a felony to request an explicit photo of an underage person, to take such a photo, to transmit such a photo, and to share such a photo. Police and district attorneys seldom want to prosecute teenagers involved in sexting, but the actions are customarily felonies—for both the boy and the girl in this scenario. If they are convicted of a sexual offense, the young people involved might have to report themselves to their community for years, if not the rest of their lives. Many young people don't think sexting is such a big deal—witness the high percentage of young people who engage in it—but it is absolutely worth warning teens about the legal risks here.

Schools and Jobs

Imagine that your son is a devoted basketball player. Since he was old enough to toddle around, he has loved to dribble and shoot hoops. Through middle school and into high school, he has starred in the local Catholic youth league. No one can stop him when he drives to the net. During high school, he added a mean shot from outside the three-point perimeter—what his friends call his trademark "dagger." During his sophomore year, it became clear that he would be a great addition to any top college team. Now, as college decisions are coming around, it looks as if he will have to choose between a big Midwestern university that has always competed for the national title and an Ivy League college looking to get into the National Collegiate Athletic Association tournament next year.

The trouble is, your son has paid more attention to his weight-lifting and his time on the court than he has paid to his social media profile. In his online social life, he has been sloppy. Like many young people his age, and particularly athletes, he likes to go out on the weekends with his friends. Sometimes, there is beer and marijuana around. On a few of his social media profiles, the pictures have begun to pile up: your son holding in his hand something that shouldn't be there. He hasn't gotten in any serious trouble, but when the college coach at his preferred school stops calling him right before he expects to get a national letter of intent, your son gets worried. Has the coach seen something? Has one of his friends forwarded some photos to the university? What has happened to that big-time full scholarship he has worked for, literally his whole life? Were a few fun photos worth giving up this opportunity?

A similar story might be true of a promising young artist, musician, or scientist who wants to go to a competitive college. It also applies to any job-seeker: leaving a trail of explicit photos on publicly accessible websites is probably not going to help a young person's cause in a tight labor market. Unfortunately, young people don't tend to think through these ramifications in the moment. They fail to realize the persistence of these images and texts and to anticipate that the posts might change contexts. Something that seems funny and harmless today might prove devastating years later, in another context. So what's a parent to do?

Start early, for sure. Talk about privacy with your kids beginning when they are quite young. Before they start to use social media extensively, talk through the consequences of sharing too much information. Use clear and understandable examples they can relate to, and adjust those examples as they get older.

A simple rule you might consider adopting in your home comes courtesy of US law. The Children's Online Privacy Protection Act of 1998 requires online services that collect, use, or disclose information collected from young people to comply with a series of rules.[9] The cutoff for this federal law is age thirteen. Many people think that this law means that it is illegal for kids to use social media before they turn thirteen. That might not be the worst misunderstanding, but it's not quite what the law says. The law actually regulates the online services—say, Snapchat, Facebook, and YouTube—rather than the young people themselves. Its purpose is to protect young people from having their data shared in ways they can't understand or control before they turn thirteen. In effect, the law prevents most social media sites from allowing children younger than thirteen to sign up for the service—at least in theory.

In a 2011 study, John and his colleagues danah boyd, Eszter Hargittai, and Jason Schultz found that a large percentage (68 percent) of a national sample of parents actually helped their children sign up for social media services before the kids turn thirteen.[10] That's more than two-thirds of parents surveyed! These parents knowingly helped their children lie about their age to sign up for, say, Facebook. In effect, the adults are helping their children waive the protections that the US government has created for them.

We recommend that you stick with the age-thirteen rule. Tell the tweens in your house that the rules are very clear on this front: Facebook, Instagram, YouTube, Snapchat, and Twitter all require you to be thirteen to sign up. Period. (As of this writing, each of the top seven most popular social media services require users to affirm that they are at least thirteen years old before they can sign up. They also tend to make clear that it is a violation of their terms of service for anyone to help someone set up an account before they turn thirteen.)

If you make a different choice about allowing your children to sign up for a social media site earlier than age thirteen, then please be sure to talk about the basics of information privacy with them. One rule of thumb that we often use is the newspaper test. Use whatever newspaper (or TV news program) is popular with their friends or family members as your example. Urge your children to think about whether they would be comfortable if anything they share online were shared that same night on the news show or the front page of the newspaper. If they would be happy with that picture or that text showing up for all to see, then fine, you could say, go ahead and post it. If they would be embarrassed for their grandparents, their cousins, or their best friend to see it on TV or the front page, then they shouldn't type it into a device to begin with. If you think the idea of news media wouldn't click with your child, try a different tack. Perhaps your child really loves a grandmother. You could ask, "What if your post was also shared in an email that your grandmother got to read?"

Another rule of thumb to share with young people involves an analogy using tattoos. You could discuss how, when people are young, they sometimes get a tattoo that they later regret. It's not impossible to have the tattoo removed, you could explain, but it's very difficult.

The same thing applies to sharing information about yourself online. If you share a picture or text that you think is cool when you are fourteen but that you find embarrassing by the time you're eighteen, it's going to be very hard to get that digital tattoo off your back, arm, or leg. While a young person would no doubt have difficulty imagining being a fifty-year-old professional who regrets a teenage tattoo, the same child might find it easier to imagine going from one school to the next. Do children want their "old selves" to travel with them to the new school? Or do they want a fresh start when they get to high school or to college or a first job? Or to a new community as a young adult? The more careful kids are with sharing information about themselves when they are young, the more flexibility they will have later on, when they are presenting themselves to others during key transitions in life.

To be clear, rules of thumb of this sort provide only rough guidance; they aren't perfect and they often come with important limitations. The two rules outlined here, for example, might help a child manage the reputational effects of sharing personal information, but they would not prevent a tech company from collecting that information, trading it with data brokers, and using it to create a digital dossier of your teenager over time. These data are likely to be used in the future to shape the child's life as a consumer and maybe even as a citizen.

Sharing Information and Modeling

Most important of all, we must look back at ourselves. The modeling part is always so important. Adults are often as bad as, if not sometimes worse than, young people in terms of sharing too much, especially through dating apps. Kids watch us like hawks, more than we think they do. We have to clean up our own acts and be smarter than we are today if we want them to be smart about their own digital privacy.

Think, too, about your own role in sharing data about your kids. Adults are too often getting kids started with sharing information and images before the kids can decide themselves how much to share online. How can we expect our kids to do better than we do if we fail to manage not only our own privacy but also theirs? We need to maintain credibility as parents and put ourselves in a position to offer good commonsense privacy advice to our kids and their friends.

The bottom line is this: Yes, young people can make poor decisions about their data privacy. Yes, companies are set up to exploit them and their data. Yes, governments are increasingly building a surveillance state to track their movements. And yes, parents are part of the problem because we are rarely more sophisticated than our children, and we often make the matter worse by sharing too much data about our own kids. Schools need to do a better job of educating young people—and not becoming part of the problem as they increasingly adopt ed tech (educational technology) and collect and analyze more and more student data to personalize learning experiences. The way forward involves a combination of better awareness about data privacy, skill-building at all ages, more public-spirited corporate citizenship, and smart new forms of regulation. The way forward starts with our own decision making and the way we raise our children in our homes.

COMMON QUESTIONS

If the claim that kids don't care about privacy is a myth, how then do they think about it?

Research we've conducted in collaboration with Sandra Cortesi at the Berkman Klein Center's Youth and Media project at Harvard University shows that many young people have developed rather sophisticated strategies to address what they consider key privacy issues and to curate their reputations, often deploying a mixed approach. Some young people change the privacy settings on their social media accounts to restrict access by adults. Some change their names on their accounts so that their friends can view their posts but others can't connect the posts to them personally. Perhaps most surprisingly to many adults is the amount of thought that at least certain groups of young people spend when deciding what to share and over what channels. Young people sometimes also deliberately use ambiguous, confusing, or misleading information to protect their privacy online. While many young users have developed such privacy-friendly strategies to manage their reputations, they typically have little awareness or control over how their data are collected and used by the companies—a persistent problem that also plagues adults and that points to the need for stronger legal protection of privacy in the digital age.

What kinds of mistakes do young people typically make when it comes to their privacy?

Young people commonly make a range of mistakes regarding their privacy, just as adults do. Kids often forget that the materials they post online can be moved from one context to another, for instance. They post something, thinking that only one group of peers might see it, only to have the words or image appear in another context for an audience that they had not considered. Perhaps a peer copied and pasted it; perhaps someone had the image on a phone and then got in trouble—who knows? These twin elements of persistence and context are important to discuss with young people.

The disinhibition effect leads young people to share and post material that they later come to regret. In the heat of the moment, they release something that they later want desperately to pull back but can't. Sometimes it is an intimate or revealing photo of themselves. Or they post a deeply held but offensive-to-others belief that they harbor. Or perhaps they make a funny but mean statement about a peer. Without seeing the other person face-to-face, a young person (or an adult) can be prone to sharing something that they should not.

What do you think about parents posting baby pictures?

We don't judge parents' decisions made in the excitement of a new child's birth, but we do urge caution. John's family waited to post pictures of the kids on social media until they were in their teens and consented to the posts. It's important to take the long view and realize just how much information will be online and shared as data about our kids through what will be a long lifetime. Wouldn't it be sufficient for now to share the baby pictures just in a controlled way, through a link to Shutterfly or Google Photos or even just as a text message, rather than posting publicly to Facebook? If you really want to put the baby pictures on Facebook, consider not tagging the images with the names of your children for now. You can always add those tags later. There are many ways to limit the implications of sharing baby pictures even as you wish to share the joy.

You may also have to deal with your well-meaning relatives posting about your kids online. A loving aunt or uncle might post a series of pictures with tags and comments that talk about your kids in relation to their own. Or they might make an innocent-yet-revealing note on a social media post ("So, when does Amanda start kindergarten?"). We believe it is completely fine to give your relatives a call or send them a back-channel note to ask them not to post about your kids in public until your kids have chosen to be shared about. Feel free to point them to this book or to the reams of research on digital privacy to back up your kind and reasonable request! To learn more, check out Leah Plunkett's informative book written entirely on this topic: *Sharenthood: Why We Should Think Before We Talk About Our Kids Online.*

Does privacy really matter? I don't have anything to hide, so why should I care about my privacy or the privacy of my kids?

Some people believe that they have nothing to hide. But for all of us, privacy does matter. It matters today and it will matter in the future. When it comes to your children's personal information, you have to avoid making any decisions that they will later wish that you hadn't.

The disclosure of private information can produce a wide range of problems. Among the most common crimes in the world, the simple and immediate concern of identity theft can affect people of all ages. Identity theft can impose enormous costs of time and money for its victims. The thieves use small amounts of personal information, such as your name and mailing address, to cobble together a profile of someone and then commit their crime. They might steal money or even commit other crimes using the false identity.

When it comes to your own children, consider the unknowns of the future. Information that you or they share about themselves in digital formats may be impossible to remove and may remain in the public domain forever. Whether that's an embarrassing image, statement, or incident, this information will potentially be accessible to everyone, forever. In the United States and many other countries, there is no universal right to delete information about oneself. The European Union has established a "right to be forgotten" and other extensive privacy controls, and the state of California somewhat follows Europe's lead with its Online Eraser Law and the California Consumer Privacy Act. But even well-written laws may not prevent the future harms that might come about from oversharing information about your children at a young age.

KEY TAKEAWAYS

Young people do care about privacy. They mostly care about keeping information away from you and other adults! That doesn't mean that they are completely unaware of the issues or that they don't care about privacy in general, as parents often fear.

Young people make lots of mistakes about their privacy. They tend to forget that the information they share today may show up tomorrow in other places and contexts—and that they may regret this reemergence. Their brains are not yet fully formed, they tend to like risk-taking, and they are usually not so great at thinking through long-term consequences.

Recall that you are likely part of the problem. Many adults are just as bad as young people at oversharing information via devices. Think about dating sites and what adults share on them. And adults' Facebook profiles have been diligently compiled over several years (the platform is now more than fifteen years old). As a result, we seldom make the best role models.

Adults also share too much about their own kids. Think about all the photos you may have posted of your infant or children before they had a say in the matter! Before you go any further, have a chat with the children in your care. Ask them what they want, if they are old enough for that conversation.

Young people are navigating a much more complicated world today than even a decade or so ago. Most millennial parents will have a good sense of what their children are facing, since these parents will have grown up in a digital era. But screen usage rates continue to rise, and the ubiquity of data and devices is growing, not receding—so these issues are intensifying over time.

Spend the time to talk about data privacy concerns with your children year after year. The circumstances change for them each year, and the world around them is changing rapidly. Connected parents need to be on the team with their children when it comes to data privacy. Consider the long term: no generation has yet lived a full life that has been recorded in digital format as those born after, say, 1982 will have done. Whether the issue of privacy arises in the household, at school, online, or in another situation, our children must have the chance to learn and think about this issue at a young age, when they can establish the skills they need for an entire lifetime in a digital age.

PART II

SOME TOPICS PARENTS
WORRY ABOUT MOST

CHAPTER FOUR

Safety

KATY, A GUIDANCE counselor at a large public school, got an urgent call about one of her students.

"Katy, do you have a few minutes?" Darrell, the principal, asked. He needed her help right away.

"Of course, Darrell. What can I do for you?"

"It's not for me. I worry that one of our kids could be in danger and I need you to reach out to her."

"Sure. I'm here for her. And for you. What happened?"

"I don't want to say her name out loud right now, but I'll text it to you. She has posted a profile on Skout—have you heard of it?"

"Yes—a dating app, right?"

"Right. And her friends tell me she has attracted a lot of attention."

"I bet," Katy said. "Not all good?"

"Not all good. I have an idea that she has apparently met a much older man on the app, and they may have been meeting after school."

"Uh-huh. I get it. How do you know this?"

"The good news is that she has friends who are worried about her. One of them came to me. I don't want her to freak out when the principal calls, but I do want to get to her right away. I am worried that she doesn't know this person well enough to be meeting him. She could be in real danger."

"I agree," Katy said. "I'll find her this afternoon before school gets out. And I'll loop in her parents at the appropriate moment. Don't worry, Darrell. We're on it. And apparently, so are her friends."

THERE IS NO greater fear for parents than the possibility that something terrible would happen to their child. We know; we have had those sleepless nights worrying about our kids, too. We worry that they will suffer harm in an untold range of ways. The digital era has added a few extra things to worry about.

Risks that relate to social media rank high on many parents' lists of worries about their children these days. We have put a few of these worries up front in this chapter. In particular, we consider the risks of physical or psychological harm that kids may face. Physical and psychological harm can, of course, be related, but they are also different in some important ways.

Over the past few decades, a large group of professionals has emerged to lead the way on online safety. These professionals can be our partners in this effort to keep our kids safe online. Increasingly, communities such as schools, youth centers, libraries, and camps have technical staff who understand the safety risks that young people are running and can help keep them safe. Law enforcement at the local, state, and federal level has also become very sophisticated in its approaches. Many companies, too, have made meaningful commitments to keep children safe in their online lives. Part of being a connected parent is figuring out the right people with whom to partner to keep the young people in your life safe from harm.

WHAT THE RESEARCH SHOWS

In considering the safety of children, we consider both physical and psychological harm. Our discussion of physical harm focuses on the possibility that a young person might meet someone online and then, by agreement or otherwise, end up meeting in person and getting hurt. The most common forms of physical harm to young people are caused by people they know—most likely a classmate, an educator, or a family member—but for the purpose of this chapter, we focus on physical-harm scenarios in which technology plays a relevant role. In our discussion of psychological harm, we refer to the safety risks to a young person's psychological well-being because of screen time interactions or material that the child might encounter online.

Physical Harm

Many parents worry that things have become more dangerous over time for children. The fear, often stoked by the media, is that danger to children has skyrocketed because of social media and other new technologies. But remarkably, the data *do not support* this claim of an increased risk of physical harm from predators.[1]

What *has* changed, and what the data *do* support, is that those who seek to harm young people have turned their attention to public spaces online rather than public spaces offline.[2] Whereas a sexual predator might have once hung around a public park in your town or city, the person might today troll some of the equivalent public parks of the internet and social media. Often, these predators are lurking in the seamiest of places online. Other times, they might be lurking in the chat section of an online game or on a mainstream dating app.

The story about the high school student that Darrell and Katy were worried about could have been about a young person posting information on dating apps such as Tinder or Grindr, seeking a connection and knowing that it might well have a sexual component to it. While most dating applications are meant for people aged eighteen and over, the apps are often used by younger people who lie about their ages. Data show that very often, young people know that they are running some risk when they are engaging online with those who might do them harm. Kids are attracted to risks and often think they can handle them. Unfortunately, they might not then reach out to adults and others who can help them when the risk becomes too great.

Psychological Harm

The other type of harm that kids regularly face online is psychological. There's no question that young people are capable of bullying or harassment in general. And that observation turns out to be true online, too.

One issue vigorously debated is whether young people are more likely to bully one another online than offline. That turns out to be a difficult question. Much of the answer turns on a series of variables that researchers cannot easily control. It's tricky, for instance, to find communities of young people who are not online and who are willing to be part of a control group in a research study. In any event, we probably don't need to find the definitive answer to that question to address the larger issues involved: that our children do face psychological risks online and that our kids can also be the perpetrators of harm to others. And as we have seen in other aspects of online life, cyberbullying is related to other issues that the child is experiencing offline, including school problems, antisocial behavior, and substance abuse.

Researchers have shown that it is most effective not to look solely at cyberbullying per se but rather to see it as bullying that can happen either online, offline, or often as a combination of both.[3] The underlying issues are the same.[4] The harm can be a little bit different, however. Consider the reach of bullying that happens online compared with the same slurs hurled at a student in a hallway with just a few other students present to hear. Very often, bullies attack young people online as well as face-to-face. Research has also shown that students who experience bullying online or offline were more likely to report suicidal thoughts and attempts.[5]

Parents have a major role in shaping the likelihood that a student becomes a bully in the first place. Research has repeatedly shown that those who carry out cyberbullying report that their parents do not monitor their activities effectively.[6] The same research shows that these children have worse relationships with their parents than do children uninvolved in cyberbullying.

While young people of all genders experience bullying, some studies have shown that girls are more likely than boys to experience bullying online. According to a nationally representative study conducted by Sameer Hinduja and Justin Patchin in the United States in 2016, adolescent girls were a bit more likely to have experienced cyberbullying in their lifetimes than boys were (36.7 percent versus 30.5 percent).[7]

Researchers have also studied at length the effect of harassment on LGBTQ+ (the plus represents the inclusion of wide spectrums of gender identity and acceptance)—those sympathetic youth both online and offline. The world of social media can be a boon for those who are exploring their gender and sexuality, as they can do so in ways that are relatively safe and anonymous in online communities. But social media can also be an environment where LGBTQ+ youth experience hazing, bullying, and other harassment, all of which are sometimes combined with negative offline experiences. For instance, GLSEN (originally called the Gay, Lesbian & Straight Education Network), an organization focused on supporting young people, has shown that 42 percent of LGBTQ+ youth have experienced bullying. That compares with about 25 to 33 percent reported by youth overall (across genders) in most studies. GLSEN's data (from 2013) also show that LGBTQ+ students are three times as likely as other youth to experience bullying in online environments. The nature of the school community and a friend group have a strong connection to the experiences of LGBTQ+ youth in this regard; stronger, more positive school communities can reduce the incidence and depth of harm to young people, both online and offline.[8]

DISINHIBITION AND BULLYING

One substantial difference between online and offline bullying is directly related to the disinhibition effect. We described this phenomenon in Chapter 2 and reintroduce it here, because disinhibition has a huge impact on online bullying and harassment. As described earlier, the disinhibition effect is the tendency of people to say and do online some things that they would not do face-to-face. In other words, people may act less inhibited when using devices than they would in other types of encounters.

You will probably recognize this complex-sounding notion from your own life. Adults suffer from this problem, to be sure; we've all probably wished that we could take back an email we sent or a post we made on social media in a moment of anger.

Consider the disinhibition effect combined with some of the key traits of teenagers, for example, and you will see quickly why this idea belongs in a chapter devoted to harm, including psychological harm, to children. We know that the teenaged brain is literally not as developed as the adult brain. The frontal lobes of the teenaged brain are present, but they are not yet fully connected. Teenagers have less "white matter," known as myelin, than adults have. As a result, their brains can act sluggishly when it comes to decision making. In that key moment of anger or drama, a teenager's brain may function in such a way as to cause harm to another person. This observation is not meant to take young people off the hook for the consequences of their actions, but it does help explain how they may act in a less inhibited way than they should.

THE CONNECTED PARENTS' APPROACH

By now, you'll have a sense of where we are coming from with respect to the advice in this book. Our guiding philosophy of connected parenting suggests that you don't try to ban the technology from your children's lives forever for fear that something bad might happen to them. It's a little like saying they can't go outside or cross the street because of the many risks that they will inevitably run. At the same time, young people do face real risks as they grow up in an increasingly digitally mediated world. The connected-parenting approach calls on us to ensure that our children develop the skills they need to keep themselves safe, with our help and guidance.

Young people who have resiliency, strong peer relationships, and good support from parents, teachers, and mentors can navigate the online world without running an unreasonable set of risks. We wish they didn't have to face risks—and we wish that people never did bad things to children—but young people must hear from us as adults about the nature and the extent of the possible risks they can run. And we must show them these risks with evidence and in a manner they can understand and connect with.

Parents who express fears in ways unsupported by facts and evidence may forfeit the child's trust that they can offer informed advice. Children need to have people they can turn to when they are in risky situations. Realistically, those people will sometimes be friends of their own age rather than the adults in their lives. Either way, we need to equip as many kids as we can with positive, constructive knowledge about online behaviors. Once informed, they can help spread advice with other young people when they need it most.

OUR RECOMMENDATIONS

There are no shortcuts to help your children stay safe. That was true a generation or two ago, and it is just as true today, in this digital era. As parents, we get a certain amount of time with our children when they are always physically near us, and then slowly they make their way away from us. As they do so, we must impart to them the skills and knowledge they need to keep themselves safe.

This process of parenting well to keep young people safe starts at the earliest ages. Before they ever cross the street, you teach your kids to hold the hand of a trusted adult and to look both ways. When they go to the park to play, you tell them not to talk to strangers, to stay in eyesight and earshot of their parents, and not to leave the park with people they don't know. These same simple types of rules—adapted for a child's age—work in the digital realm as well. Kids who internalize these types of rules at an early age can adapt them as the technologies and circumstances shift.

The most important finding from the research and advice we've seen is that parents' common sense can help kids keep themselves safe in online and offline scenarios. Commonsense advice helps more than most parents think, it turns out. As in other situations we've covered in this book, you must remain credible and open as you deliver your advice to children.

The advice that has tended to work in the privacy setting works in the online safety arena, too. For many youth, stories about other kids, ideally ones they know but even ones they can relate to, tend to stick. Kids learn from stories. If they are bored of hearing these stories—and give you an "Oh, Dad, I've heard that a million times"—you are probably getting through to them.

Keep them (and yourself) informed of the most common types of safety risks online. Share some examples of situations where kids can get into trouble. You may be aware of some stories from your parents' groups or the larger community. You don't want to use these accounts as a scare tactic, but rather use them as a cautionary tale from which kids can learn.

Many parents are concerned about the risks their children are exposed to in all aspects of life. Bear in mind how much more frequently the harm can come from nearby than from strangers in the distance. For example, the school climate and a young person's group of friends are much more likely to be the source of online and offline safety concerns than are connections with a stranger. That's not to say that danger from strangers doesn't exist. But the *likelihood* that someone will be harmed is higher from people closer at hand. For this reason, a family's focus and advice to a child should account for these different likelihoods. In our experience, parents often overlook the most likely sources of concern.

On the following pages, we offer some tips and rules that many parents adopt. As we've said before and will repeat here, we know that circumstances vary from household to household. Your ability to monitor and enforce these rules is an essential part of the equation. Rules that you can't or won't enforce are not great ideas. Rather than making rules, you might consider them to be talking points or expectations in your house if you can't realistically enforce them for whatever reason. All that said, you might consider the approaches that follow.

General Safety Rules

- Reserve the right to log in and read the chats and messages of young children as a requirement for their getting on social media, having a phone, or playing online games. We suggested this rule in other chapters—in the context of social life and privacy—but it bears repeating. Even if you do not exercise this right and never log in to your child's account, you should be able to do so, especially with younger children. This rule entails a more complex judgment call for older teens, who are likely to consider this expectation a breach of their privacy.

- Make sure your kids are aware of support systems online. For instance, Crisis Text Line is an important resource for young people who are engaged in self-harm or are otherwise struggling with mental health issues. Just as you approach "the talk" about sex and drugs, you are much better off talking about these types of sensitive topics when things are in good shape and there is no crisis in your child's life. Children may also be able to help their peers using this knowledge that you've shared with them. The data suggest that peer-to-peer advice has more impact on adolescents than does advice from adults.

- Keep up to speed with the basics of online safety via blogs such as those maintained by the Family Online Safety Institute and by Parenting for a Digital Future. They do a great job of staying apprised of the latest concerns that kids and families face and giving commonsense, well-grounded advice for how to handle these issues. Some recent posts have covered concerns about posting selfies and about geolocation tools, which some parents love to use and others worry might do more harm than good.

- A new safety issue for the mobile era is texting while driving. Parents must have a no-tolerance policy for the young drivers in their household. This policy means that you, too, must refrain from texting while driving! In most places, it is illegal to text while driving, so the law is there to back up your warnings.

- If you adopt technological controls for your young children's use of the internet, such as Net Nanny or those offered by your internet service provider, think carefully about how long to keep them in place. Your tween—or certainly your teen—will easily break through or route around these controls. You will lose trust and credibility in the process.

Approaches Relating to Hazing, Bullying, and Other Harassment

In the digital era, bullying can occur online as well as offline and often in combination. Raise awareness in your household by asking questions and using examples from this book or from your own neighborhood or experience. You'll want to get young people talking about bullying and understanding their own potential role. As parents, we need to ensure that our children are not the source of the problem just as much as we need to protect them from harm.

- Knowing that your children will be exposed to some level of bullying online and offline—whether they are the one who bullies, the one who is bullied, or a bystander who might be able to intervene—you need to give your children examples of appropriate emotional responses. Young people will have to navigate some tricky scenarios during their tween and teen years. You may not see these virtual interactions, because they are hidden in kid world online, but that doesn't mean you can't help your child respond. In fact, inevitably, your own actions and the advice you give them will be a major part of their coping strategy as they grow up.

- Children will look to the examples you set as their initial guide for how to react. You need to be highly cognizant of how you treat others and what your children observe. Do they see you acting angrily and unkindly to the people you interact with in everyday life? If so, they are likely to base their own interactions with their peers on the model you offer them. Seeing a child mirror a parent's bad behavior can be a hard pill for any parent to swallow, but all of us need to acknowledge the important role we can play in breaking or perpetuating the cycle of bullying.

- Social-emotional skills have been linked to the idea of resiliency, an important protective factor in bullying. Several studies have demonstrated that youth with higher levels of resiliency were less likely to indicate that they have been a victim of bullying, online or offline. And for young people who have been bullied, resiliency appeared to act as a buffer from the potential damage of bullying. Students who develop greater resiliency tend to benefit from other good things as well: stronger attachment to adults, a sense of belonging to a community, and participation in more-supportive environments.[9]

- As a parent, you'll want to seek out schools that look out for the whole child. The best way to keep kids safe is to provide them with a positive environment and to help them develop resiliency. These tasks are easier said than done. But you can certainly ask hard questions about school climates. Ask how the schools focus on the social and emotional side of student growth. Ask about the philosophy of preventing hazing, bullying, and other harassment—not just the mandatory, legal approaches the school takes when something goes wrong. Ideally, the school community connects back to the positive environment you are creating in the home.

- Many online resources offer tips and tools to help address bullying. Young people who are music fans might turn to Lady Gaga's Born This Way Foundation, which has developed research-based materials and messaging online to help reduce the incidence of bullying and to promote strong, positive youth leadership and communities. Lady Gaga and her mother, Cynthia Germanotta, have created programs to promote kindness among youth and to encourage young people to support one another in times of crisis. We have been among their partners in these efforts to address bullying and recommend the materials and programs they offer young people.

Social Media and Intimate Relationships

Intimate relationships between young people have always been a delicate matter, but never more so than today. The use of social media as a part of their romantic life has added yet another twist. Thanks to some great researchers, parents can understand those complexities a bit, though that doesn't make it much easier to know how to help the kids involved. If your children are anything like ours, talking to you about their romantic lives is not at the top of their priority list.

- Recognize for starters that kids may date people that they met initially online. As many as a quarter of thirteen- to seventeen-year-olds who dated have done so or have hooked up (which can refer to a range of intimate encounters) with someone they first connected with online, according to a Pew Research Center study.[10] This online-first connection, whether or not it involves romance, does not strike our kids as scary or inappropriate, though it does to us as parents. We need to help our kids tell the difference between a potentially dangerous liaison, say, with a predatory adult, and the more commonplace hookup between teenagers. Knowing these basic facts, again, is an essential starting point for a helpful conversation with your child.

- Consider applying a rule that your children under eighteen stay off dating apps. These apps and websites are generally geared toward adults and are much more appropriate for older users. We have seen too many instances where young people pretended to be older and more sophisticated than they were. Older people can and do take advantage of young people who lack the maturity to fully weigh the risks and make measured decisions about dating people they've met online. Much of the time, young people who end up in sexual encounters with older people have been either seeking sex or appear to the older person to be seeking sex. In all these cases, the law and common sense make it plain that the underage person cannot in fact consent to sex.

- We need to be sure that our kids also understand the new risks they run when they share intimate images and texts online. Whether the sharing happens in the context of a relationship or otherwise, a meaningful percentage of young people—roughly one-quarter of teens in the United States, research suggests—engage in some form of sexting during their teenage years. In many states in the United States, this activity can be treated as a felony. While it rarely is treated this way—police and prosecutors do not wish to fill their jails with teenagers—the risk is still present for young people. Be sure to raise awareness about the realities and consequences of sexting up front when you are talking about relationships with your child.

As in other areas of connected parenting, you can't outsource to a school or an app your responsibility to keep your children safe. Others—especially teachers, mentors, and coaches in your kids' life—can and should help, but you need to play a positive and open-minded role. Most of all, you want to do all you can to be there, or to ensure that a good friend or trusted adult is, when your child reaches out for help in a moment of crisis.

COMMON QUESTIONS

I've seen TV shows suggesting that young people are at greater risk than ever from sexual predators because of technology. Is that true?

No. The risk of sexual predation has not soared during the past few decades, despite what the most sensational shows and headlines might lead you to believe.

There is, however, real risk to young people in certain activities online. These risks include sexual predation. Some people who wish to harm young people in this way do use online environments as their modern-day public park in which to lure young people into off-line encounters. The data and experiences of law enforcement show that these encounters often stem from chat environments related to sex; dating applications, some of which are visibly edgier than others; and chat environments related to gaming and other activities. The greatest risk of sexual misconduct still comes from connections with people the survivors already know (date rape and related risks).

The same advice we have always given young people about interacting with people they don't know well still works—and is perhaps more important than ever—in this technologically complex era.

What are some of the best online resources devoted to online safety?

The good news about online safety is that many devoted people are focused on the issue. There are great resources that you can turn to. Many of the social media sites and technology companies are also investing more in doing a better job of keeping kids safe in their online interactions.

There are plenty of websites that we think are effective. Organizations such as the Family Online Safety Institute and Common Sense Media update their materials regularly. The advice is generally sound and, well, commonsensical. We also check out what technology journalist Larry Magid posts at two organizations he founded or cofounded, ConnectSafely.org and SafeKids.org, and the work of Anne Collier at NetFamilyNews.org. For young people who are in crisis, Crisis Text Line can be a literal lifesaver.

Companies have also ramped up their internet safety efforts for kids. Google, which certainly collects loads of information about all of us, has developed a good website called "Be Internet Awesome," which has videos, games, and exercises that may serve your family well. We also follow what the Facebook global online safety team posts from time to time. Microsoft's Digital Literacy and Digital Skills Resources website is also a good place to turn for youth, families, and educators. These company-produced materials are certainly somewhat promotional; it always helps to keep a critical eye toward how to safely use various sites. Still, these materials are often very well done and worth exploring.

KEY TAKEAWAYS

The data show both good news and bad news about the digital era and kids' safety. The good news is this: young people are not at greater risk these days than they have been in the past. Despite what you might have come to believe, most research shows that the incidence of harm to children by adults they don't know—"stranger danger"—has been decreasing over the past few decades, not increasing. The bad news: the risk of this harm is still there. The risk has merely shifted environments. Digital environments can be hard to navigate safely, especially in cases where the app or the website is focused on sex or risk-taking.

Bullying is widespread, as it has been for a long time. It takes place online and offline, over screens and over lunch. Rather than use terms like *cyberbullying* and *offline bullying*, we prefer to describe the behavior as simply *bullying* since it often occurs across environments and platforms. All bullying is all connected in the minds of our kids; it should be considered the same way by connected parents, too. LGBTQ+ youth are more likely to be bullied than youth who do not identify as LGBTQ+.

Broad-based efforts—such as school courses on digital citizenship—can be helpful but seldom reach the kids who need the advice the most. A conundrum of the digital safety realm is that the kids who are at the greatest risk tend to be those who are looking for that risk. They often know that they are risking at least some degree of harm—and that's what's attractive to them.

There are many resources to help the connected parent, from effective government websites to nonprofits and private foundations that are dedicated to promoting kind, positive, safe relationships among young people online and offline. These resources can help prompt ongoing conversations between adults and young people and among peer groups. While adults are crucial to keeping kids safe, a child's peers are the most persuasive advocates for safe and healthy behaviors.

CHAPTER FIVE

Anxiety

Two teens, Andrea and Lauren, are texting one Saturday night. They are checking in before heading to the school dance:

Andrea: OMG she looks amazing in that dress

Lauren: wait who? What r u wearing tonight?

Andrea: Itzelt. Did you see her Insta? Her dress is perfect in that pic. She looks amazing

Lauren: no didnt see it will check it out. What about u what will u wear?

Andrea: not sure. i'm rethinking everything now after i saw that pic of Itzelt at her pre-party. To which we were clearly not invited

Lauren: ???

Andrea: i can't wear what i was going to wear if Itzelt is wearing that

Lauren: u r crazy. U will look amazing in whatever u wear

Andrea: ughhhhhh. And where is she hanging out in that pic?

Lauren: don't know. Not with me. Not with u. C u at the dance
Andrea: i am going to be soooooo late. And underdressed. Or overdressed. Maybe i shouldn't bother going

BEFORE THE BOOM in social media, the common refrain was "On the internet, no one knows you are a dog."

Today, a popular line has a very different tone: "On social media, everyone looks like they are having the best day, every day."

As researchers, educators, and parents, both of us hear that kind of language from youth all the time. Social media can make young people feel as if they were constantly surrounded by friends having the best time, in the finest weather, with their best-looking friends. Every day is a good-hair day—maybe not for them, but for everyone else. The proof is all around them, coming at them in their various feeds all day long. The opportunities for acute cases of FOMO—the fear of missing out—are essentially endless in a world of Instagram, Snapchat, and Facebook.

If you've spent much time at all on social media, you've likely had the experience of marveling at the exquisitely crafted profiles of friends and celebrities. You probably have former high school classmates you only know today through images of their stylish vacations and smiling children at the beach. You might follow the accounts of celebrities who curate their image with enormous care, only showing the best-staged, most appealing versions of their experiences. Think of the perfectly set dining room tables, the lush flowers, and the stunning outfits that celebrities present on their Instagram feeds.

If you've never used VSCO, an app for editing and sharing images, take a look. The interface allows users to manipulate and post stunning photography. It offers easy-to-use presets and editing tools on your mobile phone to make beautiful photos and videos, and the app then shares your posts with the VSCO community. Young people often use VSCO as a way to curate the most beautiful pictures of themselves and their lives. Even beyond the app, VSCO has become a thing by inspiring new communities that, like the VSCO girl movement, share a particular aesthetic—including featured products— over social media. The same dynamic plays out on more-popular sites such as Instagram and Snapchat, as the text string between Andrea and Lauren demonstrates.

Consider how a young person who uses apps like VSCO, Instagram, or Snapchat might feel. For young people who are insecure about their personal appearance, the online world can be an especially treacherous environment to navigate. To the extent that these beautiful photos appear to describe a life that is dramatically more appealing than the life they are experiencing, a service like Instagram can bring up feelings of being less attractive, athletic, fun, social, and so on, feeding into feelings of loneliness, anxiety, and low self-esteem. Conversely, the expectation to have perfect lighting in your photos, witty captions, and strategic hashtags to present a socially desirable self can also be a source of stress.

At the same time, for some young people who have posted striking images of themselves and their most cherished experiences, that Insta account or VSCO page can serve as an important source of identity development, creativity, and self-expression. Unlike other social media, VSCO does not offer metrics such as likes, follower counts, and comments that track influence; the lack of tracking might take the pressure off what users post. Even with services like Instagram, where likes are a currency, the likes and approbation in the comments thread below a post can, for some, feed a sense of connectedness to their community and sense of well-being.

It is also a common practice among young people to have multiple accounts to share different aspects of their identities, especially on Instagram these days. For many youth, so-called rinstas (short for "real instas") are their default account on Instagram. On these accounts, young people often curate their online public persona carefully. By contrast, *finstas* ("fake instas") or *sinstas* ("secret instas") are secondary accounts that are often less curated and less performative and are shared only with their closest friends.

Both these experiences of social media—a student's unfavorable self-comparison with others and a student whose self-esteem is bolstered by others' likes—are commonplace for today's adolescents. Social media tends to amplify many background conditions. Adolescents with low self-esteem may grow more anxious and depressed the more time they spend comparing themselves with their peers online. Others who seek to explore different aspects of their identity and connect with affinity groups may find these same environments to be very positive to their well-being and development.

The incidence of young people diagnosed with anxiety has increased by 20 percent in the years from 2007 to 2012, according to the National Survey of Children's Health. The same study showed an 0.2 percent increase in diagnoses of depression.[1] Much less clear is the cause of this growing anxiety among our youth. How much of this increase has to do with digital life is not yet understood, but for some young people, it is definitely a factor.

We suggest that parents avoid jumping to a facile conclusion about a link between anxiety and technology—a link that may not exist. Still, a growing number of studies support what you may have anticipated as a parent: some aspects of social media feed into a sense of vulnerability in young people, especially during adolescence. For young people who are already feeling as though they are "less than" others for one reason or another, the polished images of an Instagram feed, an engaging Snapchat story, or a beautifully crafted VSCO account can exacerbate the problem. All this is on top of social media feeds that often feature negative stories or content that might otherwise exhaust its users and make them feel stressed out and frustrated.

WHAT THE RESEARCH SHOWS

The numbers for anxiety, depression, and suicide are high among adolescents. A recent study from the Centers for Disease Control and Prevention (CDC) shows that, in any given year, 20 percent of children in the United States between the ages of three and seventeen—about 15 million—have a diagnosable mental, emotional, or behavioral disorder. Of these young people affected, only about 20 percent are diagnosed or receive care.[2] Statistics from the Youth Risk Behavior Survey revealed that 17.2 percent of youth seriously considered suicide in 2017. Close to 14 percent of youth surveyed made a plan to take their own lives.[3] In 2017, the CDC also reported that suicide was the second leading cause of death for youth between the ages of ten and twenty-four.[4]

A 2019 study by Juliana Menasce Horowitz and Nikki Graf at the Pew Research Center states that 70 percent of US youth aged thirteen to seventeen believe that anxiety and depression are a major problem among their peers.[5] The highest-pressure factors mentioned in the survey include the pressures to have good grades, to be involved in extracurricular activities, to look good, and to fit in socially. The last two pressures have the potential for a strong online connection.

According to a 2018 Pew Research Center study that asked teens about their experiences on social media, 45 percent of the surveyed teens said they felt overwhelmed by all the drama on social media, while 26 percent said that social media made them feel worse about their own lives (and 4 percent mentioned that these sites made them feel "a lot" worse). Nearly half (43 percent) indicated that they felt pressured to post content that made them look good, and 37 percent felt pressured to share things that would get a lot of likes and comments.[6]

As today's adolescents spend more time using technology and interacting through screens than ever before, does this mean that there is a *causal* relationship or merely a correlation between tech usage and anxiety? In *Nature*, one of the top scientific journals in the world, researcher Candice Odgers addressed this precise question head-on. She concluded: "More and better data are crucial. But studies so far do not support fears that digital devices are driving the downfall of a generation. What online activities might be doing, however, is reflecting and even worsening existing vulnerabilities."[7]

A wide range of studies support this conclusion. One key finding: while the rates of Internet usage and screen time are similar in much of Europe, a review of 131 studies has shown that the rates of anxiety and depression among young people have not risen as much as in the United States. The authors of this study, focusing on German-speaking and British community members, found that "in contrast to North American results, anxiety, depression, and neuroticism showed no increase in the two European populations" between 1964 and 2015.[8] The latest studies also provide clues for parents and educators to consider when they are trying to help young people avoid the worst effects of social media.

A study of young people aged fourteen to twenty-two conducted by Vicky Rideout and Susannah Fox offers some perhaps counterintuitive findings: "Young people with moderate to severe depressive symptoms report having heightened responses to social media—both positive and negative—compared to those without symptoms of depression."[9]

While all of us have good reason to be worried about the increasing numbers of young people reported to suffer from anxiety, studies like this remind us to be cautious about concluding that digital technology and social media are responsible for it.

Variety of Experiences on Different Social Media Sites

A study by the Royal Society for Public Health in 2017 asked young people (aged fourteen to twenty-four) to rank a series of popular social media sites according to their effect on youth well-being. In this study, YouTube came out as the most positive in terms of effect on young people, whereas Snapchat and Instagram came out in net-negative territory. The young people surveyed suggested that the use of some social media sites led them to feel more anxious, depressed, and concerned about their body image. On the flip side, the respondents reported that social media can connect young people to others who support them, provide access to other stories and information that can help their well-being, and provide important outlets for self-expression and development of their personal and social identities. These findings underscore that young people react differently to various services and experiences online.[10]

A meta-study of sixty-five research publications on Facebook has suggested that social media usage is consistently correlated with a series of social and emotional problems. Facebook, both the most popular and the most-studied social network site globally, boasted over 2.5 billion monthly users in 2019. According to two Australian researchers, Rachel Frost and Debra Rickwood, frequent Facebook usage was associated with technology addiction, anxiety, depression, body image issues, disordered eating, alcohol use, and other mental health problems.[11]

Facebook use has a complex relationship with anxiety. Frost and Rickwood found that extensive use of Facebook has been shown to trigger anxiety among some users, exacerbate or lead to extended bouts of anxiety for those with preexisting anxiety, or reduce anxiety when social connectedness benefits are realized.[12] Some of the young people studied demonstrated brooding, rumination, and comparison of self to others. The strength of the findings varied with age, gender, personality, passive and active use of the platform, and many other factors (and many of these studies included adults as well as young people). As most other studies show, the authors of this meta-study concluded that the adverse outcomes they list are the worst for those who exhibit "addictive use of Facebook."

Inequalities: The Digital Divide, the Participation Gap,
and Gender Differences

Inequalities persist online. Students who are born into families with higher socioeconomic status tend to have more positive online experiences than do those born into lower socioeconomic status families, as the work of Nicole Zillien, Eszter Hargittai, and others has documented.[13] Students from wealthier families tend to have parents who are helping the students to mediate and contextualize their online experiences. The wealthier students usually engage in more-active forms of online engagement than do kids from less wealthy families. Students from less wealthy families report a larger number of negative experiences online than their wealthier counterparts do. The online experience is one more way in which children from wealthier families have a stronger chance of success than those from families with fewer resources.

Young people have also demonstrated different online usage along racial lines in the United States. Research has shown that African American and Latinx youth are more likely to spend more time on screens and to experience somewhat different things online than their white counterparts do.[14] While concerns about the digital divide have often focused on questions of access, the nature of those concerns for many educators has flipped. The concern today is often that white children are more likely to be encouraged to play with old-school toys and engage in face-to-face interaction while children from African American and Latinx families are more likely to be educated via screens using suboptimal methods of instruction.

Many psychologists who study youth and social media also point to the differences between boys in girls in their reactions to online experiences. Girls are more likely to have body-image concerns, and some social media sites can exacerbate these concerns. Youth who feel insecure about their appearance may compete with one another in online environments—for example, the counting and comparing of likes on an Instagram post. This practice can lead to further insecurity for those who feel unsuccessful in the competition. Studies have consistently shown that teens with low social-emotional well-being experience more of the negative effects of social media than do youth with high social-emotional well-being.

The Lengthening of Adolescence—in Both Directions

Most scholars agree that the stretch of adolescence in a young person's life lasts longer than it did in the past. This period in life—the often-turbulent years between the end of childhood and the beginning of adulthood—has hard-to-define boundaries. One reason for the definitional challenge is that the notion of adolescence combines various factors, including the social and emotional as well as those related to physical development.

As ill-defined as the term may be, many researchers and teachers agree that adolescence may start earlier than you expect and may last longer than it has in the past. What about the kids who seem to be growing up faster in some ways at an earlier age, especially girls aged ten and eleven? This early physical maturity may be truly happening among some children. Epidemiologists point to data showing an earlier onset to puberty, especially in China and the United States, which can lead to challenges for families that are unprepared for these changes when they come on fast.[15]

On the other end, young people have been delaying activities traditionally associated with adulthood in many cultures. Over the past fifty years or so, people have been getting married, having children, and taking on full-time employment at later and later periods in life. That old chestnut about more kids returning home to live with mom and dad after college? There's some truth to it—along with the many other reasons driving postgraduates to move back home, such as the lingering effects of the 2008 recession and the COVID-19 pandemic, stagnant wages, higher home prices, and the shifting job market.

The definition of *adolescent* is not mere semantics. It can matter a great deal for several important policy reasons. In the criminal justice system, the state must decide who is competent to stand trial and to take responsibility for their decisions. The length of adolescence can matter for the health-care system, in terms of how resources are deployed, and in education. The economy, too, is plainly affected by these changing decisions that young people are making. On the younger end of this spectrum, tweens are consumers in their own right earlier on; on the other end, the housing and job markets are affected by later starting points among young people.

Adolescence is a period of high anxiety for many young people. While the exact cause of these recent shifts remains unknown, the combination of a longer adolescence and the prevalence of social media has ultimately meant that the period of anxious growing and learning is longer for many young people today. No doubt our parenting choices play into that mix as well.

THE CONNECTED PARENTS' APPROACH

Fears, worries, and other anxious feelings are a normal part of childhood. Every child goes through phases of relative anxiety, such as the feeling a child has after watching a scary movie or before an important exam. This type of temporary anxiety is usually harmless—and parents can do much to help. Our children need to know that we believe in them, especially when they are anxious about their self-worth and their place in the world.

When it comes to anxiety and technology, the young people in our lives need to know that *we know* they can lead happy, fulfilled lives that involve both digital and face-to-face interactions with others. We need to help them address the fundamental causes and possible consequences of their anxiety. Social media usage is undeniably relevant in this discussion, but the usage itself is unlikely be the root cause when all the facts about a young person's condition are known over time.

One of the most important things we can do as parents and educators is support our children when they succeed and ensure they know that we will still support them when they fail. As we think about our own use of social media, we should ask ourselves some questions: Are we presenting ourselves and our own lives as perfect? How do we reveal our shortcomings and vulnerabilities to our children, to normalize imperfection and to model resilience in the face of challenges?

Our children need to know that the near-perfect collections of images and experiences they observe on many social media sites are exactly what they are: screen grabs of someone's experiences but only a part of a full life. We learn more from our mistakes and our shortcomings than from our successes. We need to reinforce that messaging with our children despite what they are likely encountering online.

Sometimes the reassurance and comfort that parents can provide are not enough to help children move past their fears and anxieties. If a child gets stuck in or overwhelmed with worries, and when these thoughts begin to interfere with daily functions like falling asleep, going to school, playing with friends, parents need to ask for professional help. These symptoms might be signs of an anxiety *disorder*, which can have serious negative consequences without appropriate treatment.

OUR RECOMMENDATIONS

The clearest finding in the research on anxiety and online life is that the use of technology by young people can exacerbate other differences and challenges in their lives. This finding points directly toward a parenting approach that seeks to get at these underlying issues that our children face. We need to help children put in perspective what they are seeing and experiencing online, and we must do it in ways that are constructive instead of destructive.

Children's pervasive use of social media and the high incidence of youth anxiety make a convincing case for connected parenting. We frame these issues in two essential ways: First, technology itself is not the problem; technology can't (yet) do anything on its own. Still, as a powerful, multifaceted tool, technology is *connected* to many habits and deep issues that young people face. A young person's technology usage can illuminate other underlying issues and sometimes make problems worse, in turn causing additional problems.

Second, the way that young people are using technology gives rise to the need for parents to connect to their children in important new ways. It has always been a good idea for parents to bond with their children; nature requires it, in fact. The *type* of connection we have with young people in our lives is changing, though, in a technological era. On the one hand, many parents give young people much independence in how they are permitted to use these powerful new tools, with little explanation or support. Parents take this hands-off approach partly because they may not understand the tools as well as their children do. On the other hand, many parents seek to control their children through the technology itself, such as tracking their movements using find-my-phone apps and related tools.

The connected-parenting philosophy calls on us to play a meaningful role in the lives of our children and technology but not to try to control them using technology. As parents, we must familiarize ourselves with, and use, the same technologies that our kids are using, if we are to become informed and credible guides. By staying connected with their experiences and practices, we as parents will have a better chance of engaging constructively with our children. As we've described throughout this book, the idea that parents can entirely control what their kids are doing online is implausible; plenty of evidence and experience shows that attempts at control aren't going to work and will always backfire once your children reach adolescence.

The data on youth, anxiety, and technology help reframe the advice we ought to heed when it comes to technology use. For many young people, things are going just fine. If that's so, there is no reason to panic if they spend a bit more time on social media or playing video games than you'd like. For young people who are otherwise healthy and thriving, we should strive to help them keep the balance that they are setting for themselves. In fact, for young people who are broadly in good shape, a growing number of studies has shown that time online—including on social media—tends to *enhance* their relationships, not detract from them.

The deep concern comes into play with respect to young people who are struggling with anxiety and other challenges. For these young people, extensive technology usage can lead to additional problems. Over time, we will probably learn more about the specific problems that technology use can exacerbate, but in the meantime, there are several steps that all of us parents can take in connecting more directly to our children.

As we have stressed over and over, you have to talk to the young people in your life about the issues on their mind. Even when— especially when—they seem sullen and withdrawn from adults and friends, you need to help connect them with a supportive adult. This support can come from you the parent, another family member, a teacher, a coach, or another mentor. If you are not the one that your child will talk to about a certain topic, swallow your pride and find another trusted adult to try.

As soon as your child begins to engage regularly with social media—we hope, as discussed, not before age thirteen—the work of parenting becomes more complicated. The stresses children face today are different from those that most of us faced as children. If you imagine that your child is going to grow up exactly as you did, you are bound to be disappointed.

Even as you shouldn't try to replicate the exact growing experiences you had, your job is to give the children in your life some perspective on what they are seeing. For instance, young people are tempted to publish only the beautiful parts of their life online. While understandable, this practice makes things harder for themselves and their peers. A carefully curated Facebook, Instagram, or Tumblr account can make the life of a teen look only glamorous, always interesting, and endlessly worthy of envy by peers. Also encourage your children to think about what their own social media practices might be doing to others. The main point is to maintain a supportive parent–child relationship that encourages disclosure and opportunities for discussion. Social media phenomena such as the #NoFilter, #NoMakeup, and #NaturalHair movements might offer starting points for such conversations.

In the big picture, we urge you to stay involved in the online and offline activities of your children without being a snowplow parent who always makes the road ahead of them smooth. Avoid overly restrictive or coercive monitoring, but do help them by setting limits that will turn into great long-term habits.

In that spirit, here are a few connected-parenting ideas that can help to prevent or mitigate anxious feelings shaped by the use of digital technology:

- *Encourage breaks from social media for children experiencing high anxiety or depressive symptoms.* For anyone having these symptoms, psychologists and researchers point to the advantages of taking periodic breaks from social media. Students also have reported to researchers that these breaks, though not necessarily desirable in the moment, can prove helpful. (What's tricky about the data is that studies also show that social media can also increase feelings of well-being in some young people. Nothing's simple.)

- *Insist on device-free time.* Both of us are fans of regular periods of device-free time for young people, whatever that might mean. The periods can mean family board games in the evenings, family dinners, times of day when phones have to be put away, or trips of any sort (even just to the store) that involve leaving devices behind. An obvious practice, as we've mentioned earlier, is to turn all devices off at least thirty minutes—and ideally an hour—before bedtime.

- *Get your children outdoors.* Have them put away their phones, laptops, tablets, and gaming consoles. One of the best things you can give your kids is a love of activities that do not involve screens. For kids who love sports, athletics are a natural way for them to be outside—shooting hoops or tossing a Frisbee or football. Others might get excited about hiking or spending time in the city park. Making outdoor time a part of the family routine can help with the "nature deficit disorder" that some people fear affects this generation.

- *Talk regularly to your child about feelings of anxiety and depression if one or more family members in your household have either of these disorders.* If you see that the issue is truly problematic, get professional help. Diagnosis, early treatment, and close monitoring are crucial to a young person's well-being.

Don't delay addressing it if there's an issue. Don't stigmatize these feelings or the discussion of social and emotional hardship. As noted earlier, studies have shown that as little as 20 percent of the cases of concern are even diagnosed or addressed.

- *Model constructive ways of dealing with anxiety.* Share with your children your own feelings of social pressure and anxiety. Seeing that those feelings are common can help them cope on their own. Help them learn to live with their anxiety, even when they're anxious. Remember too that they are almost certainly watching what you post online. If your posts and images are all incredibly polished, your children may feel pressured to appear just as polished.

- *Remember that your child's anxiety—at least in part—may have to do with issues connected to you as a parent.* Your children might feel anxious about school performance, pressure to be involved in extracurricular activities, fitting in socially, and other issues. If your children seem overly anxious, express confidence that they are going to be okay and will be able to manage their anxiety. Remind your kids that the more often they face the issues that cause anxiety, the more chances they have to overcome those challenges and to diminish their fears overall. This assurance might help to give your children confidence that your expectations are realistic and that you're not going to ask them to do anything unreasonable.

- *Familiarize yourself with the most popular apps and tools— or at least the ones the children in your life use.* Today, these digital tools mean YouTube, Instagram, Snapchat, and Facebook. You don't have to spend a ton of time on these sites to get the gist of them. In fact, your demonstrating the ability to "eat just one" (to borrow a line from the famous Lay's potato chip commercial) will itself be valuable for your children to observe. But you need to keep yourself credible as you ask them about their lives and seek to help them manage what they are seeing and experiencing. You might also ask the children in your life what app they use most of all, in case a less popular site such as VSCO is where they are spending a lot of their time.

- *Emphasize expressive activities that are not dependent on technology.* For the youngest children, think about creative play that involves everyday objects such as pots and pans, blocks, and the simplest of toys. As they get older, young people who love theater, music, or dance have natural expressive outlets that don't require technology. Public libraries can also be great sources of activities for young people. Story time still draws crowds in thousands of local libraries around the world every week. It turns out that teenagers are some of the biggest library users. Librarians can be great teachers, often very well versed in the kinds of creative play and work that do not have to involve technology (and those that do, too!).

- *Support them in their identity play—and keep an eye on it where you can.* Your child might also be among those who present one image of themselves in one account and quite another in another setting. Sometimes, this practice is a healthy, positive form of identity play in which the young person is trying on some different ways of presenting in the world. For instance, a student who wonders how she or he would be received if they came out as trans or gay might try out a new identity in a social media space before formally coming out in a face-to-face environment. As young people become more aware of the effects of race and ethnic differences, typically during adolescence, they often explore these aspects of their identity in online social media. Some young people and those who study them closely also report benefits from identity play and experimentation on Instagram.

- *Keep an eye out for fake instas and the like.* For some young people, the practice of identity play can also take on a different, less constructive twist. The simplest form of this identity play is the creation of two Instagram accounts for the same person: an insta and a finsta. An insta is ordinarily the truthful and positive account that students create for themselves; their finsta—or fake insta—can be an alternate identity, often harsher and edgier, sometimes to the point of cruelty to themselves or others.

The goal of these efforts is to keep our children healthy and safe by helping them build the skills they need to navigate this increasingly complicated world, just as they must offline. Along the way, we support our children as they establish habits of balance and engagement in the physical and natural world. As young people build resilience and understanding, they will thrive in this more complex, hybrid world of online and offline interactions.

KEY TAKEAWAYS

There are signs that young people are more anxious today than in the past. Moreover, they are also clearly spending more time on social media. These two observations might understandably be connected in one's mind, but the deep research conducted on this topic doesn't prove a connection between children's anxiety and time spent on social media.

The young people who spend the most time on social media appear to be the most at risk from increased anxiety. Excessive use of social media can almost certainly exacerbate social and emotional concerns for those who have other problems, such as depression or eating disorders. Teens with low social-emotional well-being experience more of the negative effects of social media than do youth with high social and emotional well-being.

For young people who are otherwise thriving, moderate use of social media tends to add to their sense of well-being, not detract from it.

The pattern of inequity that is so stark today between children of different socioeconomic groups is likely to play out in the context of social media use. The benefits of screen time often accrue more extensively to children from wealthier families, and unfortunately, the downsides are more likely to affect those from lower socioeconomic backgrounds.

Kids will benefit from a combination of limits, support, and conversation. It will be easier for some families than for others to provide this level of guidance, but all caregivers should try to keep connected to the children in their life. The common sense that you can share when a young person is stressed out about what they are seeing on social media can go a long way. Following your children and their friends online, with their permission, can also help you open up conversations about what they are seeing and experiencing.

Dealing with your child's anxiety is an especially difficult area of parenting. There are no simple ways to keep your children from experiencing heightened anxiety as they see the polished social media sites of their friends and celebrities. They need to hear from you that they are more than "just good enough" and that you care about them and their feelings. Your support, love, and hugs will go a long way.

CHAPTER 6

Addiction

JAMIR, AGE TEN, is a bit of a loner. He has a few friends at school, but they don't hang out together or play outside all that often. In the rare cases that they do get together, Jamir and his friends play video games, saying little to one another while they sit side by side on the couch. Jamir has never been a big one for saying much, but his parents are worried that he seems to be getting more and more withdrawn.

Jamir's parents are concerned for other reasons, too. He is barely getting by in school. He has no interest in any organized after-school activities like sports or music. The only thing he seems to love is being on his computer by himself in his room. As far as his parents can tell, that time is entirely spent gaming.

When his parents engage with Jamir about it, he says everything is fine. He doesn't seem terribly unhappy. He just likes video games, he says. He's got friends "in-game" with whom he chats extensively. He doesn't see those friends outside the game environment, but he says that they are important to him all the same.

There's no acute crisis in Jamir's life, but his parents can't see how the lifestyle he is leading could be a healthy one. He strikes them as a little bit tired each day, and it's a fight every night to get him to come down to join the family at dinnertime. They dread the parent–teacher conferences each fall; his teachers invariably say he's a bright boy but he's disengaged from schoolwork and from the other students.

Jamir's parents fear that he is addicted to the internet and video games. They believe that the few in-person friends he has are falling away. They wonder if Jamir is in fact on the autism spectrum and if they've somehow missed it up to this point.

Jamir's parents are at their wits' end.

THERE'S A RAGING debate that continues to this day: Can a young person be *addicted* to the internet? Is this addiction similar to substance abuse or behavioral disorders? In the United States, for the most part, the official answer from authorities is no. In other countries, particularly in East Asia, the official word is maybe or yes.

Part of the problem in finding a definitive answer has to do with the different types of technologies and forms of usage that can be investigated. *Technology addiction, internet addiction, smartphone addiction, gaming addiction*, and *social media addiction* are just a few examples of the partly overlapping, partly distinct terms used for excessive tech-related behaviors.

In addition to the variety of technologies and behaviors involved and the lack of clear-cut definitions, it is also methodologically very difficult to observe addiction from a genetic, neurological, and behavioral perspective. While advanced neuroimaging technology might provide some insights when researchers are comparing brains from compulsive users and brains from others, the criteria that are used to assess whether someone is addicted remain highly controversial.

Either way, mental health practitioners have observed that for a few young people, the excessive use of digital technology—whether it's the internet or smartphones, social media or gaming—can get in the way of their everyday lives. Vast amounts of time spent in gaming environments and binge-watching TV can become a coping mechanism for other issues that a child faces.

Whether you call it an addiction, a disorder, or just the problematic use of media and technology (our preferred term, given the uncertainties), there are times when parents have good reason to worry about the sheer amount of time that a young person spends connected to a screen. This topic relates closely to the aforementioned issue of time online, but here we consider the extreme cases. What do researchers know about how much internet, social media, and gaming use really is too much? And where can you turn when your child is showing worrying signs of excessive use?

WHAT THE RESEARCH SHOWS

Many studies have examined different forms of technology addiction, its pervasiveness, and its possible impacts on users. Relatively few of these studies, however, have focused specifically on children, including teens. One helpful overview of the research in this field, summarizing more than 180 sources, comes from the 2016 Common Sense Media report "Technology Addiction: Concern, Controversy, and Finding Balance." One of the key findings reads as follows:

> One systematic review of studies on American adolescents and college students reported a range of prevalence estimates between 0 and 26 percent. "Internet addiction" refers to a swath of excessive and compulsive technology-related behaviors resulting in negative outcomes. There remains substantial disagreement about whether Internet addiction is a new psychological disorder

or the manifestation of another disorder, how it is measured, and how prevalent it is. . . . Focusing on amount of time online is controversial, given that children and adults alike are connected all the time and given how many activities take place in online environments.[1]

In the United States—perhaps unsurprisingly, given the lack of solid evidence—most experts do not consider extensive use of the internet to be a formal addiction. For instance, the key medical resource called the *Diagnostic and Statistical Manual of Mental Disorders,* fifth edition, (DSM-V), which classifies mental and psychiatric disorders and provides extensive diagnostic criteria, does not currently include internet addiction.

That said, we share the view that some young people may have something close to an addiction—a condition often called *internet gaming disorder,* or the playing of immersive games to an unhealthy degree. Immersive games are those that make the players feel as though they are there in the place and moment of the game. The DSM-V lists internet gaming disorder as a condition that needs more research and clinical experience.

The World Health Organization has gone a step further by including "gaming disorder" in its most recent International Classification of Diseases. The organization defines this disorder as "a pattern of gaming behavior . . . characterized by impaired control over gaming, increasing priority given to gaming over other activities to the extent that gaming takes precedence over other interests and daily activities, and continuation or escalation of gaming despite the occurrence of negative consequences. For gaming disorder to be diagnosed, the behavior pattern must be of sufficient severity to result in significant impairment in personal, family, social, educational, occupational or other important areas of functioning and would normally have been evident for at least 12 months."[2]

Despite this definition, many questions remain open. Some researchers, for example, prefer to see internet gaming disorder as a substance-related disorder, as certain brain research has shown similarities between excessive internet gaming and drug use. Other researchers prefer a behavioral model that links gaming and internet addiction in general.

The behavior associated with excessive media usage often comes along with other types of concerns. Anxiety and depression are common pairings with excessive media usage. Some observers believe that those on the autism spectrum and those who have attention deficit hyperactivity disorder (ADHD) are more prone to excessive media usage. In our observation, it is fairly certain that boys are more prone to this disorder than girls.

In several East Asian countries, internet addiction is considered an acute issue. In China, Japan, Taiwan, and South Korea, internet addiction centers are more prevalent and young people are more commonly treated for this disorder. Reports from South Korea have proclaimed that as many as 10 percent of the boys in that country have a gaming addiction. Compared with parents and authorities from other countries, the adults in East Asian countries appear to be more concerned about the threat of internet addiction. Whether their concern correlates with truly higher incidences of this problem or with a different opinion on how to address similar cases is unclear from the existing data. We surmise that this higher level of concern most likely stems from a combination of two things: a strong internet gaming culture among East Asian boys in particular and a greater proclivity in East Asian health care to consider disorders as addictions than exists in Western medicine.[3]

The data on these extreme cases of internet usage and gaming are insufficient to draw a reliable overall conclusion. But from a case-by-case perspective, there is no doubt that some psychologists, physicians, and policy makers consider this disorder a severe problem for some individuals. And across the globe, these concerns are only likely to grow, since tech companies and the social media industry have strong economic incentives to hook young users to their digital devices and apps: the more time spent online, the more data can be collected and more ads displayed, which in turn means more revenues for these companies.

Our confidence in the research in this area of addiction is lower than in any other area of this book. The question of whether a person can become addicted to the use of the internet and gaming remains hotly debated by psychologists, and conclusions vary across cultures. The fact that experts in the United States do not classify it as an addiction while several highly wired East Asian countries do so makes us pause in our own assessment. In our research and teaching, we have observed young people—especially boys—for whom excessive media usage has been a real problem. They have tended to emerge from these problems over time, with good support and care, but along the way, parents have a very hard time knowing what to do. For this reason, we urge a conservative approach both to calling it an addiction and to how young people are treated when it is a concern.

THE CONNECTED PARENTS' APPROACH

Our philosophy is to take a conservative approach, even if there is no formal diagnosis of addiction—or even if authorities in the United States are correct and there's no possibility of addiction in a formal sense. Especially early on, when an intervention can have the most benefits for a young person, it is worth the effort to help them build positive media habits that will serve them their whole lives. We believe that the possibilities—and temptations—of media use will only grow during their lifetimes.

Conversely, we urge you not to use the term *addiction* lightly. It is a mistake to call every young person who spends a fair amount of time on digital technology an addict. This tendency is dangerous for a number of reasons. It can lead to overtreatment of something that may not be the concern you fear it is. It can also inadvertently downplay diagnosed medical conditions that clearly are in fact addictions. Terminology also matters from a larger societal perspective. The panic over "social media addiction," for instance, has fueled a proposal for a new law (called the Social Media Addiction Reduction Technology Act) that would restrict the use of social media platforms to a default of thirty minutes per day. While it is very unlikely that such a bill will ever pass in the US Congress or survive a constitutional review, it is a reminder of how the choice of words can affect perceptions and might shape policies.

Undeniably, some young people can handle media usage more easily than others can. Your child may be someone for whom two hours of television shows delivered over Netflix every afternoon is no problem in everyday life. Your child may be deep into the details of learning to code Ruby on Rails—a popular coding language—and may parlay that genuine interest into a career in computer programming, data science, or game design. Or perhaps your child, who suffers from trauma or is vulnerable in other ways, cannot handle spending too much time playing video games—and adult intervention is necessary. As a matter of philosophy, you need to realize that part of your job is to understand your own children in a holistic manner and not apply one-size-fits-all rules, no matter how clear and attractive they may seem.

Conversely—and perhaps unsurprisingly, given our connected-parenting approach—we also encourage you to think creatively about how digital technology can also become part of the solution. Screen time tracking apps can help adults and kids alike track how much they use their phones and tablets each day. Other apps can be used to schedule screen-free periods—or limit the time spent on social media. Checklists, learning resources, online expert forums, and support communities on the internet might also help families identify and address problematic media and technology uses.

OUR RECOMMENDATIONS

Most researchers, psychologists, and physicians agree on a recommendation based on the best available research: seek a balanced life for yourself and your child when it comes to the use of media. This balance should include time away from devices completely (the summer can be an especially fruitful time to do so as a family), fun activities that do not involve technology (board games, playing in parks, hiking on trails, biking, arts and crafts, and so forth), face-to-face interactions (around the dinner table, for instance), and explicitly single-tasking rather than multitasking as a general rule.

This balanced approach does not mean that young people can't be online with their friends at all. Nor does it mean mistaking all their activities online as addictive. For instance, the tendency of young people to be on social media for many hours a day in the background, while they also listen to music, or watch TV and respond quickly to one another's messages, is actually about their basic need to connect with one another. Of course, kids don't need to reply right away to every message to remain connected, and it's often a good idea to wait before responding. But seeing their online habit as a desire for social interaction helps show that much of what we think of as possible addiction has nothing to do with technology per se. Rather, the behavior is about a basic adolescent desire to be connected with friends, made possible in a new way by these technologies.

This deliberate search for a balanced slate of activities can prevent excessive media use. Such a balance is easier said than done, we know. But this is also good common sense, as usual, in connected parenting. The introduction of family time with old-school board games, card games, and puzzles may sound unlikely to work in your family, but try it; it may be much more successful than you expect.

Some children's problems with overuse of media will extend beyond the scope of this book and the advice that we can dispense. These case-by-case decisions to seek professional help are akin to the decisions parents must make to get a young person other kinds of help, whether it is for a possible learning difference, anxiety, or depression. We have found that caregivers are increasingly aware of the possible effects of extreme media usage.

If you are concerned about a potential disorder of this sort, you can call a trained professional for help. Some doctors at major medical centers have specialized in treating these disorders. For example, Michael Rich, a physician who calls himself a "mediatrician," practices at Boston Children's Hospital. Rich writes on his website: "We are not only seeing problems with gaming, such as that with your son, but also with social media, pornography, and what we're calling 'information-bingeing' which is open-ended searching and viewing of short-form videos, memes, hyperlinks, wikis and other internet black holes."[4] Rich and his colleagues at the Center on Media and Child Health have been treating these interconnected disorders for several years. Outside the Boston area, a small but growing number of specialists across the country may be worth seeking out.

Some psychologists have also begun to focus on this area of excessive media use, but the field is in an early stage. Local youth counselors, too, are getting more and more up to speed on how to support kids who are turning to devices as coping mechanisms. However, despite these experts focusing on this issue, the research suggests that much more needs to be done to understand both the disorder itself and the possible treatments.[5]

You can plan dedicated times and spaces for your child to unplug. A simple approach is to structure time when your child simply doesn't have access to screens and has no choice but to explore other interests (offline and face-to-face). Many summer camps, for example, require kids to leave their devices behind. That said, we think summers in general can be a great time to go device-free every year.

If you have the means and if the issue is more acute, you might explore a formal program that helps students make the transition away from such extensive gaming and media use and toward other pursuits. Some programs, such as the Unplugged program offered by Outback Therapeutic Expeditions in Utah, run for a few months. There are also specialized boarding schools for young people who need longer periods of inpatient support. These interventions can be expensive and impractical for some families, we realize, but they can be very effective.

COMMON QUESTIONS

What do you think? Is it an addiction or not?

We're not experts in addictive behavior, so to answer the question, we turn to those who are. We adopt the line that for the vast majority of young people, it's difficult to say that prolonged screen time is evidence of a chemical or behavioral compulsion like that found in drug or alcohol addiction. However, for a small number of kids, the use of technologies can take over everything else. Clinical experience suggests a link between excessive usage and certain personality traits as well as family relationship problems. Overuse appears to be especially prevalent among young boys. Many kids do tend to grow out of these habits when they get good support and when other things capture their attention over time. While we refrain from using the term *addiction*, we are comfortable with the classification of excessive gaming and internet use as a *disorder* in the most extreme cases.

At what point should we seek outside help if we fear our child has this disorder?

This disorder is like many other concerns that parents have about their children. We urge frequent dialogue between parents and the other caregivers in a child's life—including teachers, faith leaders, music instructors, and sports coaches. If you have a sense that there's reason to intervene in light of these conversations, then by all means seek out help. A school guidance counselor or psychologist may be a good place to start. Ask whether they have expertise with this disorder and related concerns; seek a referral if they do not. If your local area does not have an expert in this field, seek out a national expert for a consultation.

KEY TAKEAWAYS

There's a raging debate as to whether a person can be addicted to gaming and other aspects of digital life. We believe that the right frame of reference is to call it a *disorder* in the case of young people whose life is disrupted for an extended period by excessive media use. Parents should refrain from jumping to the conclusion that their child has a true addiction without first consulting an expert physician or psychologist.

The excessive use of media is almost certainly linked to other issues or concerns that a young person is facing. Anxiety and depression are among the most common associated conditions. Children on the autism spectrum and those with ADHD may be more prone to excessive media usage as well. Boys appear more prone to this disorder than are girls.

Prevention is, as usual, the best medicine. The connected parents' approach is to try to address the underlying issues and to identify excessive media use before it becomes a life-changing disorder.

While it is much easier said than done, helping young people to find other outlets—including outdoor activities, nontechnological board games, and other positive habits—is the best strategy before the issue becomes acute.

The best approach to your child's excessive use of media if it has affected the young person for a long time is to seek expert help. There is an emerging field of "mediatricians" and psychologists to whom you might turn and who specialize in this area of support for young people. You could also consider contacting specialists at schools, camps, and clinics that offer support for young people with the most acute challenges.

CHAPTER 7

Gaming

JACQUES, THE FATHER of two teenagers, has just prepared a late-Sunday morning breakfast for his family. The hardest part on this Sunday, however, isn't avoiding overcooking the eggs or keeping the pancakes warm. Rather, Jacques is struggling to get everyone to the breakfast table.

"Hey, Liam, breakfast is ready—please come downstairs," Jacques shouts up to his fifteen-year-old son.

No reply. After a few minutes, Jacques tries again. Same outcome: more silence. Jacques starts wondering whether Liam might be taking a shower, and he decides to start breakfast without him.

After another five minutes or so, Jacques asks his eighteen-year-old daughter, Melissa, to check up on Liam.

"Liam says he can't come right now," Melissa tells her dad. "He's in the middle of a game with his friends."

Jacques looks as his wife and wonders whether the time has come for an intervention. In his view, Liam spends far too much time immersed in hyperviolent games on his Xbox One. Liam has described spending most of his time playing his favorite online video game, *Fortnite Battle Royale*, a player-versus-player battle game for up to a hundred players. (In case you are wondering, you can play alone, in a duo, or in a squad consisting of three or four friends.) As the game progresses, the playable area within the island gradually constricts, giving the players less and less room to work with. The last player or team still alive wins the game.

Just as Jacques is about to take matters into his own hands and drag Liam downstairs, he hears Liam's bedroom door opening. The teen arrives at the table with his typical abundance of energy, nearly spilling all the glasses of orange juice onto his family members.

"Dad, Mom . . . ," he mumbles with a chocolate croissant already halfway into his mouth. "It was so cool. My friend Adrien and I were just awarded the Victory Royale after an epic battle. It was sooo cool, you should have seen it!"

Given Liam's enthusiasm and the otherwise peaceful Sunday morning, Jacques decides to let it go for now and not start another long—yet, always, to date, fruitless—conversation with Liam about playing video games. But he can't help worrying about Liam's well-being: Is he playing too much? Can games that include realistic violence, including shooting people at close range, make you more aggressive toward other people? And in addition to these concerns, is Liam simply wasting his time playing games instead of doing something more meaningful?

As PARENTS, BOTH of us have experienced situations like this one firsthand. And as authors and researchers, we have been asked these questions many, many times by parents who are worried about the possible effects of gaming on their children's well-being and health.

WHAT THE RESEARCH SHOWS

Playing video games is, and for decades has been, extremely popular among teenagers. The following 2018 data points from Pew Research are emblematic:

- Around 90 percent of American teens aged thirteen to seventeen say they play video games on a computer, game console, or cell phone.
- Some 97 percent of American teen boys play video games on some kind of device, and 92 percent have access to a video game console.
- About 83 percent of American teen girls play video games, and 75 percent have access to video game consoles.[1]

Another survey, the Common Sense Census, tracks media use by tweens and teens and illustrates how different gaming devices attract different audiences. For instance, games on mobile phones are played by both genders, whereas computer games are reportedly most popular among white boys. The survey also gives a sense of the amount of time teenagers spend on a given day playing mobile, video, or computer games—although these numbers should be taken with a grain of salt since teens often overestimate the time they spend online. According to the survey, "on any given day, one in 10 tween boys and one in seven teen boys plays . . . games for more than four hours. Among teen boys, 6 percent play video games for more than four hours, 3 percent play computer games that long, and 1 percent play mobile games (the rest play a combination of games)." According to the same study, 35 percent of teenage boys and 18 percent of girls state that they enjoy playing "a lot," while (perhaps surprisingly to some parents) only 3 percent and 1 percent respectively say it is their "favorite activity."[2]

"Gaming," of course, covers a broad range of activities. The data suggest that gamers often play a variety of games. While recent US surveys don't delve into details about the various genres played by children and youth, Pew surveys of adults indicate that the most popular types of video games include, in order of most to least popular: puzzles, strategy, adventure, shooter, role-playing, and simulation games.[3] Survey data from outside the United States indicate that first- and third-person shooter games (like *Fortnite Battle Royale* in Liam's example), sports games (e.g., NHL, NBA, or FIFA), open-world games (*Minecraft*, *Watch Dogs*, etc.), action-adventure games (e.g., *Assassin's Creed*, *Far Cry*, *Uncharted*), and racing games are the most popular genres among twelve- to nineteen-year-olds (with some gender variations).[4]

Given the popularity of mobile, video, and computer games and their persistence in our culture, what questions should we be asking, and where is the evidence strong enough to help us draw conclusions? What do we know about the positive and negative effects that video games can have on our children? What do the data say about violent video games? Can video games increase or decrease feelings of loneliness? Can games teach young people skills that are useful in the digital economy? And what should we do when we don't have reliable data on certain questions?

We will address each of these questions in turn in the next section. The good news is that a wealth of research has been conducted over the past few decades to better understand the effects of mobile, video, and computer games on people. This research will help us ground our advice in evidence. The depth of knowledge, however, varies across the different areas of concern, populations, and geographic locations. In some controversial areas, such as aggression or addiction, the most recent data suggest trends, but experts disagree on what larger conclusions to draw from them. Overall, the state of research on games and their effects on children is nuanced and complex, which makes it harder to draw conclusions with high degrees of confidence. Despite these drawbacks, a look at the research can be helpful.

Aggression

Parents who watch their kids playing games obsessively on their consoles, tablets, or mobile devices often wonder whether gaming—particularly playing violent video games—makes them more aggressive in their attitudes or, even more worrisome, in their behavior. The court of public opinion seem to have reached the verdict: According to a 2017 survey from the Pew Research Center, a vast majority of adults in the United States believe that the violence in video games contributes either a great deal or a fair amount to gun violence in this country.[5] Fortunately, the evidence suggests a more nuanced and less grim picture. Let's consider the most important fact up front: There is no evidence establishing a general causal link between game playing and physical violence among young people.

Given the strong yet largely unfounded public perceptions around children, gaming, and violence, let's take a slightly more detailed look at some of the available evidence:

- A literature review by the Australian attorney general's department concluded in 2010 that significant "harmful effects from VVGs [violent video games] have not been persuasively proven or disproven. There is some consensus that VVGs may be harmful to certain populations, such as people with aggressive and psychotic personality traits. Overall, most studies have consistently shown a small statistical effect of VVG exposure on aggressive behaviour, but there are problems with these findings that reduce their policy relevance. Overall, . . . research into the effects of VVGs on aggression is contested and inconclusive."[6]

- In 2011 the US Supreme Court reviewed the available evidence, and a majority found that the connection between exposure to violent video games and harmful effects on children was both small and indistinguishable from effects produced by other media, such as cartoons. Two justices questioned the majority's conclusion and pointed out that the experience of playing violent video games might be different from reading a book, listening to radio, or watching a movie or TV show.[7]

- A Swedish Media Council report concluded in 2012 that there is "an extensive amount of research that demonstrates a statistical relationship between VCG [violent computer games] and aggression." But the report also clarified that this measured aggression related only to mental processes and not to actual violent behavior. In addition, the report pointed out that there was no evidence for such games to cause aggressive behavior.[8]

- In one of its general comments in 2013, the UN Committee on the Rights of the Child expressed concerns that the "increasing levels of participation, particularly among boys, in violent video games appears to be linked to aggressive behaviour as the games are highly engaging and interactive and reward violent behavior." The committee also expressed concern that when the games are played repeatedly, the effects become more dramatic, and young people become insensitive to the pain and suffering of others.[9]

- A 2015 report by the American Psychological Association found "a consistent relationship between violent video game use and increases in aggressive behavior, aggressive cogitations, and aggressive affect, and decreases in prosocial behavior (behavior that is for the good of others or the community at large), empathy, and sensitivity to aggression."[10] The work of the association's task force, however, was heavily criticized by a large group of well-known researchers in the field, and the findings of the report were challenged in light of methodological problems of the underlying research.[11] Critics of the report pointed out that only a modest correlation between violent video games and aggression can be determined on the basis of the soundest research, not causation, and that the APA report's framing would lead to overblown recommendations.[12]

- A large representative study from our colleagues at the Oxford Internet Institute was published in 2019. It tested whether the recent playing of violent video games by British kids aged fourteen to fifteen is linearly and positively related to aggressive behavior. The robust study could not confirm the hypothesis: "We found adolescents were not more or less likely to engage in aggressive or prosocial behaviours as a function of the amount of time they devoted to playing video games." And here's the key takeaway: "We argue this study speaks to the key question of whether adolescents' violent video game play has a measurable effect on real-world aggressive behaviour. On the basis of our evidence, the answer is no. This is *not* to say that some mechanics and situations in gaming do not foment angry feelings or reactions in players."[13]

Given all these analyses and their nuanced and sometimes even contradictory findings, how worried are we about (violent) games and their effects on our children? Our short answer is this: gaming is not at the top of the list of things that currently keep us sleepless in our roles as parents, teachers, and lawyers. From what we know today, the risk that playing violent video games makes young people *behave* aggressively is low, unless there are other factors at play (such as already-established aggressive personality traits) that increase this risk. That said, given what's at stake in terms of the well-being of our children and society at large, we think a series of precautionary measures can make great sense.

Social Isolation

Another concern we've repeatedly heard from parents is the fear that children who spend a lot of time playing video games become socially isolated. Again, we're happy to report that the research conducted over the past decade offers no evidence of social isolation or, for that matter, antisocial behavior in kids who play video games. A case in point is a 2016 study drawing from the School Children Mental Health in Europe project, which was conducted in six European countries and involved more than three thousand children. The researchers found that the young people who played video games for more than five hour per week were "significantly associated with . . . a *lower* prevalence of peer relationship problems and a lower prevalence of mental health difficulties."[14] The findings of this study support the results of previous research efforts over many years that demonstrate how playing video games is typically a highly social activity for most children and that the activity tends to *increase* prosocial skills and attitudes. An extensive literature review published in 2014, for example, demonstrates that playing games often comes with important social benefits. Perhaps somewhat surprisingly, the evidence suggests not only that such "helping" behavior is found in players who engage in prosocial video games, but also that even games with violent content lead to prosocial behavior as long as the games are designed to encourage *cooperative* play.[15]

Wasting Time

Even if the current data on aggression, social isolation, and addiction do not suggest that gaming is the biggest digital challenge you face as a parent, you might still wonder whether a child's spending all this time playing games isn't just one big waste of time. For starters, let's hear what young people have to say. When gaming teenagers were asked whether they think they spend too much time playing video games, the responses were mixed. According to a Pew survey mentioned earlier in this chapter, 26 percent of teens believe they spend *too much* time (perhaps an expression of the overall trend we observe that users say they spend too much time using digital technologies overall), while 22 percent feel they actually *don't play enough* video games. Interestingly, boys are more likely than other children to say that they spend too much time gaming.[16]

While these survey results are not particularly helpful in answering our questions, we might look at them the other way around by asking whether there are potential *gains* from playing video games. A growing body of research points toward a range of social, cognitive, and emotional benefits that playing games might offer to young people. For instance, researchers have found robust evidence that certain types of games—believe it or not, especially action or shooter video games—lead to enhanced cognitive performance. Commercially available action games, for example, can improve powerful spatial skills (relevant for STEM [science, technology, engineering, and math] education and careers) in ways similar to formal courses aimed at building such skills. A range of studies have examined how such games can be used to enhance perception, attention, task-switching, multitasking, and some aspects of memory. Certain types of games, such as in-game puzzles, have been associated with improved problem-solving skills, although causality remains uncertain. Other cognitive benefits associated with video gaming include enhanced creativity. And the list goes on: while empirical research with respect to motivational benefits is still under way, initial studies suggest that playing games might improve persistence in the face of failure and can contribute to an optimistic approach to life and problem-solving for some people. Similarly, studies on emotional benefits have shown a causal relationship between playing puzzle video games and improved moods or levels of anxiety among players.

Taken together, numerous studies point toward various potential benefits of video games. While questions such as the long-term effects remain open, our reading of the available evidence is clear in one point: playing games is unlikely to be "just a total waste of time." This conclusion holds up even for violent video games, although for ethical reasons, we're not proponents of this genre. The potential benefits of video games for young people have also begun to inspire the development of new types of games. We're excited about such efforts that aim to design games in ways that lead to more prosocial behavior; help with learning, skill-building, and civic engagement; and contribute to children's health and well-being, as in the case of games developed to help child cancer patients build resilience and confidence.

THE CONNECTED PARENTS' APPROACH

The data about the effects of gaming on children are not clear-cut. Important research questions are still open. Where does this leave us in terms of our connected-parenting approach? How can we manage the risk of gaming? How can we increase the likelihood that our children harness the potential benefits, rather than suffer negative consequences, if they play these games? Given the state of knowledge, the advice that follows is steeped less in the specific research findings and more in common sense and our own experience as parents and educators. Before dipping into the nuts-and-bolts of our advice, however, let's pause briefly and reflect on a number of bigger picture points.

At the outset, keep in mind that play in the past century has been recognized as an essential part of childhood. Research shows that playing games, socializing, and participating in creative activities are key to children's development, identity, and well-being. Because of the individual and societal importance of these activities, many countries around the world recognize children's right to play as a human right (it is in fact mentioned in the UN Convention on the Rights of the Child). Given the larger societal transformation from an analog to a digital environment, children's play has, not surprisingly, changed and moved toward digital games. Viewed from that angle, a ban on playing all video games, for instance, would be not only hard to enforce, but also detrimental to the interests of the child.

We need to understand digital games in the larger context of how they are used by our children. As we have seen, there's a broad range of games that vary widely in their design and features, each shaping the risk-benefit calculus. And of course, each child who plays video games does so in a specific individual and social context, which shapes the gaming experience in important ways. All these factors, as research shows, might influence the risks and benefits that come with gaming. Our philosophy is to take a holistic perspective and think about gaming, like other activities, in the larger context of a young person's life.

OUR RECOMMENDATIONS

Our advice on gaming is consistent with our advice throughout this book: take a good look at the facts, think hard about who your child is, develop a strategy for how you want to parent, and then do your very best. We can tell you what we've done with our own children and what other experts say, but in the end, your decisions will come down to what's right for your children and what's feasible in your household.

The reality is that most young people play video games with a passion. In these cases, as parents, you have to figure out how to best navigate the situation. Fortunately, you have less reason to worry about the potential negative effects of gaming on health and well-being than popular opinion suggests. Rather, focus on the family climate and culture you want to build together. In the case of both of our families, that family culture does include a place for mobile, video, and computer games.

With the goal of finding the right balance for your family in mind, we offer these recommendations to help you mitigate the risks of gaming and to encourage their benefits:

- *Inform yourself about games.* Especially when children are younger, parents are likely to choose which games can be downloaded or installed on their kids' devices. Make sure to learn about the different games and their age-appropriateness. The most useful rating product for parents and teachers was developed by a nonprofit organization called Common Sense Media. An advocacy and research group based in the United States, Common Sense Media has developed an extensive rating system that focuses on the developmental appropriateness of games and other media. Its system is more detailed than that of the Entertainment Software Ratings Board, for example. The ratings provided by Common Sense Media consider the educational value and ease of play on the positive side of the ledger as well as the violence, sexual content, and safety concerns on the negative side. The games that typically trouble parents are the most violent or sexual games, which have the greatest possibility of leading to higher levels of aggression among young people.

- *Let children be your tutors.* Ask your children whether they are willing to share with you how their favorite games work, what the stories and tasks are, what cool features the game has, and so on. In our experience, children are typically excited to give their parents a tutorial if their parents express a genuine interest and curiosity. In some cases, you might get lucky and get invited to play a game together with your youngsters. Either way, the key point is to establish an open communication channel about games and the gaming experiences of your children.

- *Encourage your child to play different types of games.* The risk that might come from playing a certain game—say, a game with violent content—can be mitigated when gaming is not a young person's sole leisure activity. Show your child how much fun it can be to play different games, whether it's an old-fashioned board game, other video games, games designed for socializing or strategizing, activities that stretch kids' creativity, or ventures that encourage exploring the outdoors. The Common Sense Media website has a very useful "best of" list that we can highly recommend. Another fun activity is to learn about these games together with your child.

- *Be supportive of collaborative games.* The research on games is clear on this point: games that require collaboration—as opposed to games that are solely about competition—come with fewer risks in terms of the possible impact on aggression. Similarly, playing games with friends or in guilds is more likely to unlock prosocial skills and helping behaviors. The benefit of collaborative play holds true for all types of games, most notably violent video games. While you need to remain vigilant when your kids play games with strangers, you can generally support collaborative games, particularly when they're played with friends. In everyday life, this recommendation might require a bit more patience when your kid is in the middle of a gaming experience with a friend and isn't instantly running to the table when dinner is ready.

- *Keep an eye on the interactions that your child is engaged with in-game.* The ways that young people can get in trouble may involve in-game interactions with people they do not know well. Watch out, too, for instances of cyberbullying by asking kids how things are going in their gaming and being attentive to extreme moodiness. As you do for social media, keep their privacy in mind. As discussed Chapter 3, kids today are very likely to share more information through commercial games than were kids in the past, and this information is then used for targeted advertisement. Finally, keep an eye on any interactions that might include the exchange of money—for instance, in the form of in-game purchases of virtual assets—to avoid unexpected financial risks.

- *Be curious about what can be learned from games.* In the data section, we have mentioned some effects games can have on cognitive performance and on skill-building. Some of these skills— sometimes referred to as twenty-first-century skills—will become even more important in the environment of the digital economy. More broadly, games can teach real-life lessons, as a 2016 *Forbes* article enumerated so eloquently: "Difficulty increases the further you progress," "No obstacles? Wrong direction," "You have more than one life," "Tutorials will save you later," or "Take advantage of the pause button," to name just a few.[17]

- *If your child is really into gaming, make the best out of it.* We have seen children who are very much into gaming—far too much into gaming, by the standards of their parents. But this passion can sometimes translate into an opportunity. For some kids, for example, gaming can be an alternative pathway for interest-driven learning when their motivation for traditional and typically standards-driven education is otherwise low. Games have sometimes also provided the starting point for creative activity and community engagement. For instance, some young players started to document and share their experiences in tutorials with their friends over digital platforms. You may find it more rewarding to explore ways you can support such creative activities and novel pathways through video games rather than banning them outright.

As always, the most important things that you can do are to model good behavior for the young people in your life and keep open a positive line of communication about tricky topics. Acknowledge the kindness and goodness that you observe among others. Encourage a positive youth culture in your school, community, and home. These broader efforts will establish the environment where young people can learn from many experiences—including gaming.

KEY TAKEAWAYS

The data are not especially clear about the effects of gaming on young people. What is clear is this: young people are playing lots of games, some of which have real benefits in terms of kids' learning and social and emotional behavior. Other games may carry risks. Among the games that could be risky are those with excessively violent or explicit sexual material. The causal link between violence in gaming and physical violence in the real world has not as yet been established clearly, though some research points to worrying signs.

The connected parent supports young people in gaming that interests them. We urge you to emphasize gaming that involves solving problems, improving your kid's social and emotional skills, and teaching creativity. There's no reason to ban gaming altogether—doing so may well be detrimental to your child's development.

Play games with your children. Learn why a game interests them, and talk about that. The conversation may lead to special insights about your children and how they are developing.

Gaming is often an important aspect of a young person's social life. The social interaction may be in person with their friends in the room or online with friends who live at a great distance from them. These relationships are likely to be very important to your child.

As in the case of social media, keep an eye on the chats that your child is engaged with in-game. The ways young people can get into trouble often involve in-game interactions with people they do not know well. Watch out, too, for instances of cyberbullying: ask your kids how things are going in their gaming, and be attentive to extreme moodiness. Keep their privacy in mind. As discussed earlier in the book, kids today are very likely to share more information about themselves with other players than kids in the past did through commercial games.

The areas that the connected parent will flag include the most violent and sexually graphic games and the excessive use of gaming that impinges on the rest of the young person's life and growth. The gaming that is so extensive that it leads to problems in a young person's life is almost certainly connected to other problems the child is facing, such as anxiety and depression.

Parents should think about digital gaming not in a vacuum but rather in the context of other things going on in a young person's life. Read to young children, and encourage them to read on their own as they grow older. Play board games, and exercise outdoors with them, as your physical ability permits. Support the positive social and emotional development of your child in ways that are outside the frame of gaming; this positive growth will ensure that the learning they do when they are gaming is likely to be constructive.

PART III

ENGAGING THE WORLD BEYOND THE HOME

CHAPTER 8

Diversity

QUINN AND THOMAS, two siblings who also happen to be best friends, are watching the Super Bowl on TV together. Like millions of other viewers, they are not only excited about the approaching halftime show, but are also watching out for the coolest commercials produced for the game.

During one of the breaks, Thomas's favorite brand runs an advertisement during which a nonbinary person—someone who doesn't identify as either male or female—appears for a short moment, while the ad's voiceover uses the singular, gender-neutral pronoun *them* to refer to the person appearing in the ad.

"Wow, did you see that?" Thomas asks his brother. Thomas is typing with both his thumbs into his phone as he talks.

"Yup," Quinn responds, "that was a clear shout-out to the LGBTQ+ community. I'm wondering what the reactions on social media will be tonight. . . . Let's keep an eye on the hashtags that start trending."

Next up is a recruitment ad for a special unit of a well-known law enforcement agency. The commercial features fit young people engaged in all sorts of drills and other physical activities. While it features faces from diverse ethnic backgrounds, the ad primarily shows women and ends with a statement about not giving in to gender stereotypes.

"I can't believe it!" Thomas shouts at the TV. "Why does everything have to be so politicized these days? That's going way too far. Why do they only have *women* in a recruitment commercial? Especially for law enforcement? You mean men can't even do *that* anymore?"

"Well, I get your point," Quinn responds. "But I think statements like these make us talk about the gender stereotypes and other biases we all have."

Quinn is flipping through the feeds on his phone, where thousands of comments in all shapes and flavors appear in response to the first ad. "I think it's great," he says, "that women are featured on the frontline in the police force to make the point that action matters and stereotypes should be challenged."

A beat later, Quinn sees in his feed that Thomas has posted two angry social media posts about how "PC everything has gotten, even during the Super Bowl. Can't I just watch a football game in peace???"

Quinn says, "Tom, what are you up to? Don't post about this stuff online. It's only going to get you in trouble."

"Well, I am troubled," Thomas says. "These commercials—this is way too much political correctness for my taste."

"Fine," Quinn says. "We can talk about it in school tomorrow. But don't make the conversation all about your boneheaded social media posts that everyone watching the Super Bowl will have seen. Let the conversation be about the ads."

The first half of the game has had little action. Neither team can move the ball down the field. Bored by the game, the two brothers keep talking about bias, sports, and Thomas's animosity toward what he calls political correctness. By the time the next set of commercials comes along, Thomas has agreed to delete his posts. Thankfully, the game picks up and they turn their full attention back to the main event.

KEEN OBSERVERS OF professional sports expected Nick Bosa to be a top draft pick in the National Football League in the spring of 2019. As a white college student, Bosa had been a leading pass-rusher for Ohio State University. Bosa had succeeded at the pinnacle of big-time college football and was looking very likely to be successful in professional football as a result. His physical stature, college statistics, and team performance all set him up to be drafted by a major NFL team in the first round.

And then controversy hit. Bosa found himself explaining his social media activity for the years leading up to the draft. During high school and college, he had posted on Twitter a variety of things that landed him in hot water during the lead-up to the draft. After word of his controversial tweets got out, the news media started to examine all the posts that Bosa had liked on Instagram. Everything he had done online under his own name—and there was a fair amount of it—would come under the scrutiny of the major national news media in the weeks leading up to the NFL draft.

Many of Bosa's controversial tweets had to do with race. He had established for himself a clear pattern of referring to the work of people of color and others not like him in derogatory terms. According to a story in the *New York Times* on April 23, 2019, Bosa had deleted a series of these tweets. The *Times* reported that Bosa had referred to Beyoncé's music as "complete trash," he described the movie *Black Panther* as the worst Marvel movie, and had referred to San Francisco's former quarterback, Colin Kaepernick, as a "clown." Bosa explained that he had scrubbed his social media accounts of these statements because there was "a chance I might end up in San Francisco."[1]

The scrutiny for Bosa did not stop with the *Times* story. A few days later, *USA Today* ran an article on an online activist's findings after the person had examined Bosa's Instagram activity. Bosa, while in high school, had liked posts that included the N-word, references to "rape and pillage," and a homophobic slur. Just as Bosa had scrubbed his Twitter account, the person who had initially posted the Instagram images deleted that account. As a result, Bosa's likes of these posts and others were no longer visible online. Even though they were no longer online, the activist had taken screenshots of Bosa's activities and the original posts and appeared to have sent them to news reporters.[2]

Bosa's story demonstrated how a person's feelings about race and diversity can intersect with social media. Bosa said little publicly about his scrubbing of his social media image. In the weeks leading up to the NFL draft, we might have imagined that Bosa had wished he had not been so quick with his tweets or his likes. But we may never know: Bosa did not post anything publicly at the time to explain his actions.

The awkward news stories seemed to have little effect on the NFL decision makers. The San Francisco 49ers drafted Bosa as the second pick in the first round, much as analysts had imagined. (The story doesn't always end that way. In 2016, top prospect Laremy Tunsil is believed to have fallen a few spots in the draft when a video of him apparently smoking marijuana surfaced on draft night. You might reasonably infer that the decision makers in the NFL worry more about substance abuse than about racial and homophobic slurs by players. You might also consider the possibility of racial bias in the NFL owners' responses.)

For Bosa himself, the story of his social media blunders may merely feel like a cautionary tale. Perhaps it will lead him to examine some of his views. He may have some explaining to do to his new teammates in the locker room. Perhaps the fan base of his new professional team in San Francisco will have some questions for him about his views. Maybe he will learn from having to take down some of what he'd written and liked as a young person as he matures.

Think about this story not from the point of view of the person who posted the derogatory comments but rather from the point of view of a young person who observed the comments. It's not hard to find much more damaging commentary on social media than what Bosa posted, as obnoxious and thoughtless as his posts and likes were. As parents, many of us may have young people in our lives who will find these comments hurtful. Other young people might see these comments and think that racially charged statements or homophobic slurs are acceptable behavior for big-time student-athletes. We need to acknowledge that the young people in our lives are observing this type of activity and interaction all the time. Very often, those posting statements like these are public figures who should be acting as role models.

The story of Quinn and Thomas that we've shared and the example of Nick Bosa both come from the world of sports, but the expression of bias occurs in every field every day. You may be familiar with the story of the young people who posted racially offensive materials to social media after they had been admitted to Harvard College in the class of 2021—only to have their offers of admission rescinded.[3] These comments are often posted by young people who are not athletes and who have nothing to do with sports. The work of diversity matters to every member of a community, regardless of the activities they love or their background.

The effect of these public comments—whatever the context—is to drive a wedge between the reader who feels harmed and the person who posted them. The intent does not matter as much as the impact of the comments. Whether the person posting these comments did so in a cavalier manner or meant to be hurtful, the effect is the same on the observer. Social media in the hands of adults and youth alike can be part of what is driving people apart. We would all be much better off by using the technology to enable members of our society to understand one another better and bring them together.

OUR CHILDREN ARE growing up in an increasingly diverse, cosmopolitan, interconnected world. Diversity comes in many forms—race, gender, religion, sexual orientation, age, class, ability, and so forth. And whether the increasing diversity means your own identity is better represented in more situations or you feel uncomfortable with the world's changing face, all students and graduates will be working with and learning from people different from themselves. This knowledge and these skills are part of what it means to be a global digital citizen in the early twenty-first century. To succeed in virtually any major workplace in the world in the coming decades, young people will need to appreciate and navigate a diverse environment. Organizations, too, must tap into diverse talents and perspectives to succeed at any scale.

Into this shifting demographic landscape enters the digital realm. Everything that our children type into a device can potentially reach billions of people around the globe. Given the young age of our children and the incomplete development of their brains, the inability to erase mistakes raises extraordinary possibilities and serious concerns. Does the use of social media and other interconnected technologies help or hinder our children as they seek to build the skills they need to thrive in an increasingly diverse world? Could digital technologies become part of the solution rather than part of the problem?

As with many other issues explored in this book, for diversity, the digital environment can—and does—cut both ways. The online environment can promote a greater opportunity for a diverse array of voices to reach an audience. Social media can lead to greater levels of mutual understanding and interconnection across walls of difference. Digital tools can enable young people to meet one another across great distances and forge long-standing and meaningful friendships.

These same tools, used maliciously, can lead to pain, mistrust, and misinformation. If you've ever spent time on Facebook or Twitter trying to have a productive conversation with people with opposing beliefs, you know how well that tends to go (which is to say, poorly). When separated by a screen, people tend to be less inhibited than when they are face-to-face. The worst instincts of young people can emerge in online environments when tensions are high. Youth (as well as adults) can post terribly hurtful images and words on social media about those who are different.

Most of the services young people use today are not structured in an optimal way to support prosocial forms of behavior. But the good news is that technologies can support a diverse community when we structure them thoughtfully, when our students learn how to use them constructively, and when we model good behaviors.

Now, when it comes to our responsibilities as role models and resources on this issue, our work is often cut out for us as parents. As we've seen throughout this book, children learn the tools of social media quicker than adults do, and kids are often immersed in the latest tools long before we have even heard of them. Ditto when it comes to diversity. Most of us grew up in more homogenous communities than our children will experience. Our children may in fact be more comfortable with people of different backgrounds than some of us parents are. Whether we grew up feeling marginalized or at the center of the society we live in, this imbalance makes it hard for some of us to teach and act as role models as well as we might like. To be effective parents, we have to lean into our discomfort, act with humility, and learn quickly.

WHAT THE RESEARCH SHOWS

The research from a range of different fields can inform how the connected parent thinks about raising young people in an increasingly diverse world.

Big Picture: Offline

The United States is growing more diverse as a society every year. Consider one important dimension of diversity: From recent censuses, experts predict that people of color will constitute the majority of Americans by 2045.[4] Experts likewise predict that, in light of demographic and economic trends, the United States is likely to encounter continued growth and prosperity through this period—a prediction challenged by the global COVID-19 pandemic. The fastest growing groups include Hispanics, Asians, and multiracial Americans. The generation of young people now coming of age is expected to be both the most diverse and the best-educated in the history of the United States. These data raise a huge question: will Americans come together to embrace this increasingly heterogeneous—and potentially highly prosperous—future or not?

The demographics in the United States are mirrored in many other parts of the world, albeit with different specific dynamics. Cities vie for the title of "most diverse in the world." Dubai claims a population with more than 80 percent of inhabitants born outside the country. Depending on which metric you use, Toronto and Brussels often claim top spots as the most diverse or the most cosmopolitan cities, along with Sydney, Auckland, Singapore, London, New York, São Paulo, Melbourne, Amsterdam, Frankfurt, and Paris.[5] While this list of cities is largely wealthy, this phenomenon reaches many corners of the globe.

Online Spaces

While many physical spaces grow more diverse along various dimensions, what about online environments? Intuitively, you might surmise that the internet reflects the diversity of the offline space. In the United States, for instance, nine in ten adults use the internet.[6] According to data from the International Telecommunication Union, almost half of the world's population used the internet by the end of 2018.[7] From an individual user's perspective, the vast reach of the internet and the billions of people it connects give the user ample opportunity to learn about different viewpoints and interact with people from other backgrounds.

However, the picture is less rosy than these numbers suggest. At the global level, for example, it has proven to be very hard to close the digital divide in the less privileged parts of the world. Even in the highly connected United States, internet adoption and participation gaps based on age, income, education, and community type remain.

To make things more complicated, diversity varies greatly across different online platforms and forums. Studies that have looked at Wikipedia content and examined which countries, regions, cultures, and societies are represented have broadly concluded that the active Wikipedia community is based mostly in Europe and the United States.[8] Similarly, studies of a leading internet photo-sharing platform, Flickr, revealed a disproportionate number of photos of locations in Europe and North America.[9] Even in online spaces where diversity exists, individual users often prefer to connect with folks that look and think alike. Again and again, researchers from different disciplines have argued that people's preferences, the inner workings of the internet economy, and powerful algorithms of platforms like Facebook or Twitter drive us into echo chambers or "filter bubbles."

Regardless of the ongoing debate about the internet's net effects on diversity, there is some hope when it comes to youth and social media, at least when we consider the beliefs of teenage social media users in the United States as expressed in a 2018 Pew study. Pew reports that a majority of teens believe social media helps people their age to diversify their networks, to broaden their viewpoints, and to become involved with social issues. Roughly two-thirds of teens say social networking sites help teens interact with people from different backgrounds (69 percent), while a similar amount credits social media with helping teens find different points of view (67 percent) or helping teens show their support for causes (66 percent).[10] These statistics suggest that the internet and social media can play a positive role in diversity and inclusion in the experiences of young people. However, these positive effects of digital technology are often, unfortunately, unequally distributed among different populations and groups.

Inequalities

Many societies also suffer from growing levels of inequality. This inequality often tracks other forms of racial, ethnic, gender, and religious differences. Young people from different socioeconomic backgrounds are having very different experiences online; the same holds true for youth of color, girls, immigrants, and so forth. Within diverse communities, the use of technology by young people has disparate effects.

One important pattern is that those with lower socioeconomic status tend to benefit less from the promise of new technology than do those with higher socioeconomic status. Studies also show that young people who face high levels of adversity in their lives at large tend to suffer the most from the ill effects of technology. Other studies have consistently shown that students who have experienced offline forms of victimization report that they are subjected to similar negative experiences online, such as bullying and harassment. Researchers looking at young people in North Carolina showed that those with lower socioeconomic status were more likely to report that social media usage led to other types of problems, such as face-to-face confrontations and fighting.[11]

One 2014 study of thirty-five hundred European youth found a clear link between higher socioeconomic status and the likelihood that parents sought to "actively mediate" the online activities of their young children. The active mediation fell along the lines of the connected-parenting model that we suggest. The parents talked about online practices, modeled and suggested ways to use the internet safely, and used technology alongside their children.[12] A study of low-income preschool-age children showed that young people from lower socioeconomic households were more likely than not to have a television in their bedroom and that about one in eight had "high" levels of screen time (more than four hours per day).[13] Though there is no one definitive study on the topic, a careful review of multiple credible studies suggests that young people from lower socioeconomic backgrounds are more likely to spend more time each day engaging with screens than wealthier young people are—as much as three hours a day more, potentially, and often without parents in the picture.[14]

Societal Discrimination Online

Just as the advantages of digital technologies are unequally distributed, so too are the disadvantages. Our colleague Brendesha Tynes is a leading researcher who examines the role of digital technologies in young people's development, with a focus on academic and socio-emotional outcomes. Her findings from a longitudinal study on the risks and protective factors associated with online victimization are alarming: survey results from 340 African American, Latinx, Asian, and biracial adolescents show that 42 percent of these youth have experienced at least one discriminatory incident—typically people showing a racist image online—in the first year of the study. The number increased to 58 percent in the third year of the study. And an even larger majority (68 percent) of respondents have witnessed people saying mean or rude things about another person's ethnic group online. The most frequent places for these negative experiences were social networking sites, text messaging, and platforms like YouTube.[15]

To better understand the full extent of the problem young people face, consider these hurtful online experiences in addition to earlier studies that report that up to 94 percent of African American, Latinx, and Asian youth have experienced offline racial and ethnic discrimination. Turning from abstract numbers to young people's voices, Tynes and her associates asked African American students about their worst experiences online. Here are some of them:

The worst thing that has happened to me on the internet is that someone threatened to kill me because of my race.

Almost every day on *Call of Duty: Black Ops* [a video game] I see Confederate flags, swastikas and black people hanging from trees in emblems [created by other players] and they say racist things about me and my teammates.

Me and my friends were playing Xbox and some kid joined the Xbox Live party we were in and made a lot of racist jokes I found offensive.[16]

Perhaps most troubling is the overall trend that Tynes and her colleagues found: the data show that incidents of online racial discrimination have increased from year to year. The authors factored into their findings the effect of current events, such as widespread concern over heightened racial bias during the period of the study, among other factors.

These online experiences of racial discrimination have negative implications for the mental health and other developmental outcomes of young people of color. Previous studies have shown that online racial discrimination is associated with depression, anxiety, and behavioral problems. While not focused on digital technologies in particular, a study published in 2018 is eye-opening. Researchers examined the impact of societal discrimination on young people's health among 2,572 high school students from Los Angeles between 2016 and 2017. The study not only confirmed an increase in the levels of stress and worry about social discrimination in recent years but also found that these concerns correlate with unhealthy outcomes such as increased use of cigarettes and marijuana. The relationship between changes in concerns about societal discrimination and behavioral health outcomes was the strongest among African American, Hispanic, or socioeconomically disadvantaged youth.[17]

Given the rather dramatic findings from these and other studies, the American Academy of Pediatrics published in 2019 a first-ever policy statement on racism's impact on children. Titled "The Impact of Racism on Child and Adolescent Health," this statement describes how toxic stress generated by repeated and routine experiences of racism affects a child's long-term development. The stress from racism transforms how the brain and the body respond to stress in general, and it brings about achievement gaps and mental and physical health deficiencies throughout life. The academy's policy recommendations outline a broad set of steps for pediatricians and other caregivers to better support children, parents, and families.[18] We incorporate these findings into our advice that follows.

THE CONNECTED PARENTS' APPROACH

The connected parent values diversity, equity, and inclusion and encourages family members to pursue them with clarity and purpose. As societies today grow increasingly diverse, it is a practical necessity for us to pursue these goals. A society must have mechanisms to handle a diversity of backgrounds and worldviews to function properly and sustainably over time.

We believe that diversity, equity, and inclusion are moral imperatives at the very top of the list of important issues for societies today and are essential from the perspective of justice. You might be tempted to think that we are politicizing this issue unnecessarily. Whatever your political views, you don't have to agree with us on the importance of these topics to agree that our young people need to develop skills to thrive in increasingly diverse schools, workplaces, and communities.

Here's the functional argument: by understanding the shifting dynamics of diversity, equity, and inclusion, our students and our communities can grow and become stronger and more resilient. Put in negative terms, the consequences of mishandling issues of race, class, gender, sexuality, and other forms of difference for young people can be very costly in this digital age. Controversies of this sort go viral very quickly. Students who make a mistake in what they post online can affect how they are perceived for years to come when someone, including college admissions administrators or potential employers, googles their name.

Above all, we have a shared responsibility to protect the well-being of our children. If we fail to respect each other, if we expose our children to societal discrimination online, it harms young people in the long run. The evidence is clear: the increased levels of stress and worry about social discrimination experienced by many young people from different backgrounds can have a negative impact on their mental and physical health and can create problems for society at large. Both from the perspective of parents and as citizens, we need to work together to prevent such harmful real-world outcomes by ensuring that children from all backgrounds are treated fairly and can live a healthy life.

As in other arenas of life, digital tech and social media play a complicating role in the lives of young people when it comes to diversity, equity, and inclusion. The technology can support a young person who is making connections with people of different backgrounds far more effectively and efficiently than in the past. But the stakes are higher. There is more risk and the possibility of more return. The young people in our lives can use technology for good, but they can also use it to make things much, much worse, for themselves and for others.

OUR RECOMMENDATIONS

As parents, all of us can help our children develop in many dimensions. We think first of making sure they are safe, that they eat right, get sleep, and exercise—the health and safety dimension. We seek to instill in children our values, a moral code to live by: in other words, the character dimension of their development. For many parents, the academic angle is important, too. Some families strive to move to the neighborhood of a city or town with the most fitting local school option for their children. Parents encourage, cajole, and bribe kids to do their homework. Ideally, as parents we give children the love and support they need when they are struggling in school and high fives when they do well on the big test or poster-board project in science class. To the extent that we have the time and resources, we shuttle our children to the activities that will enrich their lives outside school: play dates, basketball practice, tuba lessons, swimming lessons, camp, and just about any other thing they can dream up to do.

But do we spend time helping them prepare for the increasingly diverse world in which they will learn and work? Too few of us do so, particularly those of us from overrepresented groups. It's time to change that.

Our advice is to consider how we help our children gain the skills to live in a diverse, equitable, and inclusive world. Just as young people need our help in learning about diversity, equity, and inclusion, they also often have much to offer us. On some issues, young people are far ahead of those of us who are older. As in other areas of parenting, we have to figure out when to lead and when to follow their lead.

The Why of Diversity, Equity, and Inclusion in Parenting

The simplest argument for why we should focus on diversity, equity, and inclusion in bringing up our children is justice. A strong society is a just society, one in which access and opportunity are spread equitably across the population. True equality has never been a reality in America, and it is unlikely to have been realized anywhere in human history. It remains a worthy aspiration and a bedrock idea in democratic political systems. The path toward attaining this state of true equality winds through each home, school, and community. We're aware that many will agree with this perspective on justice and many will not.

Set aside the justice dimension for a moment. The argument for parents focusing on diversity is functional, too. Perhaps you disagree with us about what a just society looks like. In any case, your child will certainly grow up in an increasingly heterogeneous society. Whether you think the United States will have a majority population of people of color in 2040, 2050, or 2060, the racial demographic is undoubtedly becoming more diverse. A similar pattern is playing out in Germany, Canada, the United Kingdom, and many other countries. There are more mixed-race children born every year. The number of people born outside of the country in which they then live keeps growing every decade as immigration continues in every corner of the globe. It will be harder and harder, if not impossible, for today's young people to wall themselves off from people different from them.

In schools, students will be more likely to have teachers and peers who are different from them. In the workplace, once they graduate, these same students will need to work on teams that are more diverse than in the past. That will be the case whether the field is food service, retail, technology development, business, law, finance, government, nonprofit, or any other line of work. From our perspective, this trajectory is a positive one; whether or not you agree, these changes are afoot.

There are other reasons, too, why diversity is important in the twenty-first century. Bringing together people from different walks of life and with a multitude of experiences will help us generate new ideas and novel approaches to some of the hardest problems of our time. The ability to communicate with people and cultures that we are initially unfamiliar will help us better understand the world and become caring global citizens—and enrich our lives in often-unexpected ways.

For all these reasons, we believe it is a good idea to guide your children in the right direction on the issue of diversity, equity, and inclusion in their online and face-to-face encounters.

Modeling

The example that we provide to our children is essential to this story. The young people in our lives are watching us all the time, whether we know it or not—or like it or not. They are watching how we interact with other people, whether we laugh about a racist joke, who our friends are, how we treat waitstaff in restaurants, and the degree to which we have inclusive skills. If we're Latinx, do we laugh at a racist joke about our black neighbors? If we're African American, do we ask a girl with Asian heritage, "Where are you *really* from?" Do we act upset if we see two men holding hands, or do we unconsciously step away from a person who uses a wheelchair? Do we stick to our group of gay friends rather than expand to groups unlike us? Before we move on to helping our children, we have to put on the "oxygen masks" for ourselves and develop our own skills.

Some workplaces make these issues a central topic for professional development. There are amazing books, blogs, and podcasts devoted to many aspects of diversity, equity, and inclusion. However we go about it, we need to start with our own skills and behaviors.

Saying "Oops" and "Sorry"—and Doing Better

As teachers and parents, both of us have had steep learning curves in our lives. No one is born naturally good at the practice of diversity, equity, and inclusion. Both of us have undergone weeks of training at work, read stacks of books, and held conversations in which we heard and learned about the experiences of others. And still, we have work to do. Children need to see that we adults are also learners and that we can make mistakes. An extremely powerful form of teaching is to show vulnerability and to own up to our own failures.

Many people—especially those in positions of power or who come from a racial majority group—report worrying that when they talk about diversity, they will say the wrong thing and offend someone. It's true. Very often, in these hard conversations, someone will say something that will offend someone else. It's okay. It's inevitable. And the moment ought to be seen as an opportunity to learn and grow rather than a terrible problem to be avoided at all costs. In many cases, silence from parents on issues of diversity, including race, creates a taboo that children pick up from very young ages. For example, if a child is shamed and silenced for bringing up race out of innocence or ignorance, rather than being brought into a larger "teaching moment" and conversation to build their skills, this can bring about lasting damage.

Today, a comment that offends by revealing a prejudiced attitude toward a marginalized group, often unconsciously or unintentionally, is called a *microaggression*. As we have inherited and grown up in a society with built-in prejudices, biases, and inequities, all of us may have absorbed some of these views, and so we all risk revealing these views and causing harm in the form of microaggressions. There are, of course, bad actors who deliberately seek to inflict pain on others, but in most cases, well-intentioned people have difficulty, and frankly a lack of education, when it comes to speaking across difference. As our communities and societies grow more diverse, the chances of making mistakes when we are speaking with people from different viewpoints and backgrounds is only likely to grow. We will need to come up with good ways to handle them when they inevitably occur.

Combine the high likelihood of mistakes with the online environment: when you post on social media, the potential audience is vast. Perhaps the post is accessible globally to nearly every person who can access the internet. That's billions of people! If they can read the language in which the post appears, or can translate it, there is an extraordinary possibility that you could be causing offense to somebody out there. Perhaps a lot of somebodies.

It is never comfortable to have someone tell you that you've caused offense. If you've spent much time online, you know that it happens all the time. While it would be best not to cause offense or not to have cultural blind spots in the first place, it is difficult, if not impossible, to speak across differences without making mistakes. What then becomes most important is whether you learn from these experiences and actively try to become more inclusive in your values, actions, and speech.

An area of growth for both of us as authors has been how to act more inclusively and equitably with people who are transgender, genderqueer, or transitioning in gender in our communities. As directors of a research center and a high school, we have had responsibility for making some obvious changes to our facilities, for instance. Rather than having restrooms marked "Women" and "Men," our workplaces now have all-gender restrooms. The school that John has led now has an all-gender dormitory and all-gender locker rooms. These are important changes to make, but they are not the whole story.

A few years ago, John was writing about issues related to gender and sexuality on his Facebook page. In a post, he used the term "transgendered." The response from the online community was quick and clear: that was not the right term to use. His use of "transgendered" caused offense, as noted both in the comments thread and in direct messaging that lit up his account. His first reaction was to feel the hot shame of messing up and hurting someone's feelings.

The best reaction in these circumstances is to say "oops" and "sorry" and to ask for help. People on John's Facebook page were more than happy to help. The better term, one person explained, was *transgender*. The rationale was simple: "transgendered" is offensive insofar as it suggests that something has happened to someone. Many trans people experience their identity as inborn, not as one that they have arrived at as a choice or an event later in their lives.

Around the same time, Saeed Jones, the LGBTQ+ editor of *Buzz-Feed*, tweeted: "Also, it's 'transgender,' not 'transgendered.' 'Transgendered' is the linguistic equivalent of describing someone as 'blacked.'"[19]

After "oops" and "sorry" and taking the time to educate ourselves, we need to follow up with a real effort to do better, to try again and try harder. Our children will observe this behavior. Outside of its importance in matters of diversity, equity, inclusion, or social media, our willingness to admit our mistakes and grow from them is a great way to model what it means to be a lifelong learner.

The Bosa story at the start of the chapter is instructive, not because he thought to delete the tweets and likes about race and homophobia or because he was still drafted high in the first round. It's because there was a great opportunity to apologize, own up to the mistake, educate himself, change his behavior, and provide a positive example for a generation of aspiring NFL players. But Bosa took another course, quietly removing the posts, declining to comment much on what happened, and jockeying for his place in the NFL draft. His behavior, of course, is his prerogative. And his choices appear to have paid off for him personally, given his successful first year as an NFL player in the 2019–2020 season (yes, in San Francisco).

As parents, all of us can and should choose another course. Our children will notice.

Skills Development

The students and workers who will succeed in these increasingly diverse environments are those who have learned and mastered a series of skills associated with diversity, equity, and inclusion. The use of technology in both social and work settings is also integral to the skills that young people will need to make it in today's global, diverse, and technologically saturated environment. Digital fluency in a networked environment connecting billions of people around the globe is a brand-new expectation for those graduating from schools and entering the twenty-first-century workforce.

Students can and do learn some of these skills on their own, without our help. That said, not all kids do. Connected parents will want to take a major role in helping their children thrive in a diverse society and workforce:

- *As connected parents, we should emphasize the positive.* Engage in activities offline that will support positive online behavior. Offline and online interactions are very frequently interconnected. Model positive connections with people, regardless of the setting, and talk about the important ties that bind us to others.
- *Bring diversity to the household.* Diversity practitioners often ask those in workshops to think back to their wedding or to the most recent wedding they attended. How diverse was that group? Think about your social group and your children's circles of friends. Whether it's in sports teams, play groups, social events, or other activities, when children from diverse backgrounds are interacting, everyone has more opportunities to learn about others who have different backgrounds and identities. They'll discover commonalities; improve their diversity, equity, and inclusion skills; and broaden their horizons.

- *Stay offline when things get tense.* If you become aware that your children are engaged in a tough online interaction, especially with respect to race or other forms of difference, encourage them to step back. Direct them toward interactions that are in person, well structured, and productive. Urge them to leave online services altogether when the encounters are regularly unproductive. Much of the time, face-to-face is vastly superior to digital conversations on sensitive topics such as race, ethnicity, sexuality, and differences in ability.

- *Engage in conversations about diversity.* In open and ongoing conversations, help children understand the values of diversity, equity, and inclusion. Make visible how we can learn from people who are different from ourselves. On the flip side, discuss how discrimination is unfair and hurtful for everyone. Opportunities to engage in such discussions are all around us, both offline and online. If you're watching a Netflix show with only people from one gender with your children, for instance, ask them how they feel about it. Or if a comic book, video game, or TV advertisement involves a character from a distinct ethnic background, ask whether they think that this is an accurate portrait or one that largely relies on stereotypes. If you hear your children say something discriminatory, speak up and say what makes you uncomfortable. But don't shut the kids down. Instead, encourage them to speak about their feelings, fears, and misconceptions, and address them as well as you can. Don't forget to also engage the other adults in your children's lives in these diversity discussions.

- *Listen to, and learn from, your children.* Especially as they grow into their teens, they will be learning skills and gaining knowledge that we never had, growing up when we did. Model humility and a growth mindset—essential components of a connected-parenting approach. Both you and your children will benefit from this openness.

What you do in your jobs and daily lives outside work will be as important as any tips or tricks you might teach your children. The most powerful thing all of us might do is to find ways in our lives to be part of the solution to our divided world. Work to bridge the digital and economic divides in your communities. As teachers and as parents, both of us encourage young people to engage with others from "up and down the street" and around the world. This work can be online and offline.

Creative Engagement

Social media can be a tool in creating a more inclusive society. An institution called the Shorty Awards holds up examples of positive uses of social media. For example, the gold winner in the category of diversity and inclusion for 2018 was a campaign called "Teachers Have Better Work Stories." The creators of this social media campaign sought to attract a more diverse group of candidates to become teachers. Given the current and looming future shortage of schoolteachers in the United States, it makes sense to use online media to reach young people thinking about their careers. The problem is more complex than simply too few people going into teaching. The mix of teachers is roughly 80 percent white and 20 percent people of color in the United States, while the school-age population is more than 40 percent students of color. As we've seen from the data, the number of people of color in the United States is growing faster than the number of white people. It's not that white teachers can't instruct students of color, but rather that students of all backgrounds benefit from a diverse population of teachers. According to the creators of this campaign, teachers of color tend to set higher expectations for students of color and serve as important academically successful role models for these students.

Young people themselves can and do use social media in creative ways to foster diversity and inclusion. We mentioned the research about how many teenagers engage on social media to broaden their perspectives. In our own research on youth practices online, we have documented how young people use technology to contribute to diversity by posting their opinions on social media, sharing articles they like, and engaging in more creative forms of online news generation, such as memes—a genre of typically humorous, often visual, and always easily digestible news content and commentary. Parents can play a role in encouraging such creative and diversity-boosting practices. These strategies are especially important in an era when algorithms are increasingly recommending content that aligns with people's existing interests and beliefs.

Whether it's through social media, our friend groups, our workplaces, or our children's schools, we all have work to do as societies grow more diverse. The need is real, regardless of our race, gender, sexuality, socioeconomic status, or any other attribute. The work of diversity, equity, and inclusion belongs to every member of society. Our children are already inheriting this more diverse, cosmopolitan, and interconnected world. Let's be sure they are ready to lead it well, ideally even better than we have.

COMMON QUESTIONS

How can digital tools and spaces support positive diversity-related experiences for youth?

Adults can do a lot to encourage children to explore diverse interests and learn about other communities, both in the online and offline spheres. When children are younger, adults can use storytelling, toys, music, movies, artwork, comics, books, and the like, to give them an early sense of how diverse the world is. We can share with them how much we can learn from each other when we consider alternative perspectives and interact with people who are different from us.

Like these familiar offline techniques, digital platforms and spaces can also help young people build skills that enable them to embrace diversity, equity, and inclusion.

While much controversy exists about whether the internet locks youth (and adults alike) into echo chambers or invites them to learn about novel perspectives and voices, we believe that parents can play a key role in promoting helpful diversity experiences online. Keeping your children's age and stage of development in mind while also paying attention to safety and privacy, consider the following ideas for shared exploration: Google Maps is a fun tool through which families can go together on virtual trips around the world and experience different cultures, cities, architecture, and the like. YouTube and Instagram offer various ways to support users who want to discover trends and learn about new topics. Hashtag searches for topics of interest can help you discover new ideas and experiences. On platforms such as Twitter and Instagram, groups use a hashtag in front of a key phrase (as the well-known #MeToo movement did) to consolidate and emphasize their comments about an issue they care about. You can easily search for the topic by typing the hashtag into the search tool for the service you are using.

Why and how should parents talk about discrimination with their children?

Whether it is based on age, gender, weight, religion, income, sexual orientation, race, or ethnicity, you might struggle to discuss discrimination with your children. Sometimes you might fear that talking about differences will draw attention to them. Sometimes you might just feel uncomfortable talking about sensitive topics such as ethnicity and gender. But experts agree on this point: it is really important to have open and ongoing conversations about diversity and discrimination. If parents avoid the topic, children learn that the topic is taboo. They might be reluctant to ask questions, and they might think that the differences they notice are bigger than they are. Without an ongoing dialogue about the subject, parents cannot easily challenge biases or clear up stereotypes.

In addition to the recommendations we've offered, the American Psychological Association has some helpful ideas and guidance for talking about diversity and discrimination with children, including the following advice:

- Parents often avoid talking about hard subjects (including sex, underage drinking, and discrimination) because they're personally uncomfortable. Keep talking anyway. The discussions get easier over time.
- Use age-appropriate language, . . . and don't give kids too much information at once. The conversation will get deeper and more nuanced as they get older.
- Learn to respond to children's questions about differences and bias as they come up naturally. Help children feel that their questions are welcome, or they might come to believe that discussing differences is taboo. . . .
- Help kids learn how to deal with being the potential target of discrimination. Plan for healthy comebacks to hurtful discriminatory statements. For example: "What an unkind thing to say." "Excuse me? Could you repeat that?" "I disagree with you, and here's why . . ."
- If you hear children say something discriminatory, don't just hush them. Use the opportunity as a conversation starter to address their fears and correct their misperceptions.[20]

We encourage you to read the full set of recommendations at www .apa.org/helpcenter/kids-discrimination.

KEY TAKEAWAYS

There are many reasons why young people are interested—or should be interested—in diversity today. No matter their own race, ethnicity, gender, sexual orientation, or level of ability—no matter any other aspect of their background—they are growing up in a much more diverse, cosmopolitan world than that of any previous generation.

Young people have much to gain from learning the skills related to diversity, equity, and inclusion. The ability to connect with, relate to, empathize with, and work with people different from themselves will be a great benefit to the individual and will lead to benefits for societies at large.

On the flip side, the problems that stem from racial hatred, gender violence, anti-trans bigotry, homophobia, ableism, and all sorts of other types of biases can harm individuals involved and can tear apart communities.

These basic facts about diversity, equity, and inclusion have nothing to do with the digital world—and everything to do with the digital world. Social media, dating apps, and online forums host every form of human interaction, including the good, the bad, and the many murky interactions in between. In fact, these online environments are often terrible places for conversations about nuanced topics such as race and ethnicity.

Young people are watching everything we do as adults, and that's especially true for how we treat other people. The systemic and structural racism and bias that have afflicted many societies—including the United States—have been passed down from generation to generation. We must continue our efforts to break that cycle with this generation coming of age now and already showing signs of greater skill and comfort with diversity.

CHAPTER 9

Learning

ARE NEW TECHNOLOGIES making our children stupider than ever before? Is it possible that the *most*-educated generation in history—the one that is coming of age today—will in fact turn out to be the *worst* educated? Or conversely, is digital technology unlocking the potential for nearly unlimited, lifelong, and connected learning? And how can we make student learning as productive as possible when they must study remotely, as millions of families wondered when the COVID-19 pandemic hit suddenly in 2020? To help address these questions, we offer three anecdotes to frame the topic of youth, learning, and the digital world today.

AT THE DINNER table, on that rare occasion when everyone in the family actually sits down together, Mom asks the kids the dreaded question: "So what are you learning in school these days?"

That question basically never works in any household, and this one is no exception.

A pause. A few more mouthfuls of food. A few reluctant replies:

"Not much."

"It's fine."

"Mom . . . I really don't want to talk about it."

It is often very hard (impossible?) to get young people to talk about what they are learning—especially what they are learning in school. Parents who try to engage with their children about school are usually given what some young people call "the Heisman"—a stiff-arm inspired by the trophy given annually to the best collegiate football player.

Many parents fear that this lack of enthusiasm for learning has to do with technology. Are young people today not reading as much? Perhaps their attention spans are shorter. Maybe they don't go to the library as often as we, their parents, did back in the day.

The dinner table conversation ultimately goes nowhere. What lingers is a sense of failure on all sides. Mom is worried that her children aren't learning anything at school. The kids feel that their mom is out of touch, is in no way "woke," and is focused on the wrong things. And if they think about it a little more deeply, they might be feeling that maybe their school *is* pretty boring and a waste of time.

HERE'S A SECOND anecdote, this time from Urs's family.

Early one morning, Urs receives a highly anticipated WhatsApp message from his sixteen-year-old son, Dave. Urs has shared custody in his divorce, though his kids and their mother live across the ocean in Switzerland. In between weekend visits, they stay in close touch, thanks to technology, including this popular messaging app. Typical for his teenage son, the message is minimal, stripped to the essentials:

a screenshot of a letter addressed to his mom and informing both parents that Dave has passed the entrance exam to an advanced school that specializes in economics and business. Dave doesn't include his own commentary beyond a few party and smiley-face emoji.

Urs immediately sends back a quick note, also telegram style, and a bunch of emoji: "Sooooo cool!!! <3 <3 <3 Congratulations!! This is amazing. #prouddad!!"

Urs realizes that Dave has added his sister to the thread. Ananda attended the same advanced school and helped him prepare for the exam.

"Yessss! so so so proud of you <3 <3 <3," Ananda responds to the group chat.

"So happy! Thanks love you <3," Dave writes back immediately.

The celebratory exchange continues for a few more minutes, and Urs even sends some high-five GIFs. Urs then reminds Dave to share the good news with his grandfather, a retired psychology professor who specializes in studying people with learning disabilities.

Why do we share this anecdote? This entire story—not just that day's messages—is made possible through technology. Dave has dyslexia, a common learning disorder. Unfortunately, he has a particularly severe form, and he has struggled with language and numbers for many years. Fast-forward to more recent tales of his academic successes: it turns out that Dave has become a real pro at using the internet to deal with his learning disorder and to help keep up with other students in school.

A combination of watching an almost infinite stream of tutorials on YouTube via his iPhone, catching up on math with personalized online learning tools, researching Wikipedia, and, according to his own account, playing games, has helped Dave achieve a major academic goal. Perhaps most importantly, his use of digital technologies in his personal and social life has helped him stay motivated and to engage in learning activities that were both academically valuable and tailored to Dave's personal interests. Through digital tech, he has discovered that learning can be fun—perhaps the most important insight for his future as a student.

Dave was lucky to have parents and teachers who were supportive of what to many might seem an unconventional mode of learning.

SOME YOUNG PEOPLE are highly focused on what they can learn in a digital era. They are pushing their schools to do more, to meet them where they are, to engage them in what is new and exciting in the world.

A ninth-grader comes into John's office with a proposal. John is the head of a boarding school, founded in 1778, that is blessed with extremely bright students from around the world. This student has tracked down Apple Computer's local sales representative and, on his own, initiated an extended conversation with the rep about buying iPads for all students and teachers at the school.

This student has come to the head of school's office to make the case for his iPad idea. He has thought it all through. He offers a set of pros and cons associated with changing from print-based textbooks to the digital alternatives that are beginning to emerge on the market. He recites every detail about the benefits of iPad-based curricular materials over traditional printed texts: interactivity, easy fostering of collaborative group work, better tailoring to student ability levels, better fit with contemporary student learning styles, less pressure on the back and arms from the backpacks worn by nearly all kids on campus. His presentation is seriously impressive.

Despite all this, John isn't persuaded, and instead he takes this meeting as a teaching moment. Given the boy's logic and enthusiasm, the student is baffled as to why his school won't immediately demand that the faculty switch to teaching all courses from iPads and switch to electronic textbooks. Instead, the head of the school shares with his young charge his views on the realities of technology and teaching. An education conducted exclusively through screens won't necessarily lead to better learning for students. For example, John says, there would be greater risks of disengagement, distraction, and multitasking if students spend all their class time on iPads. Instead, students learn best when they are exposed to a variety of teaching and learning modes, including lots of face-to-face instruction and dialogue. Teachers can better gauge ways to engage a diverse student body when classes are conducted in person, John argues, and students learn best with lessons tailored for a range of learning styles.

But this episode also turns out to be a teaching moment for John. The head of the school learned plenty about how this ninth-grader likes to engage with information—and why the boy cares so much about learning using an iPad.

Consider this student's enthusiasm and the message he was sending. Certainly his passion for experiencing a different kind of teaching was a good reminder that the demand side of the learning equation (the students)—and not just the supply side (teachers and administrators)—matters most in the end. Teachers and parents know best, in many respects, and our authority and knowledge are plainly important. But we don't know everything, and children's interest and passion can be the lifeblood of any great school or household.

THE YEAR WE first published *Born Digital* (2008) was also the year when another book came out: *The Dumbest Generation* by the scholar Mark Bauerlein. At many of the book talks and school visits we conducted, we would be asked about *The Dumbest Generation* and whether we believed today's kids were in fact "dumber" than any earlier generation of kids.

Our answer then and our answer now is absolutely not. Are they learning differently? In most cases, yes, for sure—and in a wide range of ways. Are there great challenges associated with many of their habits, including digital habits? Yes again, for sure. But "dumber"? We don't think so. Neither the data nor our experiences with young people in our own focus groups, interviews, and classrooms lead to such a conclusion. We have some concerns, too, but we are far from panicking.

Parents, teachers, and principals worry that kids are not learning as well or as deeply as they have in the past. The specific fears we hear the most have to do with cheating, multitasking, and shortness of attention. These days, the worry goes, students are more likely to cheat and plagiarize than kids were in the past. Students don't pay enough attention to learning, because they are too distracted by social media, gaming, and other digital pastimes. Last, the fear goes, students lack the attention span to take in and consider serious arguments at proper length. In each of these cases, there are some reasons to worry. The good news is that teachers, parents, and other trusted adults have some tools to help address these concerns.

It's our goal to look hard at the data, make clear recommendations for how to address problems, and flip the script where appropriate to focus on the positive side of learning in the digital era. Some schools build on the excitement that young people have for this sort of learning. For some students, that excitement comes from developing the digital tools themselves. Never before have so many students been able to affect the world around them so directly as they do when they are coding today. In other cases, the technology in the hands of students enables forms of creativity that bring alive visual art, music, theater, politics, religion, history, and many other topics. For yet other students, the technology means that they can access learning materials that were previously unreachable.

The information age has meant unprecedented access to, among other things, educational materials; think of how difficult it had been in many parts of the United States to get access to books in under-resourced or remote public school districts. The internet provides free access to world-class learning materials on virtually every subject. But students need more than internet access to gain a quality education. The skills to engage with those materials, to understand them deeply, to think critically, and to produce new meaning from them are even more important.

If we as a society make the right choices and set up the right support structures, the digital transformation can bring us closer to an age-old education ideal, from the German concept of *Bildung*. According to this vision, first formulated by German scientist Alexander von Humboldt in the early nineteenth century, education should do more than simply aim to provide professional skills through schooling along a fixed path. Rather, education should also center individual learners and empower them to choose their own pathways for life-long learning across personal, social, and academic spheres of study. While the focus of this chapter is mostly on parental concerns and down-to-earth issues like academic integrity and distraction, parents should understand that digital tech—artificial-intelligence-powered digital tutors, personalized online learning platforms, virtual and augmented reality, and the like—opens up many new possibilities. If we're keeping our minds open while navigating our concerns, if we're willing to embrace the full potential of digital technology, these new opportunities will enable us as parents and educators to support the individual learner better than ever before.

WHAT THE RESEARCH SHOWS

What constitutes a quality education has been debated for centuries. Unsurprisingly, the research on education is vast and easily fills many bookshelves if not a small library. While much of the research on this topic predates the digital revolution, many of the basic insights and principles still hold up today. A comprehensive summary of the research lies outside the scope of this book. Instead, the following research topics represent the areas of concern that we've heard most often in our conversations with parents and teachers.

Brain Development

Every year, scientists are learning more and more about how young people's brains work. Neuroscientists and researchers from various disciplines are helping educators and parents understand more about the development of the teenage brain. We know for sure that young people are learning differently in a digital era.

Even up until a few decades ago, the prevailing wisdom was that the teenage brain was not much different from the adult brain. The common belief held that by about puberty, the brain had developed into more or less an adult brain, only with fewer experiences to inform decisions.

But research in the past few decades has shown that the teenage brain is nowhere near fully developed—and, for most people, is not fully formed until they are well into their twenties. Brain imaging shows that the teenage brain has a high degree of plasticity: it can change and grow very quickly. During the teenage years, development occurs primarily through the increased connectivity between regions of the brain. This process, known as myelination, leads to greater connection between parts of the brain and drives the developmental process that young people undergo.

Generally, myelination works from the back to the front of the brain. This process means that the prefrontal cortex is often the last part of the brain to develop. The prefrontal cortex is a complicated part of the body, but in short, it connects to other parts of the brain and is strongly associated with executive functioning and many key aspects of behavior, speech, and reasoning. A young person does have frontal-lobe capabilities, but they are slow to develop and the connections between the front part of the brain and other parts are often not yet highly functional. Think of those frustrating mornings when your child has forgotten to take out the recycling in time (again) or has failed to bring the right textbook to class for an open-book in-class writing assignment. It's not impossible for children to do this kind of mental work, but they often just don't make the connections in a consistent and timely fashion.

Multitasking Versus Switch-Tasking

We know much more today than in the past about the tendency of students to multitask. A majority of students tell researchers that they try to multitask while they are doing homework (from 50 to 75 percent, depending on the study and the tasks, from our observations). Texting while reading novels for English, fooling around on social media while doing math, watching Netflix while doing science, listening to music while doing an art project—students often try to get more than one thing done at a time.

The science shows us that multitasking is essentially impossible for almost anyone, let alone a teenager whose brain has not yet fully developed. When students say that they are *multitasking*, what they are really doing is *switch-tasking*. They are switching, sometimes quite quickly, between tasks. They are not really doing two tasks at the same time.

The process of switching between two activities is less efficient in part because the learner loses time in the adjustment period each time the individual changes modes. The two activities could almost always be done in less time, and with higher-quality performance, when a person focused on one task exclusively to completion, then focused on the other.

The only possible exception to this rule is listening to music. Some students apparently can listen to music while doing certain kinds of homework without losing productivity. Consider, for instance, people who prefer to work in a busy café on their computer instead of a silent reading room at a library. For some people, this white noise can seem to help. (And we admit: as authors, we have often written or edited chapters of this book with music in the background, including right now.) But texting, social media, watching TV, playing games . . . these activities can't coincide with doing homework effectively.

Cheating, Ownership, and Attribution

Among the biggest fears that parents and teachers have about young people and learning is the concern that young people are more likely to cheat than they were in the past. The connection between cheating and digital life is tenuous; no clear cause-and-effect relationship exists. But some of the methods of cheating involve digital technologies, such as copying and pasting text into term papers and bringing a smartphone into class and peeking at it under the desk.

This chapter focuses mostly on cheating that happens in school. The internet has given rise to other forms of cheating as well, including pirating music, TV shows, and movies.

Research suggests that young people do care about ownership and attribution in a general sense, but they are often confused about the rules in specific instances such as music piracy and the proper academic attribution of others' work. And sometimes they ignore the rules that they do understand. On the one hand, this behavior is consistent with other forms of age-appropriate risk-taking; on the other, adults must make clear that cheating is unacceptable and will lead to longer-term problems.

Study Habits and Libraries

Teachers polled about student research and study habits have presented mixed findings. For instance, roughly three-quarters of the teachers from the National Writing Project and Advanced Placement courses told Pew researchers that the internet and digital search tools had a mostly positive impact on their students' research habits. But 87 percent of those same teachers reported that this generation of students appears to be more distracted and has shorter attention spans. And 64 percent of the teachers said that digital technologies do more to distract than to help students with their learning.[1]

Young people use libraries more frequently than almost any other age group in a digital age. Their reading patterns may be different from adult patterns, but they read a great deal. Most of the reading that young people do is assigned by teachers, but they read a lot on their own, too. What has shifted is that some of the reading that used to be in long-form books now takes place online in shorter, more interactive formats.

Reading

There are many changes in young people's reading patterns nowadays. Some worrisome studies show a falloff in reading for fun around the age of nine—just at the age when young people ought to have acquired and solidified their reading skills to ensure future success, according to a landmark study published by the Annie E. Casey Foundation in 2010. The foundation reports that "millions of American children get to fourth grade without learning to read proficiently, and that puts them on the high school dropout track. The ability to read by third grade is critical to a child's success in school, lifelong earning potential, and their ability to contribute to the nation's economy and its security."[2] The research does not blame the digital era for these changes, but we need to grapple with the implications of these important findings.

In our experience and according to the data, boys are reading for fun less than girls are these days. According to Scholastic's "Kids & Family Reading Report," a survey of more than twenty-seven hundred students aged six to seventeen and their parents in 2016, only 52 percent of boys said they enjoyed reading books over the summer, compared with 72 percent of girls. Only 27 percent of boys said they read books for fun five days a week, compared with 37 percent of girls. Boys in the survey also reported having a harder time finding books that interested them than girls had.[3]

One of the most hotly contested questions is whether it is better to read on screens or on paper. As author Ferris Jabr wrote in *Scientific American*, "Since at least the 1980s researchers in many different fields—including psychology, computer engineering, and library and information science—have investigated such questions in more than one hundred published studies. The matter is by no means settled."[4]

Paper does seem to have some clear advantages for reading. Many students prefer to read paper copies of a text because it's easier to annotate the text by writing in the margin or underlining words on paper rather than typing those notes onto a screen. Others report feeling more comfortable with paper and demonstrate greater depth of understanding when they read on paper. Some studies have shown mixed results and various advantages of interactions on digital platforms, including the possibilities of interactivity and interconnection via hypertext links.

Sleep and Learning

Sleep is the foundation of human health and the driving force of brain maturation in adolescence. As shown in countless research studies and clearly explained by Matthew Walker in his book *Why*

We Sleep, young people especially need sleep because different parts of the brain mature at different rates during the human growth process. The tip of the frontal lobe—which enables rational thinking and critical decision making—is the last to develop. Sleep has a lot to do with this development process in adolescents.[5]

A typical daily sleep cycle goes through five 90-minute REM (rapid eye movement) and NREM (non-REM) stages. NREM sleep dominates early in the night (weeding information out), and REM in late morning hours (strengthening the synaptic connections and dreaming). REM sleep and the act of dreaming not only guard our emotional well-being but are also key to the intelligent information processing that inspires creativity and problem-solving.

When young people get too little sleep, they miss out on most or a substantial part of REM sleep. Persistent REM sleep deprivation can lead to depression, anxiety, symptoms associated with schizophrenia, and suicidality. Teens are particularly vulnerable because, unlike adults, whose average bedtime is earlier in most cultures, the timing of melatonin release in young people will not put them to sleep until two or three hours later than the time that adults retire for the night, on average.

Into this mix, add technology. Young people too often use technology right up until the time that they fall asleep. This habit can impair their sleep. A near-constant exposure to LEDs from digital devices (mobile phones, tablets, and TV screens) can delay melatonin release—which signals the onset of sleep—by up to ninety minutes.

A majority of adolescents do not receive enough sleep, according to polling by the National Sleep Foundation.[6] This same 2014 study of youth sleep patterns showed that less than half (about 45 percent) of all children slept 9 hours per night. In 2014, the American Academy of Pediatrics recommended that middle and high schools start no earlier than 8:30 a.m., allowing students the opportunity for 8.5 to 9.5 hours of sleep per night. (In response to these recommendations, and with faculty support at the high school he led, John changed the start time from 8:00 a.m. to 8:30 a.m.) Parents and students need to do their part by putting away their devices earlier in the evening and getting to bed at a reasonable hour to ensure that sleep can do its magic.

THE CONNECTED PARENTS' APPROACH

We are devotees of an educational approach called connected learning. If the term sounds familiar, it should: it's the learning analog of the connected-parenting approach we've advanced throughout this book. Connected learning promotes the stance that students benefit from work and play that is designed to be student-centered, interest-driven, project-based, informal as well as formal, and deeply engaging.[7] Connected learning establishes a framework that can serve students well, whether they are enrolled in a traditional school, are homeschooling, or have to work remotely for a period, as millions of students had to do in response to the COVID-19 pandemic.

Connected learning occurs both in the classroom and beyond it. Much of the time, when we think about education, our minds immediately click over to the image of a school with rooms filled with blackboards and orderly desks. These classroom environments can be crucial—and in the best case even magical. They are a part of the learning experiences of most young people in most societies. But classrooms are not the only learning environments. Connected learning incorporates both what happens in the classroom and what happens elsewhere, including the online environment. Dave's opening story is a case in point.

Through connected learning, various elements come together to create a learning experience that is joyful, inspiring, challenging, and productive for the young person—as well as for teachers, mentors, coaches, and parents. While this vision may be far from what many young people currently experience, why not set forth a positive view to which we all can aspire?

The connected parent focuses mostly on the advantages of the digital world with respect to learning—many of the advantages as yet untapped—while also acknowledging the potential downsides. Better yet, connected parents help their children reap the benefits of online learning and navigate around its hazards. Young people of all ages need support. They need to know that we believe in them and their ability to learn and grow from their experiences, both good and bad.

A connected parent generally supports young people's use of digital technology for learning purposes, whether it's in school, at home, or on the bus. Your acceptance of digital tools for learning, of course, doesn't mean that learning should always involve a tablet, laptop, or phone. To the contrary, as we will discuss on the next pages, learning needs no technology. But parents should not be biased and prematurely dismiss the educational value of online activities their children might find helpful and interesting. In many of our conversations with parents, for instance, we've had to explain that YouTube is not just for entertainment but also offers many highly educational channels. YouTube star John Green offers his Crash Course series covering a broad range of subjects and reaching an audience of over ten million subscribers. We also remind parents that some games are valuable when it comes to skill-building. And that platforms like Khan Academy can help kids learn math skills when they might otherwise be struggling with the lessons at school. Here as elsewhere in this book, we encourage the connected parent to take a closer look at the online activities of their children; learn more about the value the kids see in their favorite channels, games, platforms, and so forth; and support the digital tools that contribute to learning and skill-building.

Taking a nuanced and supportive approach to learning with digital technology doesn't mean that you shouldn't draw red lines at times. When it comes to cheating, there is little room for ambiguity. Naturally, some young people will make poor choices in a moment of weakness and high stress. Students should get second chances, especially during adolescence—a period when their brains are not fully formed. But parents need to make it plain to young people that there's no place for cheating in school or in life. The only good that can come from cheating is a learning experience. Parents should be sure to allow their child to learn from a bad choice when things go awry.

As parents and as teachers, both of us see it as our job to share with students and parents our very best understanding of how learning works best. Ultimately, students need to do the work on their own—the work of learning to learn. We can't do it for them; no parent or teacher can. In the end, learners need to develop a growth mindset that empowers them to seek knowledge in a variety of ways and settings. The connected-learning approach is designed to support that approach, which will serve them best in an increasingly digital world.

OUR RECOMMENDATIONS

Start with humility. Don't assume that you know better or that the way you learned things when you were growing up was better. While your child might ultimately need exactly the corrective action you initially had in mind, at least start with an open mind. The world is changing fast, and our kids are sometimes way ahead of us. Every once in a while, their approaches are actually eye-opening. As researchers, both of us are constantly on the lookout for new studies and new educational practices that shed light on how young people learn and how we can teach them better. We urge you to do the same.

The good news is that you can take many steps to set your children up for success as learners in this digital age:

- *Set up good study environments for the young people in your life.* For many homework assignments and study tasks, a good environment might mean that you should ask your child to put the cell phone aside. If it's in the room, keep it face down, as far out of sight as possible, and with the ringer off. The distractions are just too great for students to resist. In other instances, the connected-learning approach might actually require access to digital technology such as a tablet or laptop—or sometimes even the phone, for instance, if the school is working with a homework app. Make sure to have an open conversation with your child about the appropriate use of these tools and how to deal with the temptation of distractions.
- *Model good behavior.* When you are doing something that approximates studying—whether that is reading books, the newspaper, or a magazine or doing paperwork—do so in a way that you'd want your children to emulate. Ideally, keep your phone out of sight and turned off. Don't have the television on in the background. Focus on the task at hand. Young people are watching us more than we ever realize. Modeling is such a powerful force. And it's in our control, even if we admit it's not that easy, given our highly connected lifestyles.

Reading

We wish to draw special attention to the topic of reading. If there's any place where Bauerlein—the author of *The Dumbest Generation*—might have made a worrisome point, it has to do with reading.

Our response to the concern about a possible drop in reading skills: make a point to read a lot to kids when they are young. Let them see you reading books, magazines, and newspapers—whether the material is on e-readers, tablets, or in print. Listen to audiobooks on car rides and while doing chores. Make reading a part of family life. Trips to the bookstore and public library can be a family routine. Seeing you reading may make all the difference for your children. When kids become excited by reading at an early age, it can become habit-forming. Some of the best news in the Scholastic surveys, conducted regularly since 2010, is that reading aloud to children is on the rise.[8]

One of the reasons some readers prefer print books is that reading online involves the potential for greater distractions. Some e-readers offer hypertext links, embedded or linked videos, and other related content that can disrupt the flow of the customary reading experience. These related offerings in e-readers, compared with traditional books, can distract readers rather than enhance the learning experience. For people with limited means, including students with heavy educational loans and families with tight budgets, even with the upfront cost of an e-reader, borrowing books in any format or buying digital books can be a much less expensive option than purchasing print books in the long run. The limited-function e-readers that focus only on reading and shopping for books might be a good choice in this situation.

Cheating

A related concern we've heard from parents and teachers is that the use of technology leads to a copy-and-paste culture. High-profile cases, including those at elite institutions such as Harvard (where Urs teaches and John used to), suggest that technology-enabled cheating is prevalent on college campuses. Cheating is thought to be especially common in STEM-type disciplines, in which students increasingly work together on assignments for which they are required to submit their own answers (when they are not meant to be collaborating) and for which there might be clearer "right" and "wrong" answers than there are in other disciplines. These phenomena are obvious to anyone who teaches young people in a classroom or manages them in a workplace today. These fears are realistic.

On the issue of cheating, a simple exercise with your children works remarkably well. The key is to put them in the position of the creator rather than the consumer of whatever the content is. Whether it's the answers to a test or a hit song, start a conversation about what it would be like to have created something with real effort.

Would they want every other kid taking it for free, without having to credit their work or paying them anything? If they were a moviemaker who had spent years and millions of dollars making a film, would they want everyone to see the movie for free, or would they want to recoup their investment of time and money and maybe receive a bit of profit? The answer to all the kids we've talked to has been "of course," they want to be credited and paid for their hard work. For many young people, this simple exercise will at least make them stop and think before they take someone else's work.

The broader idea here is to help young people see the issue of cheating or using someone else's creations from another perspective. When they take on the role of the creator of the content, they often can see the unfairness of using it without payment or permission—whether in the case of academic plagiarism or intellectual property violations when it comes to music and movies. Our approach is to give our children and students the benefit of the doubt, to encourage them to learn and grow, and to make sure they understand that there are limits to their behavior.

At a fundamental level, cheating only holds back the students themselves. We know that some students do go online to buy term papers, essays, reading reports, and so forth. Instead—and this may sound a bit cheesy—the connected parent's approach is to stress that it is important for students to learn and to earn their grades (and in the future, their jobs and promotions) through their own hard work. Education is their own investment in themselves; cheating impoverishes their own skill sets. Cheating is obviously unfair, but in the long run, people's cheating just hurts themselves.

Fake News and the Problems with Information Quality

Too often, when our children browse through a social media feed, they are presented with plausible-looking news accounts that are packed with half-truths and outright falsehoods. In some of these cases, children may even encounter eerily convincing deep fakes—videos that use a real person's image but superimpose completely different words in the person's own voice. We need to engage with our kids about the phenomenon of fake news and the role that different types of media—including TV and social media—play in its propagation. Given that social media is such a dominant source of information for young people, parents and educators have a big role to play in educating kids about having a critical eye on the sources of this information and the different ways others may seek to manipulate their thinking and decision making.

When you were growing up, you might have turned to *Encyclopaedia Britannica* for "the answer" to a question. While that approach, too, had its limitations, it had at least the benefit of simplicity. Today's closest equivalent is Wikipedia, a great resource that is quite popular among young people. While we still recommend Wikipedia as a generally reliable source of online information—insofar as it requires that all entries include links to primary or secondary sources and its editors do a great job overall at reducing misinformation—this online encyclopedia is more vulnerable to disinformation attacks than the good old *Encyclopaedia Britannica* ever was. Furthermore, these days, the first stop for kids (and adults alike) when they have a question is typically Google, where they get responses from a broad range of sources with varying degrees of quality.

There is such a thing as a fact, even when our politicians today might encourage us to think otherwise. We need to be sure that our kids approach the news and information they receive with appropriate skepticism. They need to learn to assess sources and the cues they see online associated with news and information. This new form of literacy needs to be taught at schools, at home, and in local libraries.

Sleep

Again, do ensure that the young people in your life get sleep. Despite your exasperation as a parent or a teacher, you can't negotiate with this biological clock. It is only in adulthood that the circadian rhythm of humans shifts to make earlier bedtimes easier. So for now, your children may need your support in getting an adequate nightly dose of rest.

We favor a mix of strategies for encouraging sleep among young people. The most effective are showing them the benefits of sleep through experiments and the experiences of their own quality of life when they test out different amounts of sleep. If you can prompt students to get enough sleep and see the positive effects, they are more likely to see that a good night's sleep works and develop a positive habit around it.

Consider a family "sleep challenge" for a month. Encourage your adolescents to log their sleep every night for that month; they could use their digital devices to help keep track if they like. (A sheet of paper and a pencil work fine, too). At the end of the challenge, compare notes on how various amounts of sleep felt and whether more sleep led to improved performance in school, in their sports, and in their overall moods. It may surprise your teens how effective a positive sleep strategy can be for improving all aspects of their lives. It may surprise you, too!

A Positive Role for Technology

A knowledgeable parent or teacher can use technology to improve learning outcomes. Young people develop knowledge and skills at different rates. Technology allows us to stop moving kids along at a predetermined, cookie-cutter pace. Instead, we can focus on whether a student has mastered a particular skill first before moving on to more advanced lessons. In courses like mathematics, sciences, and language in particular, we now have the tools to personalize learning like never before, thanks to large amounts of data and smart algorithms. Students will learn more, feel better about their success, and make better use of the time they spend with their teachers in person.

Perhaps most importantly, digital technology can help our kids connect previously siloed learning spaces. With the help of technology, children can now better connect their experiences across the personal (e.g., pursuing an interest in wildlife by watching nature documentaries on YouTube), the social (e.g., playing an adventure game with friends), and academic spheres (e.g., geography class on Australia's outback) of learning. Connected learning, understood in this way, also sets the stage for lifelong learning. When our children enter adult life, they can use these skills toward continuous self-education to help them pursue information to advance their careers or to advance their own hobbies and interests.

Technology can also be a means to a specific end: the acquisition of twenty-first-century skills (we prefer to call them digital-citizenship skills) that are needed in the globalized economy. Maybe a young person starts an Instagram or YouTube account and learns how to build a community around a topic, how to interact with an audience, how to respond to criticisms, or even how to build a brand—all these lessons provide highly relevant skills in today's digital economy. Or maybe what unlocks passion in a young person is learning to write code—to bend an app or a webpage to the coder's will or whim. By learning to code, students prepare themselves for jobs that we know will be there for them when they graduate. While we often assume young people have advanced tech skills, in truth far too few kids have the tech skills that employers are seeking, like coding and computer engineering. And the split between young people with technological skills and those without too often falls along the lines of class, gender, and race.[9]

Learning is about more than mastering content; it is also about forming character. Technology can be a means to that end, too. Every day, students are faced with ethical questions as they use YouTube, Snapchat, Instagram, and Facebook. They face questions of ethics and law as they copy and paste digital materials or consult Wikipedia. They weigh what is important, true, or worth following and what is not. We can use these moments both to model good behavior and to help our children develop strong moral character. These are great topics for the dining room table at home—topics that might be more engaging than "What did you do in school today?"

Parents and schools should encourage kids to take a learn-by-doing approach in digital environments. Whether they are savvy technology users or not, young people can learn by creating digital works ranging from the utterly simple to the highly elaborate. The idea is to build on their penchant for developing online profiles and other materials on social media. Students who are interested in music can listen to anything—Drake, Beethoven, or whatever else they love—and create their own master work (or maybe not), using inexpensive software like GarageBand and iMovie. Writing, poetry, art—in each instance, a parent or teacher can orient young people in a digital space and encourage them to build something new or improve something old. In social studies or a class on politics, students could be prompted to take recordings of political campaign speeches and remix them into contexts that make the speeches meaningful to the student. In so doing, students could learn about copyrights or Creative Commons licenses. This mode of teaching students by encouraging their talents for online creativity will no doubt present challenges for many teachers who are not yet comfortable in the digital world. But the payoff can be substantial, for parent and student alike.

Technology for its own sake is not the point. It is one of several promising tools to help students and teachers meet their shared educational goals, regardless of the context in which they are teaching and learning. We can breathe new life into our homes, communities, and schools by applying technology with care. In doing so, we will redefine what we mean by excellence in learning and build much-needed bridges between formal and informal learning environments. With connected parenting, we can engage more young people in the joy of learning and better prepare them for the jobs that they will fill, or create, and for the lives of principle we hope they can lead.

COMMON QUESTIONS

Are young people learning less in schools than they used to?

It's impossible to say, but our guess is no. Nor is a comparison of then and now our starting point. Many schools are greatly improved from a generation or two ago. And free education is much more widespread in the world than in the past. That said, there are areas in which education is plainly failing in terms of preparing our students. Too many young people are leaving school without the basic skills they need to succeed in a modern economy, and too many schools in poor communities offer a weaker education than that offered in wealthier communities. The bottom line for parents is that learning is not confined to the school environment. For this reason, we emphasize connected learning and connected parenting to underscore the need for learning to occur both inside and outside of formal environments such as schools. There is so much opportunity for students to learn on their own through online sites like SesameStreet.org (for the youngest students); CodeAcademy, Khan Academy, and Girls Who Code (for school-age kids through college students); EdX and Coursera (for high-school-age students and beyond); and many more. The possibilities for creating things online, coding, and connecting with people from other cultures is unprecedented. Even if schools are not fully serving our students, the digital world offers great opportunities for learners eager to seize them.

Why don't more schools have fully developed programs to help students learn in a digital era?

We live in an era when those who lead schools and those who teach grew up primarily in an analog age. Only the youngest teachers, coaches, and principals grew up with the internet and social media as part of their childhood experience. It is natural that we teach what we know. There's a lot of good in that practice; traditional teaching, from traditional texts, is an important part of what young people learn in schools. Consider the teacher who does a great job teaching an English literature course on texts by Toni Morrison, Jane Austen, Julia Alvarez, and Zadie Smith as well as Shakespeare's plays and sonnets. Students have much to gain from these teachers and these experiences. At the same time, schools have been slow to make the transition toward teaching some of the skills and knowledge necessary for young people to thrive in a digital age. Formal programs in computer science and digital literacy skills should be offered in more schools. Some schools have strong library programs and teachers who are adept at integrating digital-era reading and critical-thinking skills into their curricular and extracurricular programming. You might consider, too, how prepared the faculty and staff are to teach in new ways when technology is required to get the job done. When the global COVID-19 pandemic hit in early 2020, schools had to shift immediately into remote learning mode. If you had school-age children then, reflect on how your school did during that period. Were the teachers ready and able to make the pivot? Many around the world were not, for a range of reasons. Those teachers and schools that were able to make the changes to remote learning quickly kept their students better on track than those that were less prepared for a whole host of reasons. It's worth asking about the policies and approaches your school might take if remote learning were to become the norm again in a hurry. When you are thinking about schooling options (e.g., the neighborhood school or a specialized one) for your children, this topic might prompt some helpful questions to put on your list.

What is digital citizenship, and how can we help young people acquire the relevant skills?

Digital citizenship can be understood as an umbrella term that captures the various skills needed to thrive and flourish in a digital society, economy, and culture. It brings together a series of related concepts—often characterized as twenty-first-century skills—that describe the skills individuals need in order to use technologies in the digital age. In a recent review, youth and media researchers have identified seventeen tech skill areas that children can develop, including gathering data; developing computational thinking; producing and publishing content; protecting one's privacy, reputation, safety, and well-being; assessing information quality; and understanding artificial intelligence. Following the connected-learning philosophy, young people can acquire these skills across different spheres of learning. Many schools are now mandated to teach at least a subset of the skills identified in the review. Dedicated after-school programs or summer camps also offer many opportunities for building digital-citizenship skills—all the way from coding camps to data science programs for youth.

Various nonprofit organizations and academic institutions also provide educational materials that can be used by educators and young people alike. An example is the Digital Citizenship+ Resource Platform by the Berkman Klein Center at Harvard University. The platform offers learning experiences codesigned by adults and youth. Last but not least, children can learn some of these skills by *doing*. Encourage them to use their own personal and social interests as a way to learn; for example, they could participate in various online activities, such as creating and sharing content, using hashtags, building online audiences, playing collaborative games, or doing in-depth research online. All of these activities also provide great material for intergenerational reflection and opportunities for parental support.

KEY TAKEAWAYS

A growing body of data about young people and learning in the digital age supplements decades of education research from analog contexts. While there are worrisome recent trends—for instance, the finding that boys are reading less than girls—the research so far also suggests that the technologies we have at our disposal today could help student learning more than those in the past have done.

A few knowledge gaps are worth highlighting, too. Our understanding of the teenage brain and how it is developing—especially in light of the stimuli of digital media—is still evolving. We have much more to learn about what works best for young people's learning over time. This area warrants further focus as technologies develop and as the ways that young people use them evolve.

We urge you to read to your kids starting at a young age and to keep encouraging them to read as they grow older. The data suggest a falloff in reading for many young people after age nine. Help your children power through this falloff period through example, encouragement, and support.

Embrace the idea of connected learning by encouraging learners to engage in a variety of ways and environments. Young people learn in many places, at many times, and in many ways. When they are driven by their own intrinsic motivation and pulled toward topics of great interest to them, they tend to do their best work. Seek out and support mentoring relationships that can support young people in these areas of interest—inside and outside of formal learning environments such as schools. Libraries, museums, after-school programs, friend groups—these can be incredibly powerful learning environments.

Ensure that the young people in your life get enough sleep! (And get enough sleep yourself while you are at it, if you can. The example you set will affect their behavior.)

Encourage (appropriately and gently!) the teachers, librarians, and mentors in your child's life to examine their teaching practices in light of the available advances in the digital era.

The skills that young people learn in digital environments now can also prepare them for college experiences and for adulthood in the digital economy and workforce. Some technical skills such as coding and computer support, often learned initially on their own or in informal environments, can lead to job placements. But a broad range of other digital skills are also important. For instance, knowing how to learn via an online course, how to interact professionally over social media, and how to communicate effectively with adults over digital channels will serve students well in the long run as they seek jobs and promotions throughout their careers. Students who have not learned these skills, or who have not even experienced a taste of these interactions, will have to make up ground if they seek to operate in the digital economy in the future.

CHAPTER 10

Civic Life

Nadya Okamoto struggled with homelessness as a young person. As a teen, she realized that one of the biggest challenges of her tough living situation was what she called "the unaddressed natural need of periods." Yes, that's right. Okamoto worried about menstruation hygiene and the need for equity in access to period-related supplies.

While in high school, Okamoto decided to do something about it. In 2014, she founded a nonprofit with a friend, Vincent Forand. Okamoto and Forand set about making it easier for those who have periods to get the supplies they needed. Her approach was simple at first, collecting donations for purchasing period products and distributing them to people who needed them in her local area. It was a decidedly low-tech approach to the "period problem," as she sometimes called it.

Okamoto realized that her digital skills could help scale her idea beyond her organization's base in Portland, Oregon. She and Forand began recruiting other young people to join their cause in other parts of the country. This effort required no massive institution with big government grants or a widespread donor base of wealthy sponsors. Their tools? Social media, shoe leather, media savvy, and an incredible passion for doing good.

Today, Period.org is a national network with young people in three hundred communities working toward a common goal. Thousands of students per year distribute period products to those in need, educate young people and adults about the problem they seek to address, and advocate for better public policy.

The ability to coordinate and support this network is a new thing for this generation, and it requires only digital skills and extremely low-cost or free software. Even thirty years ago, without an existing trove of wealth and high-profile connections, a grassroots movement would have taken years to go from one person's idea to an effort shared across a single city. Perhaps the network would have spread across the state after a few more years and then nationally over time. But the likelihood that it could have scaled over just a few short years—into what Okamoto calls "the largest youth-run nonprofit in women's health"—is implausible. The genius of what Okamoto and her friends have done is in no small part a story about mastering and taking advantage of new technologies for the public interest.

TODAY'S TECHNOLOGY-ENABLED ACTIVISM can connect young people around the world. On March 15, 2019, parents in more than a hundred countries got a phone call from their children's school, telling them that their child was absent that day. Led by a diverse group of young people, students skipped school to join in a global protest against the ravages of climate change. Estimates of the total number of protesters reached as high as 1.4 million young people worldwide. When climate activists organized again a few months later, as many as 4 million people joined climate-related strikes on September 20, 2019.

The larger movement dates back to well before the digital age, of course, but the recent chapter starts with a determined young Swedish climate activist named Greta Thunberg. Since she was fifteen in 2018, Thunberg has been protesting against climate inaction on the part of the Swedish government—and everyone else, for that matter. Her primary tools have been skipping school on Fridays, protesting in the city streets outside the Riksdag (the Swedish Parliament), and effectively using her personal brand on social media. As the mainstream press has caught on to her activism, the number of young people aware of her efforts has grown, in turn drawing more into the movement that she started, literally on her own.

In the United States, three young women banded together to organize the national walkout: thirteen-year-old Alexandria Villasenor of New York City, sixteen-year-old Isra Hirsi of Minnesota, and twelve-year-old Haven Coleman of Denver. The result of their efforts? Students walked out in all fifty states. There is very little chance that such a distributed effort could have succeeded, with essentially no cost, in an era without social media and young people skilled in its usage.

Students helped tell the story of their own global strike in unprecedented ways. The organizers of local protests posted to the usual social media outlets: Snapchat, Instagram, Twitter. They also played professional roles. *Wired* hired two teenagers to photograph the protests for the magazine that many turn to as the definitive source of news related to the digital era. Esme Bella Rice, seventeen, photographed protesters in Atlanta, and Max Buenviaje-Boyd, eighteen, photographed events in San Francisco.

While adults wring their hands that youth are not voting, students are skipping school around the world to make the case for change. While wise observers write columns in the mainstream press such as "The Problem with Greta Thunberg's Climate Activism: Her Radical Approach Is at Odds with Democracy" (a *New York Times* opinion piece by Christopher Caldwell), Thunberg and her age cohort are online making their case that the time to act is now, before it's too late. The business of making change is changing. The leaders of that change are not writing op-eds in printed newspapers. And most of them have not yet celebrated their twentieth birthday.

LET'S RAISE A generation of active, engaged citizens. The idea of civic engagement seems to have lost currency in some quarters. You've heard the concerns; perhaps you harbor them yourselves. People who fear for our communities and our democracy point out that young people seem to have lost faith in institutions. Many schools have dropped civics from the curriculum. Fewer young people seem to be voting.

These worrisome changes seem to be coming at just the wrong time. Community after community, nation after nation, and region after region seem to be coming apart at the seams. Humans seem to be focused more on what divides us than on what brings us together. Just when our societies need civic engagement more than ever, our young people seem to be leaning back, away from the civic commons.

The blame for this deterioration is often laid at the feet of technology. There's an idea that young people have become somehow more shallow, less serious-minded about their civic obligations because of Facebook, Tik Tok, and the like. Technology seems to make things worse, not better, as kids appear to be clicking their way to a better future rather than actually rolling up their sleeves. Critics denounce the idea of "clicktivism," in which students demonstrate their support for a candidate or a cause by clicking the "like" button on a social media page—and then call it a day.

This lament has some validity, to a degree. For whatever reasons, young people tend to distrust institutions, often deeply distrusting them. But that doesn't mean they are not civically engaged. Actually, quite the contrary: young people are often intensely civically engaged. As we have seen in every previous chapter, the ways youth engage in activism today differ from the activism of earlier generations—but not necessarily for the worse.

Young people's civic engagement follows a different pattern than yours did. And some elements of this pattern we need to understand better. We need to focus on the promising aspects of their practices to encourage them further along a positive path. We can also learn from today's youth; examples like Okamoto are definitely making inspiring and innovative societal impacts.

WHAT THE RESEARCH SHOWS

Researchers have shown that some young people today may be less inclined to vote but that they are more inclined to volunteer their time. Many young people have become cynical about the electoral process. They believe that the government is too far removed and slow moving compared with nongovernmental organizations, where they can make change through direct action. This trend has been shown over a thirty-year period and over shorter periods.[1]

Young people today are more likely to join protests during their college years than are college students from any time in the past half century. This statistic comes from an important survey of incoming first-year college students by the Higher Education Research Institute at UCLA, which has been administering the survey for fifty years. When asked about community engagement and helping others, entering first-year students in 2015 gave those acts a higher personal priority than any other students had in the previous twenty years, the entire period in which the questions had been asked. The survey also showed big increases in the likelihood that African American and Latinx students would be civically engaged during their college years. The researchers suggested that much of the increased likelihood of protest on college campuses stemmed from the larger movement of nationwide demonstrations after police shootings of people of color in the years leading up to this study's administration.[2]

The data also show that young people with less education are less likely to participate in civic life than those with more education. This correlation also means that engaged citizens are more likely to be white and wealthier. Those less likely to participate are more likely to have parents with less education, to have less economic security now and in the past, to live in communities with less wealth, and to be racial and ethnic minorities.

Some studies, however, show a contrary pattern. For instance, researchers at the Center for Information and Research on Civic Learning and Engagement published a series of reports, including "How to Engage Youth in Elections and Beyond" and "Five Takeaways on Social Media and the Youth Vote in 2018." Three findings the center wrote about suggested positive areas of growth in civic activism among today's youth. First, the percentage of eligible young people who turned out to vote in the US federal midterm elections rose from an estimated 21 percent in 2014 to an estimated 31 percent in 2018. This historic uptick was almost certainly the result of massive voter-registration drives, led by March for Our Lives organizers and many other student organizations. Second, young people told researchers that they were three times more likely to join a public protest than they were two years earlier. And third, young people told pollsters that their online activism translated to offline activism. Given that 90 percent of the eighteen- to twenty-nine-year-olds polled said they used social media, this finding, if sound, could prove powerful over time.[3]

The decline in voting at every age, especially in local elections, is a national crisis in the United States. These days, rarely do more than half of those eligible to vote do so in any given election. A study by researchers at Portland State University and funded by the Knight

Foundation revealed the voting patterns in mayoral elections in thirty US cities. The results were abysmal: in most cities, the turnout was around 20 percent of eligible voters. New York City mayoral elections turn out about 15 percent of eligible voters. Dallas came in dead last in the study: 6 percent of eligible citizens bothered to vote for mayor. The median age of a voter in mayoral elections? Fifty-seven.[4]

In most households with parents of young children, voting in important elections is clearly not a priority. We as parents, and our kids as they turn eighteen, can and should turn this story around. Much will turn on it.

THE CONNECTED PARENTS' APPROACH

Connected parents embrace the old-fashioned idea that an informed and engaged citizenry is good for communities. To the extent that people are able to determine what is important and take action, both individuals and the community at large will benefit. The internet and social media offer unprecedented opportunities for anyone, anywhere, to inform themselves about what is going on.

Yes, there is also the possibility of harmful misinformation. We need to impart to our children the ability to sniff out misinformation and to act on factual information. Democracies risk withering away, or being hijacked, if we don't pay close attention to this dynamic. At the moment, it feels as though we are letting down our children in this respect.

To counteract those worrisome trends, connected parents will demonstrate their commitment to civic life primarily through their own actions. Before we cast blame on our kids, we need to look at ourselves. We need to be sure that we are setting a good example before we start lecturing.

Consider also what you post to social media yourself. Your children are no doubt watching you in this regard as well. Family updates and photos from fun events are terrific. But the extent to which you engage with the important issues of the day matters, too. If your children see how important civic life is for you online and offline, they are much more likely to engage in these practices themselves, following your good lead.

OUR RECOMMENDATIONS

If we as parents aren't civically active, we can't very well expect our children to get involved in their communities. They may decide to do so even if we are apathetic, but we should not leave it to chance. Our democracy systems will be stronger with higher levels of participation by adults and young people alike.

The best way to teach civic engagement is to get your children excited about it at a young age. Ideally, make it a part of your family's story. Engage alongside your children in your community, support them in their efforts, and help them understand why civic engagement—even with and through institutions—can lead to positive change. And listen to them when they share their excitement around their preferred modes of engagement, too, even if the methods differ from your own.

Voting is, of course, a place to start. Make Election Day a special event. Take your children to the polls with you when you go to vote, and include some kind of a treat. (We are not above small forms of bribery to create lasting, positive associations.) Your enthusiasm may rub off on your children when it comes time for them to be able to vote.

As important as it is, voting is just one form of civic engagement. Talking about public issues facing your community, volunteering at the local soup kitchen, engaging with neighbors in public spaces, organizing a potluck—there are many ways to convey your belief in civic life beyond voting. There is an endless array of possibilities.

The ideas will vary by community, but here are a few that you might consider.

Engage in activism with your children, both offline and online. Make it a family activity. Spend Mother's Day or Father's Day helping to serve a meal to families in need (and maybe let your own mom or dad put their feet up).

Attend a public meeting or another local political event at least once a year. Attend an event with your kids at the local public library. Then post a picture of you all outside the library or town hall on your Instagram feed. Your children may not love it, but they will remember that you took them, that you made it a priority. And the photo will let other families know that civic engagement is a priority for your family as well.

Talk about other young people who are doing remarkable, civic-oriented things both online and offline. There is likely to be a young person doing something like what Okamoto and Forand have done in your community. Check out DoSomething.org, arguably the largest online collection of young people anywhere in the world. Make activism and organizing a topic of dinnertime conversation. Celebrate the work and achievements of young activists you admire. Your children will remember the stories that you discuss and may later strive to emulate these young leaders that you have held up for them, even if they rolled their eyes at first. Consider letting them take a day off from school with their classmates (yes, we are educators, and we are encouraging playing hooky for a good cause!) to join a protest or demonstration, such as the Friday climate strikes led globally by Thunberg and her peers.

Advocate for civics education in your school district. If the schools that your children attend don't teach anything about civic engagement, demand to know why not. If the teachers, principal, and superintendent say it's just not possible for one reason or another, find a way to supplement this aspect of your children's education.

Seek out museums, libraries, or other institutions that offer pro-gramming for young people in your community. While schools are often the best place for young people to learn history and civics, they are not the only places. Every city and town in America has a public library or access to one in the region. Every good librarian we've ever known would love to help put together something to engage young people in civic life in a community—just ask.

Perhaps your city or town has a presidential library or a special library devoted to a former senator or another public figure. More places do that you might think! Dallas has the George W. Bush Pres-idential Center on the Southern Methodist University campus. The center offers immersive experiences with Southern hospitality. ("This will always be a place that welcomes each visitor with open arms," according to former first lady Laura Bush.) And Boston is home to both the John F. Kennedy Presidential Library and Museum and the Edward M. Kennedy Institute for the United States Senate. Both institutions have entertaining tours designed for young people and aimed at teaching civic engagement. These two institutions also have strong websites with lots of online resources to access remotely. For example, your child can use the Kennedy Library's website to learn about the civil rights leaders who worked with President Kennedy.

Museums are also often a good bet. Art museums are constantly on the lookout for ways to engage young people more directly in their work, and civic life is often a great means of outreach. Hun-dreds of art museums and other partners participated in the For Freedoms project, for instance, in 2018. These museums encouraged young people to make creative forms of expression to celebrate the "Four Freedoms" of Franklin Delano Roosevelt's speech and the corresponding Norman Rockwell paintings. These ideals—freedom of speech, freedom of worship, freedom from want, and freedom from fear—sparked a nationwide expressive wave that artists Hank

Willis Thomas and Eric Gottesman called "the largest creative collaboration in U.S. history."[5] The companion website features the work of artists of all ages, many of them teenagers. If you live near Montgomery, Alabama, make a trip to the Legacy Museum: From Enslavement to Mass Incarceration. Acclaimed public interest lawyer Bryan Stevenson and his Equal Justice Initiative established this museum to teach the history of racial inequality in the United States, and he built it on the site of a former warehouse where black people were enslaved. If you can't make it in person, watch the videos on the Equal Justice Initiative website and on YouTube with your children.[6]

If you can't find civic education for your children at their schools or local libraries, seek it out online. Check out the free resources and games on iCivics (www.icivics.org), for instance, which was created by former Supreme Court Justice Sandra Day O'Connor.

Of course these ideas all sound painfully earnest. That's fair enough. But this idealism, and the belief that we all have a role in forming a "more perfect Union," is necessary for democracy to work for all Americans. What could be more important?

If we don't exercise our democratic muscles, our entire system will go soft and eventually cease to function properly. We can't complain about the state of our republic and then do nothing about it. Most of all, we should be investing in our children and ensuring that their practices are healthier than ours have been. The data suggest that they may already be on the right track.

The technological world that our kids are growing up in also reminds us how global their experience is likely to be. Support your children in becoming global citizens in this increasingly interconnected world. Some of the issues that our children are certain to face—war, trade, immigration, climate change, pandemics—cannot be solved unilaterally. With increased global awareness and engagement, children can be part of the solution to these problems. Technology can be a force to accelerate this progress, so long as all of us direct it thoughtfully and deliberately in a positive direction.

COMMON QUESTIONS

Are you concerned that students are only involved in "clicktivism" or "slacktivism"? Has shallow support online taken the place of on-the-ground participation and activism?

We have no problem with young people's involvement in online activism as long as the cause is broadly in the public interest. To be clear, we worry about forms of online engagement that might lead to harm to others; we are in no way endorsing online radicalism, hate, or violence.

We see no evidence to suggest that clicking "like" on a cause's Facebook page, retweeting a candidate's position on a topic, or signing an online petition will make young people less likely to engage in civic life offline. If anything, the evidence points in the other direction: online engagement may lead to offline engagement. We disagree with the premise of the term "slacktivism." Digital engagement in civic affairs has nothing to do with slacking off.

Online and offline forms of engagement are more or less inextricably linked at this point, anyway, in most communities. As a result, it makes less sense over time to worry about online versus offline. As many new political organizations, such as Black Lives Matter, have shown, social media is a driver of engagement and can lead to offline engagement, and vice versa. It is hard to imagine a new social or political movement that doesn't adopt an online strategy, at least to some degree, as it seeks to grow in membership, reach, and impact. The same goes for an electoral campaign, a ballot initiative, or a petition drive. Put another way: the worry that online engagement would threaten offline engagement makes less sense over time.

Don't you think this generation is just more apathetic than we were?

We don't. We can't explain exactly how it happened, but the mode of engagement for many young people has changed. We sense that there's less of a desire, for instance, to intern on Capitol Hill in Washington than perhaps there was a generation or two ago. But there's a huge appetite among young people to start their own non-profits or movements to try to address the social problems of the age. But institutional engagement still has merit, and we hope that young people can be persuaded to make change both inside and outside of traditional political institutions.

What's going on in schools? Why doesn't anyone teach civics anymore?

We share your concern on this issue. It's true: too many schools have eliminated education in civics, and it's worrisome.

But we *don't* agree that no one cares or teaches civics anymore! In fact, John taught a year-long US history course over a span of several years with a heavy dose of civics woven through. Many schools still do teach some form of civics, though not always through the history or social studies curricula. Many states, such as Illinois, have activists who are making a concerted push to reintroduce civics into the public school curriculum—with some success. In 2019, Illinois law required that "every public elementary school shall include in its 6th, 7th, or 8th grade curriculum, beginning with the 2020–2021 school year, at least one semester of civics education, which shall help young people acquire and learn to use the skills, knowledge, and attitudes that will prepare them to be competent and responsible citizens throughout their lives."[7]

Innovative efforts to teach civics also show promise in reaching young people. Each of the efforts mentioned in the preceding section is worth exploring. For instance, former Supreme Court Justice Sandra Day O'Connor devoted many years to setting up and promoting iCivics, an institution that uses online tools to engage young people in civic life. A start-up teaching endeavor by Professor David Moss has taken the Harvard Business School teaching method and adapted it for the teaching of US history, with a strong civics bent to it. Moss's effort aims to reach high-school-age students across the United States. New museums have cropped up to drive civic engagement, such as the Edward M. Kennedy Institute, which is designed to provide young visitors with an interactive experience that makes the work of the Senate relevant, important, and appealing.

The bottom line: civic education can take many forms in the digital era. The learning can certainly come from a course in a traditional class setting with a devoted teacher at the front of the room. But connected learning occurs both inside and outside of the school building and teaching hours. One thing we know: it won't happen on its own. Parents and teachers have to coax it into being and create positive pathways for the young people in their lives.

KEY TAKEAWAYS

The information about youth and civic engagement are quite clear. There are a lot of data and many good researchers on the job. Certain types of engagement, such as voting rates, are fairly easy to estimate. Other types of engagement, such as informal types of civic participation, rely on less certain methods. Nonetheless, we believe that the data do a good job overall demonstrating the direction of participation in various forms. That direction is positive!

Generally, young people today are engaged in civic life. But because they are doing so both online and offline, their participation may appear different from what previous generations would readily recognize as civic engagement.

As we've seen in other settings, what's less certain is the best way to teach young people how to use social media for civic participation. We believe in the power of connected parenting as the core approach, with schools, churches, community groups, and online efforts supplementing the civic life that starts in the home.

Don't worry about the critiques of "clicktivism" and "slacktivism." Young people are deeply engaged in civic life—and will be, in many cases, for the long run.

Schools need to stay in the game for teaching civics and encouraging civic life. Too many schools have abandoned this work; that's not great for democracy. Of course, teachers and administrators are facing various challenges. Budgets are strapped, and curricula are often overloaded. But we can't afford to cut back in this area. Where cuts have already occurred, connected parents have to turn to online resources, libraries, and after-school programs to make sure their children learn about this crucial area as they grow up.

One other area to keep an eye on: young people today tend to distrust institutions. Their distrust can translate into less direct engagement with those institutions and a preference for other modes of organizing and action. While these other modes are often wonderful, voting and other aspects of formal civic participation can matter enormously. Encourage the young people in your life to register and to vote! That means voting in local elections for mayors and city council members as well as for federal representatives and the president.

Conclusion

CONNECTED PARENTING IS not just about how to parent online. Online and offline experiences are fully connected for our children. Our approach as their parents should also be seamlessly connected.

As the two of us set out to explore this final point, we decided to write this conclusion in the form of a digital dialogue. We each took turns posing questions and answering them, using Google Docs, continuing a form of the digital back-and-forth process we used to draft and edit this entire book. In writing the book, we also met up periodically—in real space, typically over a good dinner—to discuss and improve our ideas.

Our writing process mirrored the connected-parenting approach we advocate. It's often those everyday dinnertime conversations that connect, and provide key context to, the online experiences nearly everyone has these days.

Urs: Let's start our concluding dialogue with a question for you, John: given the flood of advice parents receive

concerning their children and technology, do you think we
might risk losing sight of—and neglecting—what's going
on in their offline lives?

John: I believe in connected parenting as a guiding framework
because it makes clear that online life and offline life
are not separate for our kids—it's all just *life*. These
experiences for them are seamlessly interconnected. If
we start thinking of ourselves as "digital parents" or as
"offline parents," we are missing the boat. We need to
understand the deep interconnections between the various
environments in which our children are interacting with
one another, with information and knowledge, and with
the world at large.

The risk that you describe strikes me as very real. A
parent who is too worried about a daughter's social media
exposure might miss the underlying risks of an eating
disorder. Parents who are upset about their son's time spent
playing video games might miss his deep-seated anxieties,
his tendency toward depression, and other factors that
have nothing to do with technology. So yes, I worry that
parental fears might turn technology into a scapegoat
when a more balanced view would show it for what it is: a
tool that kids use for a variety of reasons. These tools—in
my view—can exacerbate existing concerns, from eating
disorders to social anxieties. But they just as often mask
underlying offline issues that kids are grappling with. As
connected parents, we need to stay alert and keep in mind
the big picture when it comes to our kids.

I know this concern arises after talking to worried
parents about our research over the past two decades.
Parents have asked us some interesting questions over

the years. When we're on the road talking about kids and technology, we often get asked what has changed over the time we've been working on this subject. I would be interested in hearing what you think the biggest changes have been in recent years and also where you think we ought to be looking for changes coming around the corner. (I know—that's greedy of me! I just snuck in two questions.)

Urs: Since we started our work on youth and digital media back in 2006, many things have changed rather dramatically. We've witnessed almost unimaginable technological advancements over the past few years. The rise of smartphones and apps, new cloud-based services for always-on entertainment, the proliferation of social media platforms that now even threaten our democracies, are just a few examples. In parallel, the collection and analysis of fine-grain personal data about users has become even more important for the advertisement-based business models behind some of the world's most powerful companies like Amazon, Facebook, or Google. Public awareness has changed, too. When we started, the issue of kids and tech wasn't a mainstream topic compared with today, when caregivers, educators, and politicians talk about digital citizenship and all seem worried about things like addiction or aggression. All these changes together affect how young people (and adults as well) access and use the internet, how they interact with content, and how they interact with each other.

If I had to pick one positive change, I'd highlight the enhanced role that tech plays in providing young people spaces to form—and experiment with—their personal and social identities. This is a narrative we hear a lot, particularly from youth with a LGBTQ+ background, for instance.

On the negative side, "surveillance capitalism"—an online world in which the commodity for sale is our personal data that is captured through mass surveillance of the internet—is one of the most significant sea changes that affects the next generation the strongest.

The next wave of change with unpredictable outcomes will come when this world of big data meets powerful algorithms. Right now, we see the rollout of sophisticated technologies, branded as AI, which power a broad range of new applications such as smart toys, personalized digital tutors, or youth-oriented health apps that claim to detect or even predict illnesses. While AI-based tech can do wonders, many questions around automated decision making and human autonomy, bias and discrimination, and safety and privacy currently remain open. These are definitely things that should be on our watch list over the years to come—and topics for another book perhaps.

Now, I've focused on change in my response to your question. But I'm also wondering what hasn't changed, or what is unlikely to change. As you reflect on your tenure as head of school at Phillips Academy in Andover, how would you respond to the old saying that "kids will be kids," despite all the digital frenzy?

John: I agree but only up to a point. "Kids will be kids" has value as an idea in the sense that we should not think of this generation of young people as totally disconnected from what has come before. The human condition is still the human condition. This generation of young people is linked to all who came before, just as we are to the parents who came before us. We also want to remind parents that their good common sense still has value in raising their children. Young people still need love, encouragement, work, and limits (among other things) to thrive. Young people embrace new ideas, change, excitement, and risk-taking—and we need to support them as they do so. They need the logical skills of discernment, decision making, and problem-solving as well as the emotional kills of empathy and understanding across differences. I suspect some version of these things will always be true.

"Kids will be kids" has a few downsides as an idea, though. It can constrain our thinking; parents and other caregivers ought to be on the lookout for this kind of constraint. I worry, for instance, about the mentality that says we can't change things that may need to change—or at least, that ought to change. Let's consider the related saying, "Boys will be boys." If that concept is used to normalize aggressive behavior in boyhood, it can lead to a culture that excuses escalating harm from bullying and harassment and can lead to sexual violence. Constrained thinking like this can lead to terrible consequences.

I believe that we should always have front and center the idea of human potential. Humankind faces a few existential crises that may be in the hands of our children to solve. Consider climate change, pandemics, nuclear proliferation, and endless wars around the world. If we think that nothing changes in human behavior, we might be led to believe we are doomed. If we see potential all around us—mostly in the form of our children—the world opens up in a completely different way.

Parents can and do have a role in shaping the next generation. Now, Urs, I wonder if you might reflect on your own journey as a parent. The stories and experiences that both of us bring from our own parenting will inevitably inform our work as researchers. I wonder if you'd be willing to share your experiences, parent-to-parent, with those who have made it this far in the book.

Urs: My parenting experience has been deeply shaped by the fact that Ananda (nineteen) and Dave (seventeen) have spent most of their teenage years growing up with their mother in Switzerland, while my home base in recent years has been in Boston. As a divorced parent who has shared custody and lives thousands of miles away, technology has been an important tool on many levels. At the fundamental level, apps like FaceTime, WhatsApp, Instagram, and for a while even Snapchat (although I admit I never really got into it—I guess I'm too old for it!) have helped us a great deal to stay connected. Our patchwork family would also play online games to bring us together across distance and time zones. For example, several members of our extended family were members of the same "clan" in *Clash of Clans*. Playing this interactive game together allowed the kids to interact with me (often using the in-game chat function) in their favorite environment, at their discretion, and during times that worked best for them.

From the many hours of conversation—typically over dinner during the weekends of my visits—I've learned a great deal from Dave and Ananda about their (and their friends') approaches to digital technology, and from their experiences, including the good and not-so-good ones. Many of the stories shared by my children echoed what we've heard in our focus group interviews with young people across the globe. I made it a routine during my visits to ask about the funniest videos, latest memes, newest games, favorite songs, and so forth, that they came across since we had last met. In response, they often took out their phones and showed me things online, browsing their favorite platforms and apps. These interactions offered great windows into their interconnected lives and became opportunities to practice the connected-parent approach we propose in this book.

I owe Ananda and Dave big thanks not only for being such amazing young people but also for being my personal mini focus group and my youth teachers. They have been incredibly patient and generous with me as we've worked through challenges, navigated our differences, and learned from our mistakes. Looking back over the past decade, I think it's fair to say that it has often been easier for me to write about these things as a researcher than it has been to put our own advice into practice as a parent. Or, as my daughter reminds me occasionally, "Dad, the struggle is real!"

On this personal note, I would like to turn things over to you, John. Here's my closing question: Can you recall a time when a child successfully changed your mind and helped you approach things differently—whether it was with your own children or the ones you had been responsible for as head of school?

John: I also want to take this moment to acknowledge and thank our children, Jack (eighteen) and Emeline (fifteen).

Jack and Emeline have been very patient and thoughtful as my wife, Catherine, and I have worked our way through the various stages of parenting—and we've often sought their opinions as we have journeyed together as a family.

I appreciate the premise of your question here. If we have made anything plain throughout this book, I hope it is that connected parents should be in an extended, active, two-way dialogue with the young people in their lives. Not only can we change our approaches as the technology shifts, but we should always be open to changing our minds. And we should particularly reconsider our views when our children come up with smart ideas.

I am going to use a nontechnical example to illustrate a broader point. Several years ago, Emeline and I were talking about her allowance. She was ten. As is customary in many families, we gave our young children small allowances each week. The children, Catherine, and I had had endless conversations about whether the payments should be tied to doing chores (they are not; the chores are just required as being part of our family) and what the children should be allowed to do with the money. We decided on the three-jar approach: save, spend, give (a tip of the hat to journalist and author Ron Lieber).

Emeline suggested a new rule: there should be no limit as to when and how much of their accumulated savings they could spend in a given month. Our previous rule had been that they were permitted to make only one purchase per month. The problem with this rule was that Emeline would think all month about what one thing she wanted to spend the money on. Sometimes the pressure became too great and she would ask for an advance to buy a second thing that month (nope). We thought, of course, that this restriction would teach discipline, budgeting, and self-denial.

Emeline explained that the best rule would be no limit at all, that we should simply trust our ten-year-old daughter to spend the modest savings she had banked whenever she wanted to spend it. She acknowledged that we could ban certain purchases. But she said that she would do a better job with her money if she could get out from under the one-purchase-per-month rule.

I was skeptical, to say the least. It made no sense to me that she would be better off without this constraint. But I had great admiration for this daughter of ours and the thought that went into this request. So first, I consulted with Catherine. After that, I turned to Jack, who has for many years been somehow more intuitive and wise about finances than his parents are. Both Catherine and Jack agreed that this new rule-free regime would work. So I conceded.

The rule was lifted—for a year. We figured she couldn't do too much damage with her savings between age ten and eleven. And you know what? She didn't buy anything for the longest time. I don't remember how many months it was, but it might even have been the full year before she spent anything. We were stunned. But she had known herself; she understood that the freedom she had sought would come with responsibility. And so she acted accordingly.

The lesson in this story is, of course, about listening and trusting your kids. We knew that the consequences of a mistake were not terrible. We knew we were very lucky: our kids were responsible at heart and in great shape overall. And the benefits of changing the rule at her request were potentially great. The outcome delighted us. And that experience has stuck with me as we have made other rules and adjusted them over time—in open consultation with our kids.

In this book, we've sought to translate our own research and others' into a guide for parents, offering the best advice we could draw from the evidence we've seen. Urs, could you please conclude by sharing your thoughts on the best, and the worst, parenting advice about kids and technology that you've come across over the years?

Urs: The parenting advice I've seen work best almost always combines two simple things: talking with children about their digital experiences and applying common sense.

Gaming is an area of parental concern that is a good example of how this can work: Instead of jumping to conclusions ("all games are bad," "games are a waste of time," etc.), be curious instead and let your kids show you which games they play. Let them explain how they work, and even try one out for yourself. (If you get lucky, your teenager might even be willing to play it with you!) Share your experiences with your child, and check in occasionally ("Have you reached a new level?" "Has something cool happened in your favorite game?"). Make it part of your dinner or other regular social conversations. These interactions and your own common sense will help you to judge when your kid is just fine and when you need to start worrying or even intervene.

This approach is not so different from familiar "analog" parenting strategies and how we keep an eye on activities like hanging out with friends in the park, going on vacation with a group of friends, or riding a bicycle safely in a city. In all these cases, it's an informed and holistic perspective combined with an open communication channel that is the most likely to work.

In contrast, advice to parents that is largely fear-inducing or completely detached from the realities of what kids actually do with their digital devices will probably be ineffective or even backfire. Installing surveillance software on a child's cell phone or implanting a microchip into the child (yes, people do this!), a complete ban of online activities, or taking away all devices as disciplinary measures are all examples of parental advice we've seen that I would call bad advice.

In our book, we aim to offer parents a more constructive and helpful path forward as families navigate an increasingly connected world.

The twin concepts we have stressed throughout this book have been balance and connection. As in most things in life, there's not just one answer—a complete ban or a total free-for-all. Parenting in the digital age is about constantly finding and readjusting that balance. The one constant in both parenting and digital matters is change. The best way to ensure a harmonious balance over time, as the digital environment changes, is to strive for an ongoing connection. This connection is the only approach that will sustain you and the young people in your life through the inevitable challenges to come.

In parenting, all of us are engaged in a long conversation with those in our care and with one another as parents. We don't have to (and frankly can't expect to) get every discussion right. We don't have to (and won't) get every rule or decision right. But we should stay connected. This approach will serve our kids, our fellow parents, and ourselves in matters related to the digital world and in anything else we will face together. And perhaps the connected-parenting approach will even be fun! Here's to that.

Acknowledgments

We are endlessly grateful to many people:

Sandra Cortesi, Alexandra Hasse, Andres Lombana-Bermudez, Emma Zarriello, and the entire team at the Berkman Klein Center for Internet & Society and the Youth and Media project at Harvard University, past and present; Gosia Stergios at Phillips Academy, Andover, Massachusetts; Ananda Gasser, Jack Palfrey, Itzelt Reyes, and Summer Seward for their work to build community around the ideas in this book; and the Digital Media and Learning Network, supported by the John D. and Catherine T. MacArthur Foundation for many years.

Emi Ikkanda, Lara Heimert, Melissa Veronesi, and Patricia Boyd at Basic Books and Cynthia Cannell at Cannell Agency.

The many parents, teachers, mentors, and coaches who have asked hard questions and suggested ideas as we have pursued this work; the hundreds of young people around the globe who have shared with us how they interact with digital technologies.

And of course our families. We've dedicated this book to the parents and grandparents who have done so much for us and for our kids, in such inspiring and kind ways. We couldn't have written this book without you. Thank you so much!

Further Reading

Here we offer ideas for further reading for each chapter of *The Connected Parent*. Some of the research studies listed may offer conclusions that differ from the recommendations from other studies in this book or even from our advice in the book. But we've included these studies here, because we believe that the authors have used plausible methodologies and that their findings and advice are worth your consideration. We also offer suggestions of a small handful of news stories that provide context for some of the material in various chapters. Please also refer to the bibliography section of our previous book, *Born Digital: How Children Grow Up in a Digital Age* (New York: Basic Books, 2016), for additional resources on which we have relied over time.

CHAPTER 1: SCREEN TIME

"American Academy of Pediatrics Announces New Recommendations for Children's Media Use." American Academy of Pediatrics, AAP.org, October 21, 2016. www.aap.org/en-us/about-the-aap/aap-press-room/Pages/American-Academy-of-Pediatrics-Announces-New-Recommendations-for-Childrens-Media-Use.aspx.

Anderson, Monica. "6 Takeaways About How Parents Monitor Their Teen's Digital Activities." Pew Research Center, January 7, 2016. www.pewresearch.org/fact-tank/2016/01/07/parents-teens-digital-monitoring.

Anderson, Monica, and Jingjing Jiang. "Teens, Social Media & Technology 2018." Pew Research Center, May 31, 2018. www.pewresearch.org /internet/2018/05/31/teens-social-media-technology-2018.

———. "Teens' Social Media Habits and Experiences." Pew Research Center, November 28, 2018. www.pewresearch.org/internet/2018/11/28/teens -social-media-habits-and-experiences.

Blum-Ross, Alicia, and Sonia Livingstone. "Families and Screen Time: Current Advice and Emerging Research." London School of Economics and Political Science Department of Media and Communications, July 2016. http://eprints.lse.ac.uk/66927/1/Policy%20Brief%2017-%20Families %20%20Screen%20Time.pdf.

"Children, Teens, Media, and Body Image." Common Sense Media, January 21, 2015. www.commonsensemedia.org/research/children-teens-media -and-body-image.

"The Common Sense Census: Media Use by Kids Age Zero to Eight, 2017." Common Sense Media, 2017. www.commonsensemedia.org/research/the -common-sense-census-media-use-by-kids-age-zero-to-eight-2017.

"The Common Sense Census: Media Use by Tweens and Teens, 2015." Common Sense Media, 2015. www.commonsensemedia.org/research/the -common-sense-census-media-use-by-tweens-and-teens-2015.

Freed, Richard. "The Tech Industry's War on Kids." *Medium*, March 12, 2018. https://medium.com/@richardnfreed/the-tech-industrys-psychological -war-on-kids-c452870464ce.

Frost, Rachel L., and Debra J. Rickwood. "A Systematic Review of the Mental Health Outcomes Associated with Facebook Use." *Computers in Human Behavior* 76 (November 2017): 576–600. https://doi.org/10.1016/j.chb .2017.08.001.

Kamenetz, Anya. *The Art of Screen Time: How Your Family Can Balance Digital Media and Real Life*. New York: PublicAffairs, 2018.

———. "Don't Panic! Here's How to Make Screens a Positive in Family Life." *Guardian*, February 11, 2018. www.theguardian.com/media/2018/feb /11/screen-time-kids-children-parents-new-media.

Livingstone, Sonia, Leslie Haddon, Jane Vincent, Giovanna Mascheroni, and Kjartan Ólafsson. *Net Children Go Mobile: The UK Report*. London: London School of Economics and Political Science, 2014. http://eprints .lse.ac.uk/59098/1/__lse.ac.uk_storage_LIBRARY_Secondary_libfile _shared_repository_Content_Livingstone,%20S_EU%20Kids%20

Online_Livingstone_Net_%20children_%20go_2014_Livingstone_Net _%20children_%20go_2014_author.pdf.

Lyon, David, Colin J. Bennett, Valerie M. Steeves, and Kevin D Haggerty. *Transparent Lives: Surveillance in Canada*. Edmonton: AU Press, 2014.

Orben, Amy, Tobias Dienlin, and Andrew K. Przybylski. "Social Media's Enduring Effect on Adolescent Life Satisfaction." *Proceedings of the National Academy of Sciences* 116, no. 21 (May 6, 2019): 10,226–10,228. https://doi.org/10.1073/pnas.1902058116.

Orben, Amy, and Andrew K. Przybylski. "Screens, Teens, and Psychological Well-Being: Evidence from Three Time-Use-Diary Studies." *Psychological Science*, April 2, 2019. https://doi.org/10.1177/0956797619830329.

Perrin, Andrew, and Monica Anderson. "Share of U.S. Adults Using Social Media, Including Facebook, Is Mostly Unchanged Since 2018." Pew Research Center, April 10, 2019. www.pewresearch.org/fact-tank/2019/04/10/share -of-u-s-adults-using-social-media-including-facebook-is-mostly-unchanged -since-2018.

Przybylski, Andrew K., Amy Orben, and Netta Weinstein. "How Much Is Too Much? Examining the Relationship Between Digital Screen Engagement and Psychosocial Functioning in a Confirmatory Cohort Study." *Journal of the American Academy of Child and Adolescent Psychology*, 2019. https://doi.org/10.1016/j.jaac.2019.06.017.

Przybylski, Andrew K., and Netta Weinstein. "A Large-Scale Test of the Goldilocks Hypothesis: Quantifying the Relations Between Digital-Screen Use and the Mental Well-Being of Adolescents." *Psychological Science* 28, no. 2 (January 13, 2017): 204–215. https://doi.org/10.1177/0956797 616678438.

Schofield Clark, Lynn. "Parental Mediation Theory for the Digital Age." *Communication Theory* 21, no. 4 (November 2011): 323–343. https:// doi.org/10.1111/j.1468-2885.2011.01391.x.

"Social Media, Social Life: Teens Reveal Their Experiences, 2018." Common Sense Media, 2018. https://static1.squarespace.com/static/5ba15befec4 eb7899898240d/t/5ba165a221c67cff9a6dc5b7/1537303981859/2018 _CS_SocialMediaSocialLife_FullReport-final-release_2.pdf.

Sozio, Maria, Eugenia Cristina Ponte, Inês Vitorino Sampaio, Fabio Senne, Kjartan Ólafsson, Suzana Jaíze Alves, and Camila Garroux. "Children and Internet Use: A Comparative Analysis of Brazil and Seven European Countries." EU Kids Online, July 2015. http://fabricadesites.fcsh.unl

.pt/eukidsonline/wp-content/uploads/sites/36/2017/11/Brazil-NCGM _COMPARATIVE-REPORT.pdf.

Stiglic, Neza, and Russell M. Viner. "Effects of Screentime on the Health and Well-Being of Children and Adolescents: A Systematic Review of Reviews." *BMJ Open* 9, no. 1 (2019). https://doi.org/10.1136/bmjopen-2018 -023191.

Weinberger, David. *Everyday Chaos: Technology, Complexity, and How We're Thriving in a New World of Possibility*. Boston: Harvard Business Review Press, 2019.

Weinstein, Emily. "Influences of Social Media Use on Adolescent Psychosocial Well-Being: 'OMG' or 'NBD'?" Harvard University Graduate School of Education, 2017. https://search.proquest.com/docview/1919646242 /abstract/1685FD0205BE4882PQ/1.

Willemse, I., Gregor Waller, Sarah Genner, Lilian Suter, Sabine Oppliger, Anna-Lena Huber, and Daniel Süss, "JAMES: Jugend, Aktivitäten, Medien— Erhebung Schweiz" [JAMES: Youth, Activities, Media—Survey Switzerland]. *Angewandte Psychologie*, 2014. https://digitalcollection.zhaw.ch /bitstream/11475/4290/3/2014_JAMES_Jugend_Aktivitäten_Medien _Erhebung_Schweiz_Ergebnisbericht_2014.pdf.

CHAPTER 2: SOCIAL LIFE

Anderson, Monica. "Parents, Teens and Digital Monitoring." Pew Research Center, January 7, 2016. www.pewresearch.org/internet/2016/01/07 /parents-teens-and-digital-monitoring.

Anderson, Monica, and Jingjing Jiang. "Teens, Social Media & Technology 2018." Pew Research Center, May 31, 2018. www.pewresearch.org /internet/2018/05/31/teens-social-media-technology-2018.

Blum-Ross, Alicia, and Sonia Livingstone. "Families and Screen Time: Current Advice and Emerging Research." The London School of Economics and Political Science Department of Media and Communications, July 2016. http://eprints.lse.ac.uk/66927/1/Policy%20Brief%2017-%20Families %20%20Screen%20Time.pdf.

boyd, danah. *It's Complicated: The Social Lives of Networked Teens*. New Haven: Yale University Press, 2015.

Chambers, Deborah. *Social Media and Personal Relationships: Online Intimacies and Networked Friendship*. Basingstoke: Palgrave Macmillan, 2018.

Further Reading

Dell'Antonia, KJ. "Teenagers Leading Happy, Connected Lives Online." *Motherlode Blog* (blog). *New York Times*, August 6, 2015. https://parenting.blogs.nytimes.com/2015/08/06/teenagers-leading-happy-connected-lives-online.

Dijck, José van. *The Culture of Connectivity: A Critical History of Social Media*. Oxford: Oxford University Press, 2013.

Gasser, Urs, and Sandra Cortesi. "Children's Rights and Digital Technologies: Introduction to the Discourse and Some Meta-Observations." In *Handbook of Children's Rights: Global and Multidisciplinary Perspectives*, edited by M. Ruck, M. Peterson-Badali, and M. Freeman. New York: Routledge/Taylor and Francis Group, 2017. https://papers.ssrn.com/sol3/papers.cfm?abstract_id=2768168.

Hinduja, Sameer, and Justin W. Patchin. *Bullying Beyond the Schoolyard: Preventing and Responding to Cyberbullying*. Thousand Oaks, CA: Corwin, 2015.

Hunt, Melissa G., Rachel Marx, Courtney Lipson, and Jordyn Young. "No More FOMO: Limiting Social Media Decreases Loneliness and Depression." *Journal of Social & Clinical Psychology* 37, no. 10 (2018): 751–768. https://doi.org/10.1521/jscp.2018.37.10.751.

Lenhart, Amanda, Monica Anderson, and Aaron Smith. "Teens, Technology and Romantic Relationships." Pew Research Center, October 1, 2015. www.pewresearch.org/internet/2015/10/01/teens-technology-and-romantic-relationships.

Madden, Mary, Amanda Lenhart, Sandra Cortesi, Urs Gasser, Maeve Duggan, Aaron Smith, and Meredith Beaton. "Teens, Social Media, and Privacy." Pew Research Center, May 21, 2013. www.pewresearch.org/internet/2013/05/21/teens-social-media-and-privacy.

Odgers, Candice. "Smartphones Are Bad for Some Teens, Not All." *Nature 554* (February 22, 2018): 432–435. https://doi.org/10.1038/d41586-018-02109-8.

Orben, Amy, Tobias Dienlin, and Andrew Przybylski. "Social Media's Enduring Effect on Adolescent Life Satisfaction." *Proceedings of the National Academy of Sciences* 116, no. 21 (May 6, 2019): 10,226–10,228. https://doi.org/10.1073/pnas.1902058116.

"Social Media, Social Life: Teens Reveal Their Experiences, 2018." Common Sense Media, 2019. www.commonsensemedia.org/research/social-media-social-life-2018.

Suler, John. "The Online Disinhibition Effect." *CyberPsychology & Behavior* 7, no. 3 (July 28, 2004). https://doi.org/10.1089/1094931041291295.

"Teen Voices: Dating in the Digital Age." Pew Research Center. www .pewresearch.org/internet/interactives/online-romance.

Turkle, Sherry. *Alone Together: Why We Expect More from Technology and Less from Each Other*. New York: Basic Books, 2017.

Twenge, Jean M. "Have Smartphones Destroyed a Generation?" *Atlantic*, September 2017. www.theatlantic.com/magazine/archive/2017/09/has -the-smartphone-destroyed-a-generation/534198.

"Wait Until 8th." Wait Until 8th home page. www.waituntil8th.org.

Watkins, S. Craig., with Andres Lombana-Bermudez, Alexander Cho, Jacqueline Ryan Vickery, Vivian Shaw, and Lauren Weinzimmer. *Digital Edge: How Black and Latino Youth Navigate Digital Inequality*. New York: New York University Press, 2018.

CHAPTER 3: PRIVACY

boyd, danah, and Alice E. Marwick. "Social Privacy in Networked Publics: Teens' Attitudes, Practices, and Strategies." A Decade in Internet Time: Symposium on the Dynamics of the Internet and Society, September 10, 2011. https://papers.ssrn.com/sol3/papers.cfm?abstract_id=1925128.

Davis, Katie, and Carrie James. "Tweens' Conceptions of Privacy Online: Implications for Educators." *Learning, Media and Technology* 38, no. 1 (2013): 4–25. https://doi.org/10.1080/17439884.2012.658404.

"Digital Birth: Welcome to the Online World." *BusinessWire*, October 6, 2010. www.businesswire.com/news/home/20101006006722/en/Digital-Birth -Online-World.

Lenhart, Amanda, Mary Madden, Sandra Cortesi, Urs Gasser, and Aaron Smith. "Where Teens Seek Online Privacy Advice." Pew Research Center, August 15, 2013. www.pewresearch.org/internet/2013/08/15/where -teens-seek-online-privacy-advice.

Madden, Mary, Amanda Lenhart, Sandra Cortesi, and Urs Gasser. "Teens and Mobile Apps Privacy." Pew Research Center, August 22, 2013. www.pewresearch.org/internet/2013/08/22/teens-and-mobile-apps -privacy.

Madden, Mary, Amanda Lenhart, Sandra Cortesi, Urs Gasser, Maeve Duggan, Aaron Smith, and Meredith Beaton. "Teens, Social Media, and Privacy." Pew Research Center, May 21, 2013. www.pewresearch.org /internet/2013/05/21/teens-social-media-and-privacy.

Marwick, Alice E., and danah boyd. "Networked Privacy: How Teenagers Negotiate Context in Social Media." *New Media and Society* 16, no. 7 (2014): 1,051–1,067. https://doi.org/10.1177/1461444814543995.

Plunkett, Leah. *Sharenthood: From Baby Pictures in the Cloud to a High School's Digital Surveillance System: How Adults Unwittingly Compromise Children's Privacy Online*. Cambridge, MA: MIT Press, 2019.

Steyer, James. *Talking Back to Facebook: The Common Sense Guide to Raising Kids in a Digital Age*. New York: Scribner, 2012.

CHAPTER 4: SAFETY

boyd, danah, and Eszter Hargittai. "Connected and Concerned: Variation in Parents' Online Safety Concerns." *Policy & Internet* 5, no. 3 (October 21, 2013). https://doi.org/10.1002/1944-2866.POI332.

DeSilver, Drew. "Dangers That Teens and Kids Face: A Look at the Data." *Pew Research Center* (blog), December 5, 2018. www.pewresearch.org /fact-tank/2016/01/14/dangers-that-young-people-face-a-look-at-the-data.

Finkelhor, David, Heather Turner, Sherry L. Hamby, and Kristen Kracke. "Children's Exposure to Violence: A Comprehensive National Survey." *National Survey of Children's Exposure to Violence* 24 (October 2009). https://scholars.unh.edu/ccrc/24.

Hinduja, Sameer, and Justin W. Patchin. *Bullying Beyond the Schoolyard: Preventing and Responding to Cyberbullying*. London: Corwin Press, 2014.

———. "Cultivating Youth Resilience to Prevent Bullying and Cyberbullying Victimization." *Child Abuse & Neglect* 73 (November 2017): 51–62. https://doi.org/10.1016/j.chiabu.2017.09.010.

Levy, Nathaniel, Sandra Cortesi, Urs Gasser, Edward Crowley, Meredith Beaton, June Casey, and Caroline Nolan. "Bullying in a Networked Era: A Literature Review." Berkman Center Research Publication, September 12, 2012. https://papers.ssrn.com/sol3/papers.cfm?abstract_id=2146877.

Mascheroni, Giovanna, and Kjartan Ólafsson. *Net Children Go Mobile: Risks and Opportunities*. 2nd ed. Milano: Educatt, 2014. https://doi.org /10.13140/RG.2.1.3590.8561.

O'Keeffe, Gwenn Schurgin. *CyberSafe: Protecting and Empowering Kids in the Digital World of Texting, Gaming, and Social Media*. Elk Grove Village, IL: American Academy of Pediatrics, 2011.

Strohmaier, Heidi, Megan Murphy, and David DeMatteo. "Youth Sexting: Prevalence Rates, Driving Motivations, and the Deterrent Effect of Legal Consequences." *Sexuality Research and Social Policy* 11 (2014): 245–255. https://doi.org/10.1007/s13178-014-0162-9.

Suler, John. "The Online Disinhibition Effect." *CyberPsychology & Behavior* 7, no. 3 (July 28, 2004). https://doi.org/10.1089/1094931041291295.

Wolak, Janis, David Finkelhor, Kimberly J. Mitchell, and Michele L. Ybarra. "Online 'Predators' and Their Victims: Myths, Realities, and Implications for Prevention and Treatment." *American Psychological Association* 63, no. 2 (2008): 111–128. https://doi.org/10.1037/0003-066X.63.2.111.

Yeung, Jessie. "Mom Shoots New Zealand Man Who Flew to US to Confront Teens He Met Online." *CNN*, June 27, 2018. www.cnn.com/2018/06/27/us/new-zealand-man-richmond-attack-intl/index.html.

CHAPTER 5: ANXIETY

"Dealing with Devices: The Parent-Teen Dynamic." May 3, 2016. Common Sense Media. www.commonsensemedia.org/technology-addiction-concern-controversy-and-finding-balance-infographic.

Ehmke, Rachel. "What Selfies Are Doing to Girls' Self-Esteem." Child Mind Institute, December 7, 2018. https://childmind.org/article/what-selfies-are-doing-to-girls-self-esteem.

Elhai, John D., Robert D. Dvorak, Jason C. Levine, and Brian J. Hall. "Problematic Smartphone Use: A Conceptual Overview and Systematic Review of Relations with Anxiety and Depression Psychopathology." *Journal of Affective Disorders* 207, no. 1 (January 2017): 251–259. https://doi.org/10.1016/j.jad.2016.08.030.

Frost, Rachel L., and Debra J. Rickwood. "A Systematic Review of the Mental Health Outcomes Associated with Facebook Use." *Computers in Human Behavior* 76 (November 2017): 576–600. https://doi.org/10.1016/j.chb.2017.08.001.

George, Madeleine J., and Candice L. Odgers. "Seven Fears and the Science of How Mobile Technologies May Be Influencing Adolescents in the Digital Age." *Perspectives on Psychological Science* 10, no. 6 (November 2015): 832–851. https://doi.org/10.1177/1745691615596788.

George, Madeleine J., Michael A. Russell, Roy R. Piontak, and Candice L. Odgers. "Concurrent and Subsequent Associations Between Daily Digital

Technology Use and High-Risk Adolescents' Mental Health Symptoms." *Child Development* 89, no. 1 (May 3, 2017). https://doi.org/10.1111/cdev.12819.

Hargittai, Eszter, and Yuli Patrick Hsieh. "Digital Inequality." *The Oxford Handbook of Internet Studies*, January 2013. https://doi.org/10.1093/oxfordhb/9780199589074.013.0007.

Kowalski, R. M., G. W. Giumetti, A. N. Schroeder, and M. R. Lattanner. "Bullying in the Digital Age: A Critical Review and Meta-Analysis of Cyberbullying Research Among Youth." *Psychological Bulletin* 140, no. 4 (2014): 1,073–1,137. https://doi.org/10.1037/a0035618.

Ledford, Heidi. "The Shifting Boundaries of Adolescence." *Nature* 554 (February 22, 2018): 429–431. www.nature.com/magazine-assets/d41586-018-02169-w/d41586-018-02169-w.pdf.

"National Survey of Children's Health." Data Resource Center for Child & Adolescent Health. www.childhealthdata.org/learn-about-the-nsch/NSCH.

Odgers, Candice. "Smartphones Are Bad for Some Teens, Not All." *Nature* 554 (February 22, 2018): 432–435. https://doi.org/10.1038/d41586-018-02109-8.

Orben, Amy, and Andrew K. Przybylski. "The Association Between Adolescent Well-Being and Digital Technology Use." *Nature Human Behavior* 3 (January 14, 2019): 173–182. https://doi.org/10.1038/s41562-018-0506-1.

Organisation for Economic Co-operation and Development. "Are There Differences in How Advantaged and Disadvantaged Students Use the Internet?" *PISA in Focus*, 64 (July 12, 2016). https://doi.org/10.1787/5jlv8zq6hw43-en.

Przybylski, Andrew K., and Netta Weinstein. "A Large-Scale Test of the Goldilocks Hypothesis: Quantifying the Relations Between Digital-Screen Use and the Mental Well-Being of Adolescents." *Psychological Science* 28, no. 2 (January 13, 2017): 204–215. https://doi.org/10.1177/0956797616678438.

Rideout, Victoria. "The Common Sense Census: Media Use by Tweens and Teens." Common Sense Media, 2015. www.commonsensemedia.org/research/the-common-sense-census-media-use-by-tweens-and-teens.

Rideout, Victoria, and Susannah Fox. "Digital Health Practices, Social Media Use, and Mental Well-Being Among Teens and Young Adults in the

U.S." A National Survey Sponsored by Hopelab and Well Being Trust. December 7, 2018. www.hopelab.org/report/a-national-survey-by-hopelab -and-well-being-trust-2018.

Rideout, Victoria, and Michael Robb. "The Common Sense Census: Media Use by Tweens and Teens." Common Sense Media, 2019. www .commonsensemedia.org/research/the-common-sense-census-media-use -by-tweens-and-teens-2019.

"Social Media, Social Life: Teens Reveal Their Experiences, 2018." Common Sense Media, 2019. www.commonsensemedia.org/research/social-media -social-life-2018.

Twenge, Jean M. "Have Smartphones Destroyed a Generation?" *Atlantic*, September 2017. www.theatlantic.com/magazine/archive/2017/09/has -the-smartphone-destroyed-a-generation/534198.

Young Health Movement. "#StatusOfMind: Social Media and Young People's Mental Health and Wellbeing." Royal Society for Public Health, May 2017. www.rsph.org.uk/uploads/assets/uploaded/d125b27c-0b62 -41c5-a2c0155a8887cd01.pdf.

CHAPTER 6: ADDICTION

Aarseth, E., A. Bean, H. Boonen, M. Colder Carras, M. Coulson, and Jeroen Jansz. "Scholars' Open Debate Paper on the World Health Organization ICD-11 Gaming Disorder Proposal." *Journal of Behavioral Addictions* 6, no. 3 (2017): 267–270. http://doi.org/10.1556/2006.5.2016.088.

Carr, Nicholas. "How Smartphones Hijack Our Minds." *Wall Street Journal*, October 6, 2017. www.wsj.com/articles/how-smartphones-hijack-our -minds-1507307811.

Cortesi, Sandra, Urs Gasser, Gameli Adzaho, Bruce Baikie, Jacqueline Baljeu, Matthew Battles, and Jacqueline Beauchere. "Digitally Connected: Global Perspectives on Youth and Digital Media." Berkman Center Research Publication, March 26, 2015. https://dx.doi.org/10.2139/ssrn .2585686.

Dunckley, Victoria L. *Reset Your Child's Brain: A Four-Week Plan to End Meltdowns, Raise Grades, and Boost Social Skills by Reversing the Effects of Electronic Screen-Time.* Novato, CA: New World Library, 2015.

Freed, Richard. "The Tech Industry's Psychological War on Kids." *Medium*, April 27, 2018. https://medium.com/@richardnfreed/the-tech -industrys-psychological-war-on-kids-c452870464ce.

Frost, Rachel L., and Debra J. Rickwood. "A Systematic Review of the Mental Health Outcomes Associated with Facebook Use." *Computers in Human Behavior* 76 (November 2017): 576–600. https://doi.org/10.1016/j.chb.2017.08.001.

Gentile, Douglas. "Pathological Video-Game Use Among Youth Ages 8 to 18: A National Study." *Psychological Science* 20, no. 5 (2009): 594–602. https://doi.org/10.1111/j.1467-9280.2009.02340.x.

"How Children Interact with Digital Media." *Economist*, January 3, 2019. www.economist.com/special-report/2019/01/03/how-children-interact-with-digital-media.

Ives, Mike. "Electroshock Therapy for Internet Addicts? China Vows to End It." *New York Times*, August 7, 2018. www.nytimes.com/2017/01/13/world/asia/china-internet-addiction-electroshock-therapy.html.

Jabr, Ferris. "Can You Really Be Addicted to Video Games?" *New York Times*, October 22, 2019. www.nytimes.com/2019/10/22/magazine/can-you-really-be-addicted-to-video-games.html.

Kamenetz, Anya. "Teens and Tech: Distinguishing Addiction from Habit." KQED, February 5, 2018. www.kqed.org/mindshift/50510/teens-and-tech-distinguishing-addiction-from-habit.

Kardaras, Nicholas. *Glow Kids: How Screen Addiction Is Hijacking Our Kids—and How to Break the Trance.* New York: St. Martin's Press, 2016.

Kardefelt-Winther, Daniel, Alexandre Heeren, Adriano Schimmenti, Antonius van Rooij, Pierre Maurage, Michelle Carras, Johan Edman, Alexander Blaszczynski, Yasser Khazaal, and Joël Billieux. "How Can We Conceptualize Behavioural Addiction Without Pathologizing Common Behaviours?" *Addiction* 112, no. 10 (February 15, 2017): 1,709–1,715. https://doi.org/10.1111/add.13763.

Kuss, D. J., M. D. Griffiths, L. Karila, and J. Billieux. "Internet Addiction: A Systematic Review of Epidemiological Research for the Last Decade." *Current Pharmaceutical Design* 20, no. 25 (2014): 4,026–4,052. https://doi.org/10.2174/13816128113199990617.

Kuss, D. J., M. D. Griffiths, and H. M. Pontes. "Chaos and Confusion in DSM-5 Diagnosis of Internet Gaming Disorder: Issues, Concerns, and Recommendations for Clarity in the Field." *Journal of Behavioral Addictions* 6, no. 2 (2017): 103–109. https://doi.org/10.1556/2006.5.2016.062.

Rich, Michael. "How Should Clinicians Diagnose Patients with 'Internet Addiction'?" Center on Media and Child Health, April 12, 2016. https://cmch.tv/diagnose-internet-addiction.

"Technology Addiction: Concern, Controversy, and Finding Balance." Common Sense Media, December 7, 2018. www.commonsensemedia .org/research/technology-addiction-concern-controversy-and-finding -balance.

Weinstein, Aviv, Abigail Livny, and Abraham Weizman. "New Developments in Brain Research of Internet and Gaming Disorder." *Neuroscience & Behavioral Reviews* 75 (April 2017): 314–330. https://doi.org/10.1016/j .neubiorev.2017.01.040.

Zajac, Kristyn, Meredith K. Ginley, Rocio Chang, and Nancy M. Petry. "Treatments for Internet Gaming Disorder and Internet Addiction: A Systematic Review." *Psychology of Addictive Behaviors* 31, no. 8 (2017): 979–994. https://doi.org/10.1037/adb0000315.

CHAPTER 7: GAMING

Alexandraki, Kyriaki, Vasileios Stavropoulos, Emma Anderson, Moham-mad Qasim Latifi, and Rapson Gomez. "Adolescent Pornography Use: A Systematic Literature Review of Research Trends, 2000–2017." *Current Psychiatry Reviews* 14, no. 1 (2018): 47–58. https://doi.org/10.2174 /2211556007666180606073617.

Anderson, Craig A., and Brad J. Bushman. "The Effects of Media Violence on Society." *Science* 295, no. 5564 (March 29, 2002): 2,377–2,379. https:// doi.org/10.1126/science.1070765.

Anderson, Craig A., Brad J. Bushman, Edward Donnerstein, Tom A. Hummer, and Wayne Warburton. "SPSSI Research Summary on Media Violence." *Analyses of Social Issues and Public Policy* 15, no. 1 (November 4, 2015). https://doi.org/10.1111/asap.12093.

Anderson, Craig A., Douglas A. Gentile, and Katherine E. Buckley. *Violent Video Game Effects on Children and Adolescents: Theory, Research, and Public Policy*. New York: Oxford University Press, 2007.

Anderson, Monica. "6 Takeaways About How Parents Monitor Their Teen's Digital Activities." Pew Research Center, January 7, 2016. www .pewresearch.org/fact-tank/2016/01/07/parents-teens-digital-monitoring.

Bartholow, Bruce D., and Craig A. Anderson. "Effects of Violent Video Games on Aggressive Behavior: Potential Sex Differences." *Journal of Experimental Social Psychology* 38, no. 3 (2002): 283–290. https://doi .org/10.1006/jesp.2001.1502.

Brown, Jane D., and Kelly L. L'Engle. "X-Rated: Sexual Attitudes and Behaviors Associated with U.S. Early Adolescents' Exposure to Sexually Explicit Media." *Communication Research* 36, no. 1 (February 1, 2009): 129–151. https://doi.org/10.1177/0093650208326465.

Bushman, Brad J., and Rowell J. Huesmann. "Short-Term and Long-Term Effects of Violent Media on Aggression in Children and Adults." *Archives of Pediatrics & Adolescent Medicine* 160, no. 4 (2006): 348. https://doi.org/10.1001/archpedi.160.4.348.

Byron, Tanya. *Safer Children in a Digital World: The Report of the Byron Review: Be Safe, Be Aware, Have Fun, Department for Children, Schools and Families (DCSF), Department for Culture, Media and Sport (DCMS).* Nottingham: DCSF Publications, 2008.

Children's Bureau. *Child Maltreatment 2016.* Administration on Children, Youth and Families, February 1, 2018. www.acf.hhs.gov/cb/resource/child-maltreatment-2016.

"Creating a Better Internet for Kids." European Commission, Accessibility, Multilingualism & Safer Internet Team, updated October 18, 2019. https://ec.europa.eu/digital-single-market/en/content/creating-better-internet-kids-0.

Entertainment Software Association. "ESA Annual Report 2015." Entertainment Software Association, December 4, 2015. www.theesa.com/perspectives/annual-report/esa-annual-report-2015.

Ferguson, Christopher John. "The Good, the Bad and the Ugly: A Meta-Analytic Review of Positive and Negative Effects of Violent Video Games." *Psychiatric Quarterly* 78 (October 4, 2007): 309–316. https://doi.org/10.1007/s11126-007-9056-9.

Gentile, Douglas A. *Media Violence and Children: A Complete Guide for Parents and Professionals.* 2nd ed. Santa Barbara, CA: Praeger, 2014.

Gentile, Douglas A., Dongdong Li, Angeline Khoo, Sara Prot, and Craig A. Anderson. "Mediators and Moderators of Long-Term Effects of Violent Video Games on Aggressive Behavior." *JAMA Pediatrics* 168, no. 5 (May 2014): 450–457. https://doi.org/10.1001/jamapediatrics.2014.63.

Gentile, Douglas A., Paul J. Lynch, Jennifer Ruh Linder, and David A. Walsh. "The Effects of Violent Video Game Habits on Adolescent Hostility, Aggressive Behaviors, and School Performance." *Journal of Adolescence* 27, no. 1 (February 2004): 5–22. https://doi.org/10.1016/j.adolescence.2003.10.002.

Greitemeyer, Tobias, and Dirk O. Mügge. "Video Games Do Affect Social Outcomes: A Meta-Analytic Review of the Effects of Violent and

Prosocial Video Game Play." *Personality and Social Psychology Bulletin* 40, no. 5 (January 23, 2014): 578–589. https://doi.org/10.1177/0146167213 520459.

Huesmann, L. Rowell, and Leonard D. Eron. *Television and the Aggressive Child: A Cross-National Comparison.* London: Routledge, 1986.

Kirsh, Steven J. *Children, Adolescents, and Media Violence: A Critical Look at the Research.* 2nd ed. Thousand Oaks, CA: Sage Publications, 2012.

Koletić, Goran. "Longitudinal Associations Between the Use of Sexually Explicit Material and Adolescents' Attitudes and Behaviors: A Narrative Review of Studies." *Journal of Adolescence* 57 (June 2017): 119–133. https://doi.org/10.1016/j.adolescence.2017.04.006.

Krahé, Barbara, ed., "Report on the Media Violence Commission." Media Violence Commission, International Society for Research on Aggression. *Aggressive Behavior* 38, no. 5 (2012): 335–341. https://doi.org/10.1002 /ab.21443.

Lenhard, Amanda. "Video Games, Teen Boys and Building Social Skills and Friendships." *Pew Research Center: Internet, Science & Tech* (blog), August 6, 2015. www.pewinternet.org/2015/08/06/chapter-3-video-games -are-key-elements-in-friendships-for-many-boys.

Malamuth, Neil, and Mark Huppin. "Pornography and Teenagers: The Importance of Individual Differences." *Adolescent Medicine Clinics* 16, no. 2 (2015): 315–326. https://doi.org/10.1016/j.admecli.2005.02.004.

Martins, Nicole, and Barbara J. Wilson. "Social Aggression on Television and Its Relationship to Children's Aggression in the Classroom." *Human Communication Research* 38, no. 1 (2012): 48–71. https://doi.org/10.1111 /j.1468-2958.2011.01417.x.

"Media and Violence: An Analysis of Current Research." Common Sense Media, February 13, 2013. www.commonsensemedia.org/research/media -and-violence-an-analysis-of-current-research.

Mendelsohn, Alan L., Carolyn Brockmeyer Cates, Adriana Weisleder, Samantha Berkule Johnson, Anne M. Seery, Caitlin F. Canfield, Harris S. Huberman, and Benard P. Dreyer. "Reading Aloud, Play, and Social-Emotional Development." *Pediatrics* 141, no. 5 (2018). https://doi.org/10.1542 /peds.2017-3393.

Owens, Eric W., Richard J. Behun, Jill C. Manning, and Rory C. Reid. "The Impact of Internet Pornography on Adolescents: A Review of the Research." *Sexual Addiction & Compulsivity* 19, no. 1–2 (2012): 99–122. https://doi.org/10.1080/10720162.2012.660431.

Peter, Jochen, and Patti M. Valkenburg. "Adolescents and Pornography: A Review of 20 Years of Research." *Journal of Sex Research* 53, no. 4–5 (2016): 509–531. https://doi.org/10.1080/00224499.2016.1143441.

Scharrer, Erica. "Media and Violence: An Analysis of Current Research. A Common Sense Media Research Brief." Common Sense Media, 2013. www.br-online.de/jugend/izi/english/publication/televizion/27_2014_E /Research_Bibliography_Children_TV_Violence.pdf.

Slater, Michael D., Kimberly L. Henry, Randall C. Swaim, and Lori L. Anderson. "Violent Media Content and Aggressiveness in Adolescents: A Downward Spiral Model." *Communication Research* 30, no. 6 (2003): 713–736. https://doi.org/10.1177/0093650203258281.

Warburton, Wayne, and Danya Braunstein. *Growing Up Fast and Furious: Reviewing the Impacts of Violent and Sexualised Media on Children.* Annandale, New South Wales: The Federation Press, 2012.

Ybarra, Michele L., Kimberly J. Mitchell, Merle Hamburger, Marie Diener-West, and Philip J. Leaf. "X-Rated Material and Perpetration of Sexually Aggressive Behavior Among Children and Adolescents: Is There a Link?" *Aggressive Behavior* 37, no. 1 (2011): 1–18. https://doi.org/10 .1002/ab.20367.

Ybarra, Michele L., and Richard E. Thompson. "Predicting the Emergence of Sexual Violence in Adolescence." *Prevention Science* 19, no. 4 (2018): 403–415. https://doi.org/10.1007/s11121-017-0810-4.

CHAPTER 8: DIVERSITY

Cohn, D'Vera, and Andrea Caumont. "10 Demographic Trends That Are Shaping the U.S. and the World." *Fact Tank* (blog). Pew Research Center, March 31, 2016. www.pewresearch.org/fact-tank/2016/03/31/10-demo graphic-trends-that-are-shaping-the-u-s-and-the-world.

"The Common Sense Census: Media Use by Tweens and Teens." Common Sense Media, 2018. www.commonsensemedia.org/research/the-common -sense-census-media-use-by-tweens-and-teens.

Cortesi, Sandra, and Gasser, Urs. "Youth Online and News: A Phenomenological View on Diversity." *International Journal of Communication* 9 (2015): 1,425–1,448.

Frey, William H. *Diversity Explosion: How New Racial Demographics Are Remaking America*. Washington, DC: Brookings Institution Press, 2015.

———. "Diversity Defines the Millennial Generation." *Brookings* (blog), June 28, 2016. www.brookings.edu/blog/the-avenue/2016/06/28/diversity-defines-the-millennial-generation.

———. "New Projections Point to a Majority Minority Nation in 2044." *Brookings* (blog), November 30, 2001. www.brookings.edu/blog/the-avenue/2014/12/12/new-projections-point-to-a-majority-minority-nation-in-2044.

———. "The US Will Become 'Minority White' in 2045, Census Projects." *Brookings* (blog), March 14, 2018. www.brookings.edu/blog/the-avenue/2018/03/14/the-us-will-become-minority-white-in-2045-census-projects.

Leventhal, Adam M., Junhan Cho, Nafeesa Andrabi, and Jessica Barrington-Trimis. "Association of Reported Concern About Increasing Societal Discrimination with Adverse Behavioral Health Outcomes in Late Adolescence." *JAMA Pediatrics* 172, no. 10 (2018): 924–933. https://jamanetwork.com/journals/jamapediatrics/fullarticle/2696519.

Mascheroni, Giovanna, and Kjartan Ólafsson. *Net Children Go Mobile: Risks and Opportunities*. 2nd ed. Milano: Educatt, 2014. https://doi.org/10.13140/RG.2.1.3590.8561.

Neckerman, Kathryn M. *Social Inequality*. New York: Russell Sage Foundation. 2004.

Organisation for Economic Co-operation and Development. *Students, Computers and Learning: Making the Connection*, 123–143. Pisa: OECD Publishing, 2015. https://doi.org/10.1787/9789264239555-8-en.

———. "Are There Differences in How Advantaged and Disadvantaged Students Use the Internet?" *PISA in Focus* 64 (July 12, 2016). https://doi.org/10.1787/5jlv8zq6hw43-en.

———. "How's Life in Your Region?" OECD.org, 2019. www.oecd.org/regional/how-is-life-in-your-region.htm.

———. "Inequality." OECD.org, 2019. www.oecd.org/social/inequality.htm#income.

Paschall, Katherine W., Elizabeth T. Gershoff, and Megan Kuhfeld. "A Two Decade Examination of Historical Race/Ethnicity Disparities in Academic Achievement by Poverty Status." *Journal of Youth and Adolescence* 47, no. 6 (2018): 1,164–1,177. https://doi.org/10.1007/s10964-017-0800-7.

Tynes, Brendesha M. "Online Racial Discrimination: A Growing Problem for Adolescents." *Psychological Science Agenda, Science Brief*, December 2015. www.apa.org/science/about/psa/2015/12/online-racial-discrimination.

Watkins, S. Craig, with Andres Lombana-Bermudez, Alexander Cho, Jacqueline Ryan Vickery, Vivian Shaw, and Lauren Weinzimmer. *The Digital Edge: How Black and Latino Youth Navigate Digital Inequality.* New York: New York University Press, 2018.

Williams, David R., Jourdyn A. Lawrence, and Brigette A. Davis. "Racism and Health: Evidence and Needed Research." *Annual Review of Public Health* 40 (2019): 105–125. www.annualreviews.org/doi/pdf/10.1146/annurev-publhealth-040218-043750.

CHAPTER 9: LEARNING

Adolescent Sleep Working Group, Committee on Adolescence, and Council on School Health. "School Start Times for Adolescents." American Academy of Pediatrics, Adolescence Sleep Working Group, and Council on School Health. *Pediatrics* 134, no. 3 (2014): 642–649. https://doi.org/10.1542/peds.2014-1697.

"Children, Teens, and Reading." Common Sense Media, May 12, 2014. www.commonsensemedia.org/research/children-teens-and-reading.

"The Common Sense Census: Media Use by Tweens and Teens, 2015." Common Sense Media, 2015. www.commonsensemedia.org/sites/default/files/uploads/pdfs/census_factsheet_homeworkandmultitasking.pdf.

Dunster, Gideon P., Luciano de la Iglesia, Miriam Ben-Hamo, Claire Nave, Jason G. Fleischer, Satchidananda Panda, and Horacio O. de la Iglesia. "Sleepmore in Seattle: Later School Start Times Are Associated with More Sleep and Better Performance in High School Students." *Science Advances* 4, no. 12 (2018). https://doi.org/10.1126/sciadv.aau6200.

Gasser, Urs, Sandra Cortesi, Momin M. Malik, and Ashley Lee. "Youth and Digital Media: From Credibility to Information Quality." Berkman Center Research Publication No. 2012-1. February 16, 2012. https://papers.ssrn.com/abstract=2005272.

Jabr, Ferris. "The Reading Brain in the Digital Age: The Science of Paper Versus Screens." *Scientific American*, December 7, 2018. www.scientificamerican.com/article/reading-paper-screens.

Jensen, Frances E., and Amy Ellis Nutt. 2015. *The Teenage Brain: A Neuroscientist's Survival Guide to Raising Adolescents and Young Adults*. New York: Harper, 2015.

Junco, Reynol. "In-Class Multitasking and Academic Performance." *Computers in Human Behavior* 28, no. 6 (2012): 2,236–2,243. https://doi .org/10.1016/j.chb.2012.06.031.

McCabe, Donald L., Kenneth D. Butterfield, and Linda Klebe Treviño. *Cheating in College: Why Students Do It and What Educators Can Do About It*. Baltimore: Johns Hopkins University Press, 2012.

"News and America's Kids: How Young People Perceive and Are Impacted by the News." Common Sense Media, December 7, 2018. www.common sensemedia.org/research/news-and-americas-kids.

Payne, Kathy. "High School Students Cheating Less, Survey Finds." *USA Today*, November 25, 2012. www.usatoday.com/story/news/nation/2012/11/25 /high-school-students-cheating/1719297.

Perez-Pena, Richard. "Studies Show More Students Cheat, Even High Achievers." *New York Times*, September 7, 2012. www.nytimes.com/2012/09 /08/education/studies-show-more-students-cheat-even-high-achievers .html.

"Plagiarism: Facts & Stats." Plagiarism.org, December 7, 2018. www.plagiarism .org/article/plagiarism-facts-and-stats.

Purcell, Kristen, Judy Buchanan, and Linda Friedrich. "The Impact of Digital Tools on Student Writing and How Writing Is Taught in Schools." Pew Research Center, July 16, 2013. www.pewinternet.org/2013/07/16 /the-impact-of-digital-tools-on-student-writing-and-how-writing-is -taught-in-schools.

Purcell, Kristen, Lee Rainie, Alan Heaps, Judy Buchanan, Linda Friedrich, Amanda Jacklin, Clara Chen, and Kathryn Zickuhr. 2012. "How Teens Do Research in the Digital World." Pew Internet & American Life Project, 2012. https://eric.ed.gov/?id=ED537513.

Rainie, Lee. 2014. "Teens and Libraries in Today's Digital World." Pew Research Center, April 9, 2014. www.pewinternet.org/2014/04/09/millennials -and-libraries.

Robb, Michael. "Our New Research Shows Where Kids Get Their News and How They Feel About It." Common Sense Media, March 7, 2017. www .commonsensemedia.org/blog/our-new-research-shows-where-kids-get -their-news-and-how-they-feel-about-it.

Sifferlin, Alexandra. "Why Teenage Brains Are So Hard to Understand." *Time*, December 7, 2018. http://time.com/4929170/inside-teen-teenage-brain.

"Statistics." International Center for Academic Integrity, December 7, 2018. https://academicintegrity.org/statistics.

Walker, Matthew P. *Why We Sleep: Unlocking the Power of Sleep and Dreams*. New York: Scribner, 2017.

CHAPTER 10: CIVIC LIFE

Bennett, W. Lance, ed. *Civic Life Online: Learning How Digital Media Can Engage Youth*. John D. and Catherine T. Macarthur Foundation Series on Digital Media and Learning. Cambridge, MA: MIT Press, 2008.

Caldwell, Christopher. "The Problem with Greta Thunberg's Climate Activism." *New York Times*, August 2, 2019. www.nytimes.com/2019/08/02/opinion/climate-change-greta-thunberg.html.

Center for Information and Research on Civic Learning and Engagement (CIRCLE). "Election Night 2016: 24 Million Youth Voted, Most Rejected Trump." CIRCLE, Tufts University, November 14, 2016. https://civicyouth.org/an-estimated-24-million-young-people-vote-in-2016-election.

———. "Five Takeaways on Social Media and the Youth Vote in 2018." CIRCLE, Tufts University, November 15, 2018. https://civicyouth.org/five-takeaways-on-social-media-and-the-youth-vote-in-2018.

Dautrich, Kenneth. "Future of the First Amendment: 2016 Survey of High School Students and Teachers." Knight Foundation, December 2018. https://knightfoundation.org/reports/future-of-the-first-amendment-2016-survey-of-high-school-students-and-teachers.

Dreyfuss, Emily. "The Youth Climate Strike as Seen by Teen Photographers." *Wired*, March 20, 2019. www.wired.com/story/youth-climate-strike-teen-photographers.

Dreyfuss, Emily, and Andrea Valdez. "Kids and Teens Strike Against Adults' Climate Screw-Ups." *Wired*, March 15, 2019. www.wired.com/story/kids-and-teens-strike-against-adults-climate-screw-ups.

Fingerhut, Hannah. "Millennials' Views of News Media, Religious Organizations Grow More Negative." Pew Research Center, January 4, 2016. www.pewresearch.org/fact-tank/2016/01/04/millennials-views-of-news-media-religious-organizations-grow-more-negative.

Fry, Richard. "Millennials Approach Baby Boomers as America's Largest Generation in Electorate." Pew Research Center, April 3, 2018. www.pewresearch.org/fact-tank/2018/04/03/millennials-approach-baby-boomers-as-largest-generation-in-u-s-electorate.

"Future of the First Amendment Survey." Knight Foundation, 2006–2019. www.knightfoundation.org/future-first-amendment-survey.

Gardiner, Cait, Abby Kiesa, and Alberto Medina. "Youth Volunteering on Political Campaigns." CIRCLE, Tufts University, March 17, 2020. https://circle.tufts.edu/latest-research/youth-volunteering-political-campaigns.

"How Students Engage with News: Five Takeaways for Educators, Journalists, and Librarians." *Educause*, October 16, 2018. https://library.educause.edu/resources/2018/10/how-students-engage-with-news-five-takeaways-for-educators-journalists-and-librarians.

Montanaro, Domenico. "Here's Just How Little Confidence Americans Have In Political Institutions." *All Things Considered* (NPR), January 17, 2018. www.npr.org/2018/01/17/578422668/heres-just-how-little-confidence-americans-have-in-political-institutions.

McLennan, Destiny. "The American Freshman: National Norms, Fall 2017." Research Brief, Higher Education Research Institute at UCLA, April 2019. https://heri.ucla.edu/publications-tfs.

"Public Trust in Government: 1958–2019." Pew Research Center, April 11, 2019. www.people-press.org/2019/04/11/public-trust-in-government-1958-2019.

Rouse, Stella M., and Ashley D. Ross. 2018. *The Politics of Millennials: Political Beliefs and Policy Preferences of America's Most Diverse Generation.* Ann Arbor: University of Michigan Press, 2018.

Syvertsen, Amy K., Laura Wray-Lake, Constance A. Flanagan, D. Wayne Osgood, and Laine Briddell. "Thirty Year Trends in U.S. Adolescents' Civic Engagement: A Story of Changing Participation and Educational Differences." *Journal of Research on Adolescence* 21, no. 3 (2011): 586–594. https://doi.org/10.1111/j.1532-7795.2010.00706.x.

US Census Bureau. "Young-Adult Voting: An Analysis of Presidential Elections, 1964–2012." Census.gov, April 24, 2014. www.census.gov/library/publications/2014/demo/p20-573.html.

"Who Votes for Mayor?" Portland State University and the Knight Foundation, 2016. www.whovotesformayor.org.

"Youth Poll: Harvard Public Opinion Project." Institute of Politics at Harvard University, December 2017. https://iop.harvard.edu/youth-poll/fall-2017-poll.

Notes

INTRODUCTION

1. John Palfrey and Urs Gasser, *Born Digital: Understanding the First Generation of Digital Natives* (New York: Basic Books, 2008).

2. "What Is Connected Learning?," Connected Learning Alliance, https://clalliance.org/about-connected-learning.

3. Nathaniel Popper, "Panicking About Your Kids and Their Phones? The New Research Says Don't," *New York Times*, January 17, 2020, www.nytimes.com/2020/01/17/technology/kids-smartphones-depression.html.

CHAPTER 1: SCREEN TIME

1. Oxford Internet Institute, "Moderate Use of Screen Time Can Be Good for Your Health, New Study Finds," October 22, 2019, www.oii.ox.ac.uk/news/releases/moderate-use-of-screen-time-can-be-good-for-your-health-new-study-finds.

2. Victoria Rideout and Michael B. Robb, "Social Media, Social Life: Teens Reveal Their Experiences," Common Sense Media, 2018, https://static1.squarespace.com/static/5ba15befec4eb7899898240d/t/5ba165a221c67cff9a6dc5b7/1537303981859/2018_CS_SocialMediaSocialLife_FullReport-final-release_2.pdf.

3. Monica Anderson and Jingjing Jiang, "Teens, Social Media and Technology," Internet & Technology, Pew Research Center, May 31, 2018, www .pewresearch.org/internet/2018/05/31/teens-social-media-technology-2018.

4. For the UK statistics, see Sonia Livingstone, Leslie Haddon, Jane Vincent, Giovanna Mascheroni, and Kjartan Ólafsson, *Net Children Go Mobile: The UK Report* (London: London School of Economics and Political Science, 2014), www.lse.ac.uk/media@lse/research/EUKidsOnline/EU%20Kids%20III /Reports/NCGMUKReportfinal.pdf. For the Brazilian numbers, see Maria Eugenia Sozio, Cristina Ponte, Inês Vitorino Sampaio, Fabio Senne, Kjartan Ólafsson, Suzana Jaíze Alves, Camila Garroux, Alexandre Barbosa, and Giovanna Mascheroni, "Children and Internet Use: A Comparative Analysis of Brazil and Seven European Countries," EU Kids Online, July 2015, http://fabricadesites.fcsh.unl.pt/eukidsonline/wp-content/uploads/sites/36 /2017/11/Brazil-NCGM_COMPARATIVE-REPORT.pdf.

5. Valerie Steeves, "Young Canadians in a Wired World—Phase III: Life Online," MediaSmarts, 2014, https://mediasmarts.ca/sites/mediasmarts/files /pdfs/publication-report/full/YCWWIII_Life_Online_FullReport.pdf.

6. Isabel Willemse et al., "JAMES: Jugend, Aktivitäten, Medien— Erhebung Schweiz" [JAMES: Youth, Activities, Media—Survey Switzerland], *Angewandte Psychologie*, 2014, https://digitalcollection.zhaw.ch/bitstream /11475/4290/3/2014_JAMES_Jugend_Aktivitäten_Medien_Erhebung_Schweiz _Ergebnisbericht_2014.pdf.

7. Anderson and Jiang, "Teens, Social Media & Technology."

8. Anderson and Jiang, "Teens, Social Media & Technology."

9. Anderson and Jiang, "Teens, Social Media & Technology."

10. Anderson and Jiang, "Teens, Social Media & Technology."

11. Anderson and Jiang, "Teens, Social Media & Technology."

12. Anderson and Jiang, "Teens, Social Media & Technology."

13. "Landmark Report: U.S. Teens Use an Average of Nine Hours of Media Per Day, Tweens Use Six Hours," Common Sense Media, November 3, 2015, www.commonsensemedia.org/about-us/news/press-releases/landmark -report-us-teens-use-an-average-of-nine-hours-of-media-per-day.

14. "Landmark Report: U.S. Teens."

15. "Landmark Report: U.S. Teens."

16. Anderson and Jiang, "Teens, Social Media & Technology."

17. Angus Whyte, "Common Sense Media: The Digital Census 2017," *Evolve* (blog), July 19, 2018, https://evolvetreatment.com/blog/common -sense-media-the-digital-census-2017.

18. Tanya Basu, "Two Studies Lay the Blame for Childhood Screen Time at Mom's Feet," *MIT Technology Review*, November 25, 2019, www.technologyreview.com/f/614759/two-studies-lay-the-blame-for-childhood-screen-time-at-moms-feet.

19. "Internet/Broadband Fact Sheet," Pew Research Center, www.pewresearch.org/internet/fact-sheet/internet-broadband.

20. Monica Anderson, "Parents, Teens, and Digital Monitoring," Internet & Technology, Pew Research Center, January 7, 2016, www.pewresearch.org/internet/2016/01/07/parents-teens-and-digital-monitoring.

21. David L. Hill, "Why to Avoid TV for Infants and Toddlers," Healthychildren.org, American Academy of Pediatrics, October 21, 2016, www.healthychildren.org/English/family-life/Media/Pages/Why-to-Avoid-TV-Before-Age-2.aspx.

22. Nellie Bowles, "A Dark Consensus About Screens and Kids Begins to Emerge," *New York Times*, November 13, 2018, www.nytimes.com/2018/10/26/style/phones-children-silicon-valley.html.

23. Andrew Przybylski, Amy Orben, and Netta Weinstein, "How Much Is Too Much? Examining the Relationship Between Digital Screen Engagement and Psychosocial Functioning in a Confirmatory Cohort Study," *Journal of the American Academy of Child & Adolescent Psychiatry*, June 17, 2019, https://jaacap.org/article/S0890-8567(19)31437-6/fulltext.

24. Przybylski, Orben, and Weinstein, "How Much Is Too Much?"

CHAPTER 2: SOCIAL LIFE

1. Victoria Rideout and Michael Robb, "Social Media, Social Life: Teens Reveal Their Experiences," Common Sense Media, 2018, www.commonsensemedia.org/sites/default/files/uploads/research/2018_cs_socialmediasociallife_fullreport-final-release_2_lowres.pdf.

2. "Digital Friendships: The Role of Technology in Young People's Relationships," UK Safer Internet Centre, 2018, www.saferinternet.org.uk/digital-friendships.

3. Amanda Lenhart, "Teens, Social Media & Technology Overview 2015," Pew Research Center, April 9, 2015, www.pewresearch.org/internet/2015/04/09/teens-social-media-technology-2015; Aaron Smith and Monica Anderson, "Social Media Use in 2018," Pew Research Center, March 1, 2018, www.pewresearch.org/internet/2018/03/01/social-media-use-in-2018.

4. Sandra Cortesi, "Youth Online: Diversifying Social Media Platforms and Practices," H2O, December 10, 2013, https://h2o.law.harvard.edu/text_blocks/2113.

5. "Teens' Social Media Habits and Experiences," Pew Research Center, November 27, 2018, www.pewresearch.org/internet/2018/11/28/teens-social-media-habits-and-experiences/pi_2018-11-28_teens-social-media_0-01-2.

6. "Digital Friendships."

7. Amy Orben, Tobias Dienlin, and Andrew Przybylski, "Social Media's Enduring Effect on Adolescent Life Satisfaction," *PNAS* 116, no. 21 (May 21, 2019): 10,226–10,228, www.pnas.org/content/pnas/116/21/10226.full.pdf.

8. Catherine Steiner-Adair, *The Big Disconnect: Protecting Childhood and Family Relationships in the Digital Age* (New York: Harper, 2014).

9. "Social and Emotional Skills: Well-Being, Connectedness and Success," OECD, www.oecd.org/education/school/UPDATED%20Social%20and%20Emotional%20Skills%20-%20Well-being,%20connectedness%20and%20success.pdf%20(website).pdf.

10. John Suler, "The Online Disinhibition Effect," *CyberPsychology & Behavior* 7, no. 3 (July 28, 2004): 321–326, www.liebertpub.com/doi/10.1089/1094931041291295.

11. Monica Anderson, "6 Takeaways About How Parents Monitor Their Teen's Digital Activities," Pew Research Center, January 7, 2016, www.pewresearch.org/fact-tank/2016/01/07/parents-teens-digital-monitoring.

12. Michele Lew, "A 4-Step Process for Building Student Resilience," *Edutopia*, George Lucas Educational Foundation, November 7, 2018, www.edutopia.org/article/4-step-process-building-student-resilience.

CHAPTER 3: PRIVACY

1. NASDAQ, "Facebook, Inc. Class A Common Stock (FB) Earnings Report Date," NASDAQ, 2020, www.nasdaq.com/market-activity/stocks/fb/earnings.

2. "Digital Birth: Welcome to the Online World," *Business Wire*, October 6, 2010, www.businesswire.com/news/home/20101006006722/en/Digital-Birth-Online-World.

3. Mary Madden, "Privacy, Security, and Digital Inequality: How Technology Experiences and Resources Vary by Socioeconomic Status, Race, and Ethnicity," Data and Society Research Center, September 27, 2017,

https://datasociety.net/pubs/prv/DataAndSociety_PrivacySecurityandDigital Inequality.pdf.

4. "Teens, Social Media, and Privacy," Pew Research Center, May 21, 2013, www.pewresearch.org/internet/2013/05/21/teens-social-media-and -privacy-2.

5. Monica Anderson and Jingjing Jiang, "Teens, Social Media & Technology," Internet & Technology, Pew Research Center, May 31, 2018, www .pewresearch.org/internet/2018/05/31/teens-social-media-technology-2018.

6. Anderson and Jiang, "Teens, Social Media & Technology."

7. "Teens, Social Media, and Privacy," Pew Research Center, May 21, 2013, www.pewresearch.org/internet/2013/05/21/teens-social-media-and -privacy-2.

8. Sheri Madigan, Anh Ly, Christina L. Rash, Joris Van Ouytsel, and Jeff R. Temple, "Prevalence of Multiple Forms of Sexting Behavior Among Youth: A Systematic Review and Meta-Analysis," *JAMA Pediatrics* 172, no. 4 (April 2018): 327–335, https://jamanetwork.com/journals/jamapediatrics /fullarticle/2673719.

9. "Children's Privacy," Federal Trade Commission, www.ftc.gov/tips -advice/business-center/privacy-and-security/children%27s-privacy.

10. danah boyd, Eszter Hargittai, Jason Schultz, and John Palfrey, "Why Parents Help Their Children Lie to Facebook About Age: Unintended Consequences of the 'Children's Online Privacy Protection Act,'" *First Monday* 16, no. 11 (November 7, 2011), https://journals.uic.edu/ojs/index.php/fm/article /view/3850.

CHAPTER 4: SAFETY

1. "The Facts About Online Predators Every Parent Should Know," Common Sense Media, June 25, 2017, www.commonsensemedia.org/blog /the-facts-about-online-predators-every-parent-should-know.

2. "Internet," Crimes Against Children Research Center, http://unh.edu /ccrc/internet-crimes.

3. Robin M. Kowalski and Susan P. Limber, "Psychological, Physical, and Academic Correlates of Cyberbullying and Traditional Bullying," *Journal of Adolescent Health* 53, no. 1 (July 2013): S13–S20, www.sciencedirect.com /science/article/pii/S1054139X12004132.

4. "Cyberbullying Facts," Cyberbullying Research Center, https://cyber bullying.org/facts.

5. Sameer Hinduja and Justin W. Patchin, "Connecting Adolescent Suicide to the Severity of Bullying and Cyberbullying," *Journal of School Violence*, May 14, 2018, https://cyberbullying.org/bullying-cyberbullying -suicide-among-us-youth.

6. S. P. Kiriakidis and A. Kavoura, "Cyberbullying: A Review of the Literature on Harassment Through the Internet and Other Electronic Means," *Family and Community Health* 33, no. 2 (201AD): 82–93, www.ncbi.nlm .nih.gov/pubmed/20216351; Rashmi Shetgiri, "Bullying and Victimization Among Children," *Advances in Pediatrics* 60, no. 1 (July 12, 2013): 33–51, www.ncbi.nlm.nih.gov/pmc/articles/PMC3766526/#R6.

7. Justin W. Patchin, "2016 Cyberbullying Data," Cyberbullying Research Center, November 26, 2016, https://cyberbullying.org/2016-cyberbullying -data.

8. Andy Marra, "Out Online: The Experiences of LGBT Youth on the Internet," *GLSEN*, July 10, 2013, www.glsen.org/news/out-online-experiences -lgbt-youth-internet; "Facts About Bullying," StopBullying.gov, June 10, 2019, www.stopbullying.gov/resources/facts.

9. Maria Sapouna and Dieter Wolke, "Resilience to Bullying Victimization: The Role of Individual, Family and Peer Characteristics," *Child Abuse and Neglect* 37, no. 11 (June 2013), doi: 10.1016/j.chiabu.2013.05.009.

10. Amanda Lenhart, Monica Anderson, and Aaron Smith, "Teens, Technology and Romantic Relationships," Pew Research Center, October 1, 2015, www.pewresearch.org/internet/2015/10/01/teens-technology-and -romantic-relationships.

CHAPTER 5: ANXIETY

1. "The National Survey of Children's Health," Data Resource Center for Child & Adolescent Health, www.childhealthdata.org/learn-about-the-nsch /NSCH; "Children's Mental Health: Data and Statistics," Centers for Disease Control and Prevention, April 19, 2019, www.cdc.gov/childrensmentalhealth /data.html.

2. Kate Snow and Cynthia McFadden, "Generation at Risk: America's Youngest Facing Mental Health Crisis," *NBC News*, December 10, 2017, www .nbcnews.com/health/kids-health/generation-risk-america-s-youngest-facing -mental-health-crisis-n827836; "Children's Mental Health: Data and Statistics."

3. "Youth Risk Behavior Survey," Centers for Disease Control and Prevention, www.cdc.gov/healthyyouth/data/yrbs/pdf/trendsreport.pdf.

4. CDC data cited in "Suicide," National Institute of Mental Health, April 2019, www.nimh.nih.gov/health/statistics/suicide.shtml.

5. Juliana Menasce Horowitz and Nikki Graf, "Most U.S. Teens See Anxiety and Depression as a Major Problem Among Their Peers," Pew Research Center, February 20, 2019, www.pewsocialtrends.org/2019/02/20/most-u-s-teens-see-anxiety-and-depression-as-a-major-problem-among-their-peers.

6. Monica Anderson and Jingjing Jiang, "Teens' Social Media Habits and Experiences," Pew Research Center, November 28, 2018, pewresearch.org/internet/2018/11/28/teens-social-media-habits-and-experiences.

7. Candice Odgers, "Smartphones Are Bad for Some Teens, Not All," *Nature*, February 21, 2018, www.nature.com/articles/d41586-018-02109-8#ref-CR1.

8. Jan Schürmann and Jürgen Margraf, "Age of Anxiety and Depression Revisited: A Meta-Analysis of Two European Community Samples (1964–2015)," *International Journal of Clinical and Health Psychology* 18, no. 2 (2018): 102–112, https://doi.org/10.1016/j.ijchp.2018.02.002.

9. Victoria Rideout and Susannah Fox, "Digital Health Practices, Social Media Use, and Mental Well-Being Among Teens and Young Adults in the U.S.," Hopelab and Well Being Trust, summer 2018, https://hopelab.org/reports/pdf/a-national-survey-by-hopelab-and-well-being-trust-2018.pdf.

10. "#StatusOfMind: Social Media and Young People's Mental Health and Wellbeing," Young Health Movement, May 2017, www.rsph.org.uk/uploads/assets/uploaded/d125b27c-0b62-41c5-a2c0155a8887cd01.pdf.

11. Rachel L. Frost and Debra J. Rickwood, "A Systematic Review of the Mental Health Outcomes Associated with Facebook Use," *Computers in Human Behavior* 76 (November 2017): 576–600, https://doi.org/10.1016/j.chb.2017.08.001.

12. Frost and Rickwood, "Facebook Use."

13. Nicole Zillien and Eszter Hargittai, "Digital Distinction: Status-Specific Types of Internet Usage," *Social Science Quarterly* 90, no. 2 (April 12, 2009): 274–291, https://doi.org/10.1111/j.1540-6237.2009.00617.x.

14. S. Craig Watkins, Andres Lombana-Bermudez, Alexander Cho, Jacqueline Ryan Vickery, Vivian Shaw, and Lauren Weinzimmer, *The Digital Edge: How Black and Latino Youth Navigate Digital Inequality* (New York: New York University Press, 2018).

15. Brittany Allen and Helen Waterman, "Stages of Adolescence," American Academy of Pediatrics, healthychildren.org, March 2019, www.healthychildren.org/English/ages-stages/teen/Pages/Stages-of-Adolescence.aspx.

CHAPTER 6: ADDICTION

1. "Technology Addiction: Concern, Controversy, and Finding Balance," Common Sense Media, 2016, www.commonsensemedia.org/sites/default /files/uploads/research/csm_2016_technology_addiction_research_brief _0.pdf.

2. "Gaming Disorder: Online Q&A," World Health Organization, September 2018, www.who.int/features/qa/gaming-disorder/en.

3. Juliet Ye, "China Sets Internet Addiction Standard," *Wall Street Journal* (blog), November 10, 2008, https://blogs.wsj.com/chinarealtime/2008 /11/10/china-sets-internet-addiction-standard; "Korea's Internet Addicts," *Dateline*, April 12, 2016, www.sbs.com.au/news/dateline/tvepisode/korea-s -internet-addicts.

4. Michael Rich, "Ask the Mediatrician: How Do I Know if My Tween Has Gaming Disorder?," *Thriving, Boston Children's Hospital Pediatric Health Blog* (blog), August 27, 2018, https://thriving.childrenshospital.org/gaming -disorder-tweens.

5. Kristyn Zajac, Meredith K. Ginley, Rocio Chang, and Nancy M. Petry, "Treatments for Internet Gaming Disorder and Internet Addiction: A Systematic Review," *Psychology of Addictive Behaviors* 31, no. 8 (December 1, 2018): 979–994, https://doi.org/https://dx.doi.org/10.1037/adb0000315.

CHAPTER 7: GAMING

1. Andrew Perrin, "5 Facts About Americans and Video Games," Pew Research Center, September 7, 2018, www.pewresearch.org/fact-tank/2018 /09/17/5-facts-about-americans-and-video-games.

2. "The Common Sense Census: Media Use by Tweens and Teens," Common Sense Media, 2015, www.commonsensemedia.org/sites/default/files /uploads/research/census_researchreport.pdf.

3. Perrin, "Americans and Video Games."

4. Isabel Willemse, Gregor Waller, Sarah Genner, Lilian Suter, Sabine Oppliger, Anna-Lena Huber, and Daniel Süss, "JAMES: Jugend, Aktivitäten, Medien—Erhebung Schweiz" [JAMES: Youth, Activities, Media—Survey Switzerland], *Angewandte Psychologie*, 2014, https://digitalcollection.zhaw .ch/bitstream/11475/4290/3/2014_JAMES_Jugend_Aktivitäten_Medien _Erhebung_Schweiz_Ergebnisbericht_2014.pdf.

5. Kim Parker, Juliana Horowitz, Ruth Igielnik, Baxter Oliphant, and Anna Brown, "America's Complex Relationship with Guns: An In-Depth Look at the Attitudes and Experiences of U.S. Adults," Pew Research Center, June 22, 2017, www.pewsocialtrends.org/wp-content/uploads/sites/3/2017/06 /Guns-Report-FOR-WEBSITE-PDF-6-21.pdf.

6. "Literature Review on the Impact of Playing Violent Video Games on Aggression," Australian Attorney General's Department, September 2010, www.apadivisions.org/division-46/resources/articles/video-games .pdf.

7. *Brown v. Entertainment Merchants Association*, 564 U.S. 768 (2011).

8. "Summary of *Violent Computer Games and Aggression—An Overview of the Research 2000-2011*," Swedish Media Council, January 9, 2012, www.isfe.eu/wp-content/uploads/2012/01/literature_review_violent_games _-_summary.pdf.

9. UN Committee of the Rights of the Child, "General Comment No. 17 (2013) on the Right of the Child to Rest, Leisure, Play, Recreational Activities, Cultural Life and the Arts (Art. 31)," UN Convention on the Rights of the Child § (2013), April 17, 2013, www.refworld.org/docid/51ef9bcc4 .html.

10. American Psychological Association, "Technical Report on the Review of the Violent Video Game Literature," APA Task Force on Violent Media, 2015, www.apa.org/pi/families/review-video-games.pdf.

11. "Scholars' Open Letter to the APA Task Force on Violent Media," September 26, 2013, www.scribd.com/doc/223284732/Scholar-s-Open-Letter -to-the-APA-Task-Force-On-Violent-Media-Opposing-APA-Policy-Statements -on-Violent-Media?campaign=SkimbitLtd&ad_group=87543 X1557188X8178f7d318d24207be784ac2ff241262&keyword=660149026 &source=hp_affiliate&medium=affiliate.

12. Taylor Wofford, "APA Says Video Games Make You Violent, but Critics Cry Bias," *Newsweek*, August 20, 2015, www.newsweek.com/apa -video-games-violence-364394.

13. Andrew K. Przybylski and Netta Weinstein, "Violent Video Game Engagement Is Not Associated with Adolescents' Aggressive Behaviour: Evidence from a Registered Report," Royal Society Publishing, February 13, 2019, https://royalsocietypublishing.org/doi/10.1098/rsos.171474.

14. Viviane Kovess-Masfety, et al., "Is Time Spent Playing Video Games Associated with Mental Health, Cognitive and Social Skills in Young

Children?," *Social Psychiatry and Psychiatric Epidemiology* 51, no. 3 (March 2016): 349–357, https://doi.org/10.1007/s00127-016-1179-6.

15. Isabela Granic, Adam Lobel, and Rutger C. M. E. Engels, "The Benefits of Playing Video Games," *American Psychologist* 69, no. 1 (2013): 66–78, https://doi.org/10.1037/a0034857.

16. Perrin, "5 Facts About Americans and Video Games."

17. Neil Herndon, "15 Lessons About Life We Learn from Video Games," *Forbes*, February 22, 2016, www.forbes.com/sites/archenemy/2016/02/22/15 -lessons-about-life-we-learn-from-video-games/#398e8a7253f0.

CHAPTER 8: DIVERSITY

1. Mark Tracy, "Nick Bosa Comes with the Kind of Baggage That Doesn't Matter," *New York Times*, April 23, 2019, www.nytimes.com/2019/04/23 /sports/nick-bosa-twitter-nfl-draft.html.

2. Andrew Joseph, "Nick Bosa Liked Instagram Posts Featuring Racist and Homophobic Slurs," *For the Win (USA Today)*, April 25, 2019, https://ftw.usatoday.com/2019/04/nick-bosa-instagram-racist-n-word-posts -twitter-social-media-nfl-draft.

3. Hannah Natanson, "Harvard Rescinds Acceptances for At Least Ten Students for Obscene Memes," *Harvard Crimson*, June 5, 2017, www .thecrimson.com/article/2017/6/5/2021-offers-rescinded-memes.

4. William H. Frey, "The US Will Become 'Minority White' in 2045, Census Projects." *The Avenue* (blog), Brookings, March 14, 2018, www .brookings.edu/blog/the-avenue/2018/03/14/the-us-will-become-minority -white-in-2045-census-projects.

5. "Dubai Most Cosmopolitan City Globally, 83% of Population Is Foreign-Born," *Emirates 24/7*, January 17, 2016, www.emirates247.com /news/emirates/dubai-most-cosmopolitan-city-globally-83-population-is -foreign-born-2016-01-17-1.617596.

6. "Internet/Broadband Fact Sheet," Pew Research Center, June 12, 2019, www.pewresearch.org/internet/fact-sheet/internet-broadband.

7. "New ITU Statistics Show More Than Half the World Is Now Using the Internet," *ITU News*, December 6, 2018, https://news.itu.int/itu -statistics-leaving-no-one-offline.

8. Steven J. L. Jankowski, "Wikipedia and Encyclopaedism: A Genre Analysis of Epistemological Values" (master's thesis, University of Ottawa,

Ontario, Canada, 2013), https://pierrelevyblog.files.wordpress.com/2013/05/stevejankowski_thesis_v18.pdf.

9. Mark Graham, Scott A. Hale, Monica Stephens, and Viktor Mayer-Schönberger, *Geographies of the World's Knowledge*, ed. Corinne M. Flick (London: Convoco Foundation, 2011), www.oii.ox.ac.uk/archive/downloads/publications/convoco_geographies_en.pdf.

10. Monica Anderson and Jingjing Jiang, "Teens' Social Media Habits and Experiences," Pew Research Center, November 28, 2018, pewresearch.org/internet/2018/11/28/teens-social-media-habits-and-experiences.

11. "The Common Sense Census: Media Use by Tweens and Teens," Common Sense Media, 2015, www.commonsensemedia.org/sites/default/files/uploads/research/census_researchreport.pdf.

12. Sonia Livingstone, Leslie Haddon, Jane Vincent, Giovanna Mascheroni, and Kjartan Ólafsson, *Net Children Go Mobile: The UK Report* (London: London School of Economics and Political Science, 2014), www.lse.ac.uk/media@lse/research/EUKidsOnline/EU Kids III/Reports/NCGMUKReportfinal.pdf.

13. Erica N. Fletcher, Robert C. Whitaker, and Sarah E. Anderson, "Screen Time at Home and School Among Low-Income Children Attending Head Start," *Child Indicators Research* 7, no. 2 (June 2014): 421–436, https://doi.org/10.1007/s12187-013-9212-8.

14. Victoria Rideout and Michael B. Robb, *The Common Sense Census: Media Use by Tweens and Teens* (San Francisco: Common Sense Media, 2019), www.commonsensemedia.org/sites/default/files/uploads/research/2019-census-8-to-18-full-report-updated.pdf.

15. Brendesha M. Tynes, "Online Racial Discrimination: A Growing Problem for Adolescents," *Science Brief* (American Psychological Association, Psychological Science Agenda), December 2015, www.apa.org/science/about/psa/2015/12/online-racial-discrimination.

16. Tynes, "Online Racial Discrimination."

17. Adam M. Leventhal, Junhan Cho, Nafeesa Andrabi, and Jessica Barrington-Trimis, "Increasing Societal Discrimination with Adverse Behavioral Health Outcomes in Late Adolescence," *JAMA Pediatrics* 170, no. 10 (May 9, 2018): 924–933, https://doi.org/10.1001/jamapediatrics.2018.2022.

18. Maria Trent, Danielle G. Dooley, and Jacqueline Dougé, "The Impact of Racism on Child and Adolescent Health," *Pediatrics* 144, no. 2 (August 2019), https://doi.org/https://doi.org/10.1542/peds.2019-1765.

19. Saeed Jones (@theferocity), "Also It's 'Transgender,' Not 'Transgendered.' 'Transgendered' Is the Linguistic Equivalent of Describing Someone As 'Blacked,'" Twitter, February 17, 2015, https://twitter.com/theferocity /status/567718273484333056.

20. Diane Hughes and Howard Stevenson, "Talking to Kids About Discrimination," American Psychological Association, 2020, www.apa.org /helpcenter/kids-discrimination.

CHAPTER 9: LEARNING

1. Kristen Purcell and Linda Friedrich, "The Impact of Digital Tools on Student Writing and How Writing Is Taught in Schools," Pew Research Center, July 16, 2013, www.pewresearch.org/internet/2013/07/16/the-impact -of-digital-tools-on-student-writing-and-how-writing-is-taught-in-schools.

2. Leila Fiester, with Ralph Smith, "Early Warning! Why Reading by the End of Third Grade Matters," Annie E. Casey Foundation, January 1, 2019, www.aecf .org/resources/early-warning-why-reading-by-the-end-of-third-grade-matters.

3. Paula J. Schwanenflugel and Nancy Flanagan Knapp, "What Is It with Boys and Reading?," *Psychology Today Blog*, March 31, 2018, www .psychologytoday.com/us/blog/reading-minds/201803/what-is-it-boys-and -reading; Scholastic, *Kids & Family Reading Report*, 7th ed. (New York: Scholastic, 2019), www.scholastic.com/readingreport/home.html.

4. Ferris Jabr, "The Reading Brain in the Digital Age: The Science of Paper Versus Screens," *Scientific American*, April 11, 2013, www.scientific american.com/article/reading-paper-screens.

5. Matthew P. Walker, *Why We Sleep: Unlocking the Power of Sleep and Dreams* (New York: Scribner, 2017).

6. "2014 Sleep in America Poll: Sleep in the Modern American Family," National Sleep Foundation, www.sleepfoundation.org/professionals/sleep -americar-polls/2014-sleep-modern-family.

7. "What Is Connected Learning?," Connected Learning Alliance, https:// clalliance.org/about-connected-learning.

8. Scholastic, "Kids & Family Reading Report: The Rise of Read-Aloud," 7th ed., 2019, www.scholastic.com/readingreport/rise-of-read-aloud.html.

9. Eszter Hargittai and Aaron Shaw, "Mind the Skills Gap: The Role of Internet Know-How and Gender in Differentiated Contributions to Wikipedia, Information," *Communication & Society* 18, no. 4 (2015): 424–442, https://doi.org/10.1080/1369118X.2014.957711.

CHAPTER 10: CIVIC LIFE

1. Kevin Eagan, Ellen Bara Stolzenberg, Abigail K. Bates, Melissa C. Aragon, Maria Ramirez Suchard, and Cecilia Rios-Aguilar, "The American Freshman: National Norms Fall 2015," Cooperative Institutional Research Program and the Higher Education Research Institute at UCLA, 2016, www .heri.ucla.edu/monographs/TheAmericanFreshman2015.pdf.

2. "College Students' Commitment to Activism, Political and Civic Engagement Reach All-Time Highs," UCLA Newsroom, February 10, 2016, http://newsroom.ucla.edu/releases/college-students-commitment-to-activism -political-and-civic-engagement-reach-all-time-highs.

3. "2018 Election Center," Center for Information & Research on Civic Learning and Engagement, https://civicyouth.org/quick-facts/2018-election -center.

4. "Who Votes for Mayor?," Portland State University and the Knight Foundation, 2016, www.whovotesformayor.org.

5. Patton Hindle, "For Freedoms and Kickstarter Launch a Campaign for the Largest Creative Collaboration in U.S. History," *The Kickstarter Blog*, June 4, 2018, www.kickstarter.com/blog/for-freedoms-and-kickstarter -launch-a-campaign-for-the-largest-c.

6. "The Legacy Museum: From Enslavement to Mass Incarceration," Equal Justice Initiative, https://museumandmemorial.eji.org.

7. "Illinois Civic Education Legislation," IllinoisCivics.org, Civics Education Resource Site, 2016, www.illinoiscivics.org/resources/illinois-civic -education-legislation; Public Act 101-0254, Public Act 101-0254 § (2019), http://ilga.gov/legislation/publicacts/fulltext.asp?Name=101-0254.

Index

activism
  attendance at public meetings, 223
  climate activism, 216–218
  demonstrations, 220
  DoSomething.org, 223
  menstruation-related supplies
    project, 215
  online activism's effect on offline
    activism, 220
  online and offline, 228
  positive change as a result of, 222
  starting movements, 227
  starting nonprofits, 227
  using new technologies for public
    interest, 216
  volunteering, 219
addiction
  anxiety, relationship to media usage,
    133
  attention deficit hyperactivity
    disorder (ADHD), 133, 139
  autism, 133
  boarding schools for, 138
  in boys, 133, 138
  centers for, 133
  Common Sense report, 131
  depression and excessive media
    usage, 133
  devices as coping mechanisms, 137
  excessive tech-related behaviors,
    130–131
  family relationship problems and,
    138
  internet addiction defined, 131–132
  Outback Therapeutic Expeditions,
    138
  prevalence in East Asian countries,
    133
  role of tech companies and social
    media industry in, 134
  Unplugged program, 138
ADHD (attention deficit hyperactivity
  disorder), 133, 139
adolescence, length of, 117–118

adolescent, defined, 118
Advanced Placement courses, 197
advertisements, targeted, 70, 234
African American youth
  civic engagement during college
    years, 219
  discriminatory incidents offline, 170
  discriminatory incidents online, 169
  screen time of, 116
  societal discrimination and
    behavioral health, 171
  worst experiences online, 170
AI-based technology, 234
alcohol use, association with frequent
  Facebook usage, 115
allowance anecdote, 238–239
Amazon, 233
American Academy of Pediatrics, 27,
  38, 171, 199
American Psychological Association,
  184
Annie E. Casey Foundation study of
  reading skills, 197
anxiety
  association with frequent Facebook
    usage, 115
  connection to issues with parent, 124
  effect of digital devices on, 114
  incidence of in young people,
    112–114
  modeling ways to deal with, 124
  online racial discrimination and, 170
  signs of anxiety disorder, 119
artificial intelligence. *See* AI-based
  technology
Asians
  growth of population in US, 170
  online racial and ethnic
    discrimination, 169

Assassin's Creed, 144
autism, 133, 139

baby pictures on social media,
  84–85
balanced life, 34, 54–55, 131, 136,
  156, 241
Bauerlein, Mark, 191, 203
BBC Schools, 62
behavior problems, caused by online
  racial discrimination, 170
Berkman Klein Center for Internet &
  Society, 23, 47, 82, 212
Black Lives Matter, 226
blogs
  Family Online Safety Institute,
    100
  Parenting for a Digital Future
    (Livingstone), 3, 100
Born Digital (Palfrey and Gasser), 4–5,
  191
Bosa, Nick, 161–162
boyd, danah, 79
brain development
  knowledge about, 213
  of prefrontal cortex, 194–195
  in teenagers, 96
Brussels, 166
Buenviaje-Boyd, Max, 217
bullying
  Born This Way Foundation, 102
  bully's relationship with parents,
    95
  cyberbullying, 31, 49, 94–96, 153,
    156
  developing resiliency, 102
  disinhibition and, 96
  girls' experiences with cyberbullying,
    95

Index

GLSEN data, 96
LGBTQ+ youth and, 95–96
parents' advice, 101
suicidal thoughts and attempts, 95
Bush, Laura, 224

Caldwell, Christopher, 217
California Consumer Privacy Act, 85
California privacy controls, 85
Canada, access to devices in, 19
Carnegie Library of Pittsburgh, 63
Center for Information and Research on Civic Learning and Engagement reports, 220
Center on Media and Child Health, 137
Centers for Disease Control and Prevention (CDC), 113
chat environments, 105
cheating
  on college campuses, 204
  earning one's own grades, 205
  pirating on internet, 196
  taking someone else's work, 205
Children's Online Privacy Protection Act of 1998, 79
China
  earlier onset of puberty in, 117
  internet addiction centers in, 133
cigarette usage, 171
civic engagement
  activism, 223
  attendance at public meetings, 223
  civics education in school districts, 223, 227
  clicktivism, 218

climate activism, 216–218
demonstrations, 220
DoSomething.org, 223
global issues, 225
Illinois law requiring civics education in schools, 227
Knight Foundation, 220–221
local library as resource, 224
menstruation-related supplies project, 215
online activism's effect on offline activism, 220, 226
online and offline, 228
parents' commitment to, 222
positive change as a result, 222
presidential libraries as resource, 224
starting movements, 227
starting nonprofits, 227
talking about other young people's involvement in, 223
using new technologies for public interest, 216
volunteering, 219, 222
voting, 222, 229
voting patterns in mayoral elections, 221
young people's disinclination to vote, 219
young people's distrust of institutions, 218–219, 229
Clash of Clans, 236
clicktivism, 218
climate activists, 216–217
CodeAcademy, 210
Coleman, Haven, 217
Common Sense Census, 143
Common Sense Media, 3, 18, 20, 22, 36, 45, 152

Index

communication
  about issues on young people's
    minds, 121–122
  data privacy, 75
  games and gaming experiences, 153,
    240
  information sharing, 71, 75
  keeping channels open, 5–6
  longevity of social media posts, 79,
    86
  monitoring online behavior, 31
  online safety, 97
  online social life, 55–56, 66
  rules, 32
computer access, 19
connected learning
  Connected Learning Alliance, 8
  defined, 200
  educational value of online activities,
    201
  focus on advantages of digital world,
    201
  MacArthur Foundation, 8
  multiple learning environments, 200,
    213
  vision of learning experience,
    200–201
The Connected Parent
  organization of chapters, 8–12
  philosophy of, 5–8
Cortesi, Sandra, 47, 82
Coursera, 210–211
COVID-19 pandemic
  college postgraduates moving back
    home, 118
  connected learning, 200
  studying remotely, 187
  virtual schoolwork, 34
Crash Course series, 201

Crisis Text Line, 18, 100
Curious George, 36

date rape, 105
dating applications, 103, 105
depression, 112–115, 133, 170
devices, access to
  in Canada, 19
  smartphones, 45
  in Switzerland, 19
  in United Kingdom, 19
  in United States, 19
Diagnostic and Statistical Manual of
    Mental Disorders (DMS-V),
    132
digital citizenship
  defined, 212
  educational materials for teachers
    and students, 212
  tech skills for children, 212
Digital Citizenship+ Resource
    Platform, 212
digital education in schools
  faculty background in computer
    skills, 211, 214
  faculty preparation for, 211
  lack of computer science and digital
    literacy skills, 211
"Digital Friendships" report, 45
digital media
  benefits of, 24
  counterproductive activities, 24
  ubiquity and power of, 6, 21
Digital Public Library of America,
    63
discrimination
  offline racial and ethnic
    discrimination, 170
  online racial discrimination, 170

relationship between societal discrimination and behavioral health, 171

sexual orientation, 183

talking about, 183—184

www.apa.org/helpcenter/ kids-discrimination, 184

disinhibition effect, 51, 83, 96

disordered eating, association with frequent Facebook usage, 115

diversity

Bosa, Nick, 161–162

in cities, 166

digital tool usage for unity or divisiveness, 164–165, 173

diversity-boosting practices, 182

diversity-related experiences, 182

Google Maps, 183

"The Impact of Racism on Child and Adolescent Health" (American Academy of Pediatrics), 171

importance of, 175

Instagram, promotion of diversity experiences on, 183

learning from mistakes, 176

micro aggression, 176

modeling positive behaviors, 165

negative experiences on social networking sites, 169

offensive posts on social media, 159–163, 177

parental modeling of acceptance of, 165, 175

people of color as fastest-growing group in America, 166

racial and ethnic discrimination offline, 170

racial and ethnic discrimination online, 169

racial demographic increase, 174

societal discrimination, impact on young people's health, 170–171

in teaching staffs, 181

toxic stress and children's long-term development, 171

victimization online, 169

world-wide internet usage, 167

worst experiences online, 170

www.apa.org/helpcenter/ kids-discrimination, 184

Dora the Explorer, 36

DoSomething.org, 223

Dubai, 166

The Dumbest Generation (Bauerlein), 191, 203

e-readers, 204

echo chambers, 167, 183

Edward M. Kennedy Institute for the United States Senate, 224, 228

EdX, 210

emoji, 46

Equal Justice Initiative, 225

ethnic discrimination, 171

European Union, privacy controls of, 85

Facebook

age requirement, 80

alcohol usage and, 115

anxiety and, 115

curated posts, 53, 122

disordered eating and, 115

ethical questions, 209

filter bubbles and, 167

mental health problems, 115–116

as popular platform, 46–47

revenue for one quarter in 2019, 70

targeted advertising, 233

fake news, 206

Far Cry, 144

filter bubbles, 167

finsta, 48, 112

Flickr, 167

For Freedoms project, 224

Forand, Vincent, 215

Fortnite Battle Royale, 144

Fox, Susannah, 114

"free" services, 70

Frost, Rachel, 115

game console access, 19

gaming

antisocial behaviors, 148

as aspect of young person's social life, 155

audience attraction to different devices, 143

chat environments, 105

children's right to play as a human right, 151

Clash of Clans, 236

development of new types of games, 150

effects on children's well-being and health, 142

gains from playing video games, 148–149

gaming disorder, defined, 132

internet gaming disorder, 132

as pathway for interest-driven learning, 154

prosocial behaviors, 147, 150

sexually graphic games, 155–156

social isolation, 148

as starting point for creative activity and community engagement, 154

statistics, 143

gaming, popular types of

action-adventure, 144

open-world, 144

puzzles, 144

racing, 144

role-playing, 144

shooter, 144

simulation, 144

sports, 144

strategy, 144

gaming research

American Psychological Association, 146–147

Australian attorney general's department, 145

on links between aggressive or prosocial behaviors and violent video games, 145–149

Oxford Internet Institute, 147

Pew Survey, 149

School Children Mental Health in Europe project, 148

Supreme Court, US, 146

Swedish Media Council report, 146

UN Committee on the Rights of the Child, 146

George W. Bush Presidential Center, 224

Germanotta, Cynthia, 102

Girls Who Code, 210

Goldilocks principle, 18, 35, 38

Google

Be Internet Awesome, 105

Google Docs, 231

Google Maps, 183

Google Photos, 84

problems caused by oversharing online, 76

revenue for one quarter in 2019, 70

targeted advertising, 233

Gottesman, Eric, 225
Graf, Nikki, 113
Green, John, 201
Grindr, 94
group chats, 46

Hargittai, Eszter, 79, 116
hashtag searches, 183
Hinduja, Sameer, 95
Hirsi, Isra, 217
Hispanic youth, effect of societal
    discrimination on, 171
homework time rules, 62, 67
Horowitz, Juliana Menasce, 113
Humboldt, Alexander von, 193

identity theft, 85
Illinois law requiring civics education
    in schools, 227
inequalities in online experiences, 168
information
    bingeing, 137
    distinguishing fact from
        misinformation, 221
    sales of, 70
    sharing, 72–75
Instagram
    activism, 217
    age requirement, 80
    curated posts, 53, 110–112, 122
    ethical questions, 209
    identity play, 125–126
    multiple accounts, 48
    owner of, 47, 70
    parental monitoring of, 124–125
    popularity of, 74
    ranking, 21, 115
    sale of targeted information, 70
    trends and new topics, 183

International Classification of Diseases
    (WHO), 132
International Telecommunication
    Union, 167
internet
    addiction, 131–132
    addiction centers, 133
    broadband service access, 22
    economy of, 71
    gaming disorder, 132
    gender differences in reactions to
        online experiences, 116–117
    online engagement of wealthier and
        less wealthy students, 116
    racial differences in usage of, 116
    social-emotional well-being in
        reactions to online experiences,
        117
    usage of, 19–20

Jabr, Ferris, 198
Japan, prevalence of internet addiction
    centers in, 133
John F. Kennedy Presidential Library
    and Museum, 224
Jones, Saeed, 178

Khan Academy, 62, 201, 210
"Kids & Family Reading Report
    (Scholastic), 198
Knight Foundation, 220–221

Lady Gaga, 102
Latinx youth
    civic engagement during college
        years, 219
    racist incidents offline, 170
    racist incidents online, 169
    screen time, 116

learning
  acquisition of twenty-first-century
    skills, 208
  benefits and potential of technology,
    7–8, 23–24, 193
  connecting with previously siloed
    learning spaces, 208
  data on reading habits, 198
  digital platforms' advantages for
    reading, 198
  digital skills, 214
  ethics and law issues, 209
  fake news *vs.* truth, 206
  learn-by-doing approach in digital
    environments, 209
  learning from mistakes, 202
  library use, 197
  multiple learning environments, 210
  paper reading material *vs.* screens,
    198
  personalized learning, 208
  preparation for jobs of the future,
    208
  reading patterns, 197
  technology as tool to meet
    educational goals, 210
  See also cheating; connected learning
LEDs, effect on melatonin release, 199
Legacy Museum: From Enslavement to
    Mass Incarceration, 225
LGBTQ+, 95–96, 106, 234
Lieber, Ron, 238
Livingstone, Sonia, 3

MacArthur Foundation, 8
Magrid, Larry, 105
marijuana usage, 171
mediatricians, 140
melatonin, 199

menstruation hygiene project, 215
Messenger, 46, 73
micro aggression, 176
Minecraft, 36
mobile phones
  games on, 143
  ownership by teens, 18–19
  uses of, 18
modeling good practices
  big five skills, 50
  bullying, 101–102
  dealing with anxiety, 124
  information privacy, 71
  lifelong learning, 178
  moral behavior, 59, 155
  positive connections with people,
    179
  resilience, 119
  sharing information, 72, 81–82
  support for diversity, 165
monitoring
  accessing child's accounts, 58–59,
    99
  maintaining child's trust, 58
  online behaviors, 31
  technical tools, 57, 100–101
Moss, David, 228
multitasking, 63, 195
multitasking experiment, 63–64
myelination, 194
MySpace, 46

National Geographic, 62
National Sleep Foundation, 199
National Survey of Children's Health,
    112
National Writing Project, 197
Net Nanny, 100
neuroticism, 114

newspaper test, 80
nonverbal disabled context, 50

O'Connor, Sandra Day, 225, 228
Odgers, Candice, 114
Okamoto, Nadya, 215
Online Eraser Law, 85
open mind, 180
Outback Therapeutic Expeditions, 138

parenting, children's social activities and
    balancing social media with other aspects of life, 25, 34, 54–55, 75, 121
    building positive media habits, 66, 134
    diversity-boosting practices, 182
    helping develop positive relationships, 65
    helping develop skills to thrive in diverse environments, 172, 179–181
    helping find outlets other than internet, 126, 140
    identity play, 125–126
    keeping an eye on in-game interactions, 153–154, 156
    limiting time spent on social media, 135
    See also monitoring; social life
parenting, gaming activities and
    collaborative games, 153
    gaming and social life, 155
    keeping an eye on in-game interactions, 153–154, 156
    playing different types of online games, 153

    playing online games with children, 155
parenting, internet knowledge and
    being informed and credible, 66–67, 124–125, 152–153
    curiosity about what can be learned from games, 154
    encouraging diversity-related experiences, 182
    factors in, 10–11
    filling in learning gaps, 65
    identity play, 125–126
    interacting with own children through social media, 236
    keeping an eye on in-game interactions, 153–154, 156
    keeping an eye out for fake instas, 126
    personal information sharing, 75–76
    sharing data about own kids, 82, 84–86
    support systems online for kids, 100
parenting in digital age
    allowing children to learn from mistakes, 176
    discussing discrimination, 183
    family time, 136–137
    fears about children's learning, 192
    having an open mind, 202
    homework time rules, 62, 67
    listening and trusting your kids, 239
    putting online experiences in perspective, 120
    reading to young kids, 203
    scheduling screen-free periods, 135
    screen time tracking apps, 135
    seeking professional help, 137, 139
    setting up study environments, 203
    sharing data about kids, 84–85, 86

Index

parenting in digital age (*continued*)

  sleep, 207

  socioeconomic status and parental involvement, 169

  supporting children in success and failure, 119

  turning technology into scapegoat, 232

  worries, 9

  See also civic engagement; communication; modeling; social life

Patchin, Justin, 95

PBS Kids, 62

personal data, sales of, 71

Pew Research Center subjects

  access to digital devices, 18–20

  broadband at home, 22

  dating, 103

  digital technologies, 197

  experiences on social media, 113–114

  Facebook ranking, 47

  Facebook use by teens, 74

  gaming statistics, 143

  link between gaming and physical violence, 145

  monitoring, 57

  preference for Snapchat, 73–74

  teens' view of social media, 48–49, 167–168

  video games popular with adults, 144

platforms, popular, 45

Plunkett, Leah, 84

predators online

  "Be Internet Awesome," 105

  Connect Safely.org, 105

  data about, 93–94

  dating, 104–105

Family Online Safety Institute, 105

SafeKids.org, 105

sexual predation, 105

presidential libraries

  Edward M. Kennedy Institute for the United States Senate, 224, 228

  George W. Bush Presidential Center, 224

  John F. Kennedy Presidential Library and Museum, 224

privacy

  asking for advice on, 74

  Children's Online Privacy Protection Act of 1998, 79

  college applications, 78

  concerns about, 75

  data privacy, 75

  identity theft, 85

  information sharing, 71, 75

  job-seeking, 79

  mistakes made by young people, 83–84

  newspaper test, 80

  parental modeling, 81–82

  personal information sharing by young people, 74–75

  privacy-friendly strategies, 83

  sexting, 76–77

  tattoo analogy, 80–81

prosocial behaviors, 147, 150

puberty, onset of, 117

racism

  cycle of, 185

  discriminatory incidents offline, 170

  discriminatory incidents online, 169

  "The Impact of Racism on Child and Adolescent Health" (American Academy of Pediatrics), 171

toxic stress effect on children's long-term development, 171
Reddit, 47
resiliency, 102
Rice, Esme Bella, 217
Rich, Michael, 137
Rickwood, Debra, 115
Rideout, Vicky, 114
rinsta, 111–112
Rockwell, Norman, 224
Roosevelt, Franklin Delano, 224
Royal Society for Public Health, ranking of media sites by young people, 115
rules
   changing, 239
   enforcing, 99
   exceptions to, 33
   homework, 62
   modeling, 39, 64, 71, 81–82
   screen time, 24, 27–32
   sharing personal information, 81

safety
   geolocation tools, 100
   online resources, 105–106
   peer group conversations about, 107
   predators, 93
   rules, 98, 99–101
   school climate, 102
   selfies, 100
   stranger danger, 98, 99, 106
   technological controls, 100–101
   texting while driving, 100
Scholastic survey, on reading aloud to children, 204
Schultz, Jason, 79
Scientific American magazine, 198
Scratch, 36

screen time
   benefits of, 17, 23–24, 39
   community contracts, 37
   counterproductive activities, 24
   disadvantages of high levels of, 23
   discussing online activities, 24–26
   family contracts, 37
   guidelines for age groups, 27–32. *See also* screen time guidelines
   link between socioeconomic status and levels of screen time, 169
   mobile phones, 18–19
   norm in US, 16
   parents as role models, 38
   recommended types of, 36
   rule-setting consistency, 34–35
   setting limits, 24–27, 32
   sleep and, 33, 36–37
   technological controls, 39
screen time guidelines
   birth to 18 months old, 27–29
   18 months to two years, 28
   two- to five-year-olds, 28
   six- to twelve-year-olds, 30
   thirteen- to fifteen-year-olds, 31–32
   sixteen-year-olds and older, 32
selfies, 46, 100
Sesame Street, 36
SesameStreet.org, 210
sexting
   legal risks of, 77
   prevalence of, 76–77
   sharing without permission, 77
sexual orientation
   discrimination, 183
   LGBTQ+ issues, 95–96, 106, 234
sexual predation online, 105
sexually graphic games, 155–156

Index

Sharenthood: Why We Should Think Before We Talk About Our Kids Online (Plunkett), 85

Shorty Awards, 181

sinsta, 112

skills needed to thrive in diverse environments, 172

slacktivism, 226

sleep
  challenge, 207
  cycle, 199
  effect of excessive media on, 33
  getting enough, 213
  patterns of young people, 199
  REM sleep deprivation, 199
  Why We Sleep (Walker), 198–199

smartphones
  access to, 45
  ownership, 45
  uses of, 18–19

Snapchat
  age requirement, 80
  effect on well-being, 115
  ethical questions, 209
  as "free" service, 70
  organization of protests, 217
  popularity of, 21, 45, 73
  ranking among social media services, 47

social life
  avoiding risky habits, 44
  awareness of long-term public dissemination of interactions, 52, 61
  building moral compass, 59
  building resilience, 60
  communicating with friends, 45
  connecting through social media, 43
  discussing disinhibition effect, 60–61
  expressing themselves online, 46
  gaming as aspect of young person's social life, 155
  guidelines on screen time, 43
  identity, 48, 125–126
  inclusion in group chats, 46
  multiple identities, 48
  platform diversification, 47
  receiving response to messages, 46
  research on, 44–45
  sexuality or gender, 48
  social life defined, 44
  social media usage, 45
  strategies for dealing with challenges, 52
  understanding consequences of public interactions, 52

social media
  anxiety and suicides among young people, 52–53
  balance, 53–55
  benefits of, 49
  big five model of skills, 50
  breaks from, 123
  comments, 111
  curated images on, 110
  as desire for social interaction, 136
  development of sophisticated strategies, 50
  dual nature of, 21, 56
  face-to-face activities, 61, 123
  follower counts, 111
  homework time, 62
  likes, 111

multiple accounts, 111
multitasking, 63–64
offensive posts on, 177
online experiences, 49
as predictor of life satisfaction
    among adolescent users, 49
societal discrimination, 171
socioeconomically disadvantaged
    youth, effect of societal
    discrimination on, 171
South Korea, gaming addictions in
Steiner-Adair, Catherine, 50
Stevenson, Bryan, 225
suicide, 52–53, 65, 113
surveillance capitalism, 234
switch-tasking, 195
Switzerland, access to devices in, 19

Taiwan, prevalence of internet
    addiction centers in, 133
tattoo analogy, 80–81
technology
    activism, technology-enabled, 216
    AI-based technology, 234
    benefits and potential of, 7–8
    cheating, technology-enabled, 204
    excessive tech-related behaviors,
        130–131
    limiting exposure to, 27, 29
    negative aspects of, 234
    positive aspects of, 233
    as scapegoat, 232
    skill areas, 212
    supporting a diverse community,
        165, 168
    technological controls, 100–101
    as tool to meet educational goals,
        210

using new technologies for public
    interest, 216
"Technology Addiction: Concern,
    Controversy, and Finding
    Balance," 131
television. *See* TV
Thomas, Hank Willis, 225
Thunberg, Greta, 217
Tinder, 94
Toronto, 166
transgender, 178
Tumblr, curated posts in, 47, 122
Tunsil, Laremy, 162
TV access, 22
TV programs for children
    Curious George, 36
    Dora the Explorer, 36
    Minecraft, 36, 144
    Sesame Street, 36
Twitter, 47, 80, 167, 183, 217
Tynes, Brendesha, 169

UK Safer Internet Centre report on
    digital friendships, 45, 49
UN Convention on the Rights of the
    Child, 151
Uncharted, 144
United Kingdom, access to devices in,
    19
United States
    access to devices in, 19
    earlier onset of puberty in, 117
Unplugged program, 138

Villasenor, Alexandria, 217
volunteering, 219, 222
voting, 222, 229
VSCO, 110–111, 125

Walker, Matthew, 198
websites
American Academy of Pediatrics, 3
BBC Schools, 62
Be Internet Awesome, 105
Born This Way Foundation, 102
Common Sense Media, 3, 18, 20, 22, 36, 105, 153
ConnectSafely.org, 105
Digital Skills Resources, 106
DoSomething.org, 223
Edward M. Kennedy Institute for the United States Senate, 224
Equal Justice Initiative, 225
Facebook global online safety team posts, 106
Family Online Safety Institute, 3, 105
For Freedoms project, 224
Google's "Be Internet Awesome," 105
iCivics (www.icivics.org), 225, 228
Microsoft's Digital Literacy, 106
Period.org, 216
SafeKids.org, 105
SesameStreet.org, 210
supplements to classroom learning, 62–63
www.apa.org/helpcenter/kids-discrimination, 184
WeChat, 47
WhatsApp, 45, 47, 188
Wikipedia, 63, 167, 206

Wired, hiring of teenagers to photograph protests, 217
World Health Organization (WHO), 132

young people
anxiety, 52–53, 112–114
constrained thinking about, 235
delay of activities associated with adulthood, 117
disinclination to vote, 219
distrust of institutions, 218–219, 229
effects of gaming on, 155
impact of societal discrimination on, 170–171
needs of, 235
personal information sharing, 74–75
ranking of media sites by, 115
sleep patterns, 199
suicides, 52–53
Youth and Media Lab, 73
Youth and Media Project, Berkman Klein Center, 82
Youth Risk Behavior Survey, 113
YouTube
age requirement, 80
educational channels, 201, 208
effect on well-being, 115
Equal Justice Initiative, 225
ethical questions, 209
as "free" service, 70
owner of, 70
popularity of, 45, 47

Zillien, Nicole, 116

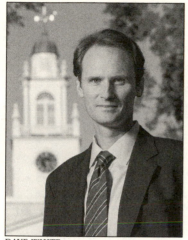

DAVE WHITE

JOHN PALFREY is president of the John D. and Catherine T. MacArthur Foundation and a former faculty director of the Berkman Klein Center for Internet & Society at Harvard University. He previously served as head of school at Phillips Academy in Andover, Massachusetts. He lives in Chicago.

URS GASSER is executive director of the Berkman Klein Center for Internet & Society and a professor of practice at Harvard University. He lives in Cambridge, Massachusetts.

ANNE GABRIEL-JÜRGENS